THE ESSENTIAL KITCHEN GARDENER

frieda arkin

ILLUSTRATIONS BY
CONSTANCE ARKIN DEL NERO

the
essential
kitchen
gardener

A Donald Hutter Book
HENRY HOLT AND COMPANY
NEW YORK

Published by Henry Holt and Company, Inc.,
115 West 18th Street, New York, New York 10011.
Published in Canada by Fitzhenry & Whiteside Limited,
195 Allstate Parkway, Markham, Ontario L3R 4T8.

Library of Congress Cataloging-in-Publication Data
Arkin, Frieda.
The essential kitchen gardener / Frieda Arkin ; illustrations by
Constance Arkin del Nero.—1st ed.
p.   cm.
"A Donald Hutter book."
ISBN 0-8050-1188-9
1. Vegetable gardening—Dictionaries.   2. Organic gardening—
Dictionaries.   3. Fruit-culture—Dictionaries.   4. Herb gardening—
Dictionaries.   5. Vegetables—Dictionaries.   6. Fruit—
Dictionaries.   7. Herbs—Dictionaries.   8. Garden pests—Biological
control—Dictionaries.   I. Title.
SB324.3.A75   1990
635'.03—dc20   89-27389
                                                    CIP

Henry Holt books are available at special discounts
for bulk purchases for sales promotions, premiums,
fund-raising, or educational use. Special editions
or book excerpts can also be created to specification.

For details contact:
Special Sales Director
Henry Holt and Company, Inc.
115 West 18th Street
New York, New York 10011

FIRST EDITION

Designed by Kate Nichols
Printed in the United States of America
Recognizing the importance of preserving the written word,
Henry Holt and Company, Inc., by policy, prints all of its
first editions on acid-free paper.∞

10   9   8   7   6   5   4   3   2   1

I'd like to dedicate this book to the ordinary, home variety of gardeners, people who ask little more than that the seeds or seedlings they put into the earth with such hope reward them with good fruits for their table. There's no particular mystique surrounding gardening. It requires no green thumbs, no mystical rapport with the earth. Nor is successful gardening difficult. Like any other rewarding undertaking, it requires common sense and some specific knowledge—exactly what I have done my best to put into this book.

Contents

Acknowledgments

I should like to thank all those enthusiastic friends and neighbors who so willingly brought me the gardening hints and tips they have for years sworn by, many of which I have adopted.

And also my thanks to Donna Scanlon, of the Cooperative Extension Service, Essex Agricultural and Technical Institute, Hathorne, Massachusetts, for her many instances of sensible gardening advice.

And also my thanks to the many, many magazines devoted to gardening or containing occasional articles on gardening, which I have been reading for years with delight. They have stirred me to many garden tests and experiments. Among these are *Country Journal, Harrowsmith, Horticulture, House & Garden, New England Gardener, Organic Gardening,* and *Yankee.*

A Few Words First

When I moved to the country eight years ago, what I didn't know about gardening would have filled a book. This is the book. I don't mean to say that it contains everything (certainly not everything botanical) about every vegetable, herb, and berry you might grow—but it does contain everything essential to a vegetable gardener. It's the book I wish I had had when I lifted my first spadeful of soil. I would have been spared the grief of miniature vegetables, and pepper plants without peppers, and carrots whose entire glory was above the soil.

This book is for the common home gardener who wants to put seeds in the soil and reap a plentiful harvest from them for healthful eating. It's a book for people without a greenhouse, a hotbed, or a cold frame.

Yet there are people who like the idea of starting seeds on a windowsill while blizzards are howling outside (doing so does seem to bring the spring a little nearer). For them I have in some cases included directions for windowsill culture of early seedlings. But I don't recommend it, since special equipment is usually needed, and lots of steady care. And the fact is, most vegetables do excellently when grown from seeds planted outdoors at the proper time. If you absolutely insist on getting a leg up early in the spring, plant shops and nurseries now offer well-started seedlings of more and more varieties of garden fruits and vegetables, ready to go straight into your garden.

Now, you may not have heard of some of the garden and kitchen tips I've recommended in this book. Every one that I've used has worked. And though others may not yet have got into the literature, loads of gardeners and cooks swear by them year after year. Give them a try.

I have also done my best to present information on the chief diseases and pests that can afflict the plants in your garden. There seem to be many, but take heart: This doesn't mean that every vegetable, herb, or berry you grow will necessarily be attacked by any of them.

With regard to treatment, you'll see that I lean to organic, or botanical, methods of combating diseases, insects, and weeds, as well as the physical removal of pests when feasible. It isn't necessary for most home gardeners to use, on their own plants, the poisonous, synthetic chemicals employed by most commercial growers. Indeed, avoiding these chemicals is one of the reasons for growing your own fruits and vegetables.

I have many reservations about these poisonous chemicals and am all for soft-pedaling their use until their safety can be established. There is, first of all, the problem of handling them safely. Some are harmful when their fumes are inhaled, or acutely toxic when they come in contact with the skin. They can be fatal if swallowed. The leaves of young plants can be "burned" by their use, and the plants themselves may be dwarfed. Some plants are injured by arsenicals. And although poison sprays should never be applied to fruits and vegetables before harvesting—since the chemicals remain on the plants for some time—residues from earlier spraying can still be found on some of the fruits and vegetables we eat. Furthermore, repeated small doses of some of these poisons, when ingested, can either sensitize the body or accumulate within the body with unpredictable future consequences.

In addition, most of these poisons can endanger children, pets, and other animals. They are often acutely toxic to fish, birds, and helpful insects, such as chalcid wasps and bees. Many have side effects on other garden components, such as the soil and nearby vulnerable plants. Last, many of the pests these sprays aim for are able to build up resistance to them, and the whole process has to start over again, with the introduction of new poisons whose long-term effects cannot yet be known.

On the other hand, botanical insecticides when used properly, natural controls, and poison-free methods of eliminating pests are not dangerous to humans yet are quite effective in ridding home gardens of enemies to plants. Because the sprays are not persistent, you don't have to worry about precautions concerning the number of days between their use and harvest. The organic and natural products recommended in this book are all sold in conventional spray form and are available under several trade names. Not only that—many of them you can make yourself (see *Repellents*).

It's true that biological controls may not totally exterminate all garden pests; some mechanical measures may have to be added. Hand picking of many types of bugs is entirely feasible; traps for slugs and squash bugs are easily constructed; and insect traps and dormant oil sprays are effective (although they don't discriminate between good and bad insects).

Many plants contain insect-repellent substances and not only are relatively safe from garden pests themselves but, when used as companion plants with vulnerable crops, can lessen the degree of local infestation. Interplanting with the following can help ward off many predaceous insects: asters, chrysanthemums, coreopsis, cosmos, costmary, feverfew, leaf sage, marigolds, pennyroyal, savory, tansy, thyme, and wormwood.

And there are many insects that destroy garden pests. The eggs of some of these (and the insects themselves, such as ladybugs) can be bought from many nurseries. Naturally occurring ones in your vicinity can often be lured to and kept in your garden by ensuring them a supply of flower nectar and water. Besides your usual garden flowers, grow the following plants for these beneficial insects: buckwheat, carrots, daisies of all varieties, dill, goldenrod, Jerusalem artichokes, and parsley.

There are ways to minimize pest and disease incursions in your garden. Don't leave rotting fruits on the ground—grubs and maggots grow in them and use them for breeding sites. Practice plant rotation to keep enemies of a particular host plant from proliferating in the same spot next season. And till up your garden soil in late fall to expose insect eggs to winter frosts.

Last, on the following pages you will find an easy-to-read graph that will enable you to see at a glance when, depending on where you live, it's safe for you to plant every vegetable, herb, or berry in your garden.

Good harvests to you!

Where to Plant When

The following (overleaf) graph gives you at a glance a picture of the start of your growing season, depending on your area within the continental United States. Pick your state (or section of your state). You will see:

1. A line of minus signs indicating when *not* to plant
2. A wavy line indicating a period of transition; this time frame will vary within the state due to altitude and other geographical fluctuations
3. A line of plus signs indicating when it is generally safe to plant

Some states show no variability (Connecticut, for example). This means that the time period for the last frost will be fairly stable throughout the state. The states with the greatest variability—Texas, Arizona, and California—have each been subdivided into two regions for more accurate delineation.

WHERE TO PLANT WHEN

STATE	JAN.	FEB.	MAR.	APR.	
S.W. ARIZONA					
S. CALIFORNIA					
S. TEXAS					
FLORIDA					
LOUISIANA					
MISSISSIPPI					
S. CAROLINA					
ALABAMA					
GEORGIA					
ARKANSAS					
N. CAROLINA					
CALIF. Coastal Ranges					
MASSACHUSETTS					
RHODE ISLAND					
ILLINOIS					
TENNESSEE					
CONNECTICUT					
DELAWARE					
VIRGINIA					
MARYLAND					
OKLAHOMA					
KENTUCKY					
MISSOURI					
ARIZ. Colorado Plateau					
N. TEXAS					
KANSAS					

LEGEND
- - - - Frost; Don't Plant
~~~~ Transition
+ + + Safe Planting

STATE	MAR.	APR.	MAY	JUNE	

Graph Developed by Rosario Del Nero

The following symbols are used throughout this book to identify entries other than those that deal with plant species:

: Garden Pests and Plant Diseases

: Soil Control and Cultivation

THE
ESSENTIAL KITCHEN
GARDENER,
A TO Z

Alternaria Disease 🐞

Also called alternaria leafspot and early blight, alternaria disease is caused by a fungus that attacks many vegetables and fruits, including cabbages and tomatoes, in the garden and during storage. The spores of the fungus are windborne and require moisture and warmth for germination. They often enter fruits or vegetables through cracks, bruises, and nicks.

Manifestation
• Ringed brown spots appear on leaves, which turn yellow and drop off. Young fruit may also drop, and dark spots may develop on the stem ends of more mature fruit.

To Combat
• Store only sound, unbruised vegetables and fruits. In the garden, good air circulation is your best weapon: Don't overcrowd plants.

Amaranth Spinach

See *Tampala*

Anise

An easy-to-grow, hardy, annual herb of the carrot family, anise has leaves and seeds that taste like licorice. The fresh leaves can be picked throughout the growing season and served in salads. The seeds, harvested in the fall, are used in cookies and candies.

Anise seeds are slow to germinate, and the plant requires a 120-day season if grown for its seeds. It grows to 2 feet in height. Once established, it generally reseeds itself for years. Anise doesn't transplant well.

When to Plant
• Plant anise seeds as soon as the soil is warm.

Where to Plant
• Anise likes to grow in fertile, well-drained, light soil (pH 6 to 7), in full sun.

How to Plant
• Plant seeds ½ inch deep, 1 inch apart, in rows 2 to 3 feet apart.

Germination Time
• Anise seeds take 28 days to germinate.

Care During Growth
• Thin to 3 or 4 plants per foot when seedlings are 4 inches tall. Since the plants tend to fall over easily, hill them with dirt as they grow.

Maturation Time
• Plants are mature in 75 days.

Harvesting
• Leaves can be picked for salads and flavorings throughout the growing season.
• The umbels (seed-bearing clusters) turn from green to brown and become dry in the fall; the seeds are then ripe. Keep your eye on them— you don't want the seeds to fall to the ground before you've collected them.

Kitchen Tips
• Mash fresh anise leaves up in some butter or margarine and freeze them. The result makes a delicious spread for canapés.
• For maximum flavor when you're using anise seeds in a cake, pudding, or other dish, crush them between sheets of waxed paper with a rolling pin.

Anthracnose

A fungal disease chiefly attacking blackberry and raspberry plants, as well as beans and tomatoes, anthracnose is usually a minor pest.

Manifestation
• Purple-edged white or gray blotches appear on the bark of berry bushes. On fruits, small purple spots gradually enlarge, turn gray, and become sunken.

To Combat
• Since black raspberries are more susceptible than reds, separate black and red varieties by at least 100 feet.
• Cut out and burn all infected berry canes.

• If anthracnose appears on beans or tomatoes, break the continuity of the disease in your garden by practicing crop rotation—don't sow the same plant in the same place for 2 to 3 years.

Ants 🐜

Ants are seldom, themselves, a great nuisance in the garden. Occasionally their burrowing may loosen the soil around young plants and cause them to die, but the chief damage ants do is to nurture aphids and mealybugs for the honeydew they excrete. But bear in mind that ants aerate the soil by their burrowings and improve its drainage capacity.

To Combat
• Pennyroyal planted around garden beds deters ants. So do bonemeal, camphor, and oil of cloves.

• Baltimore orioles are great ant eaters.

. . .

Aphids 🐜

See also *Corn-root aphids*; *Green peach aphids*

Also called plant lice, aphids are soft-bodied sucking insects that extract the vital juices from plants. They exude a sweet substance called honeydew that ants love; consequently, ants move aphids from plant to plant and protect them. Aphids also spread mold and virus diseases.

Aphids can be black, green, pink, red, or yellow. Their tiny eggs are black and oval. Aphids are fast-breeding, particularly in cold, damp weather. A heavy infestation, untreated, can kill a plant. Although aphids attack almost all plants, they are especially attracted to beans and cole crops (broccoli, Brussels sprouts, cabbage, cauliflower, celery, collards, horseradish, kale, kohlrabi, mustard, nasturtiums, peppers, potatoes, radishes, rutabagas, squashes, and turnips). Some carry diseases that infect raspberry bushes.

Manifestation
• Aphids are frequently found on young growth, and on the undersides of leaves. Infested leaves turn yellow or stippled, curl, and wilt. Growth becomes stunted or plants die back, and

honeydew they excrete frequently attracts a soot-colored mold.

To Combat

• Aphids are attracted to chickweed, so rid your garden of this plant.

• As soon as you see the first sign of aphids, remove them with cotton swabs dipped in alcohol, or dislodge them with a strong stream of water from the hose.

• Aphids are strongly attracted to the color yellow. You can trap and drown many of them by setting a yellow plastic pan, three-quarters full of water, in your garden.

• Sprays

Mix 1 part mint leaves with 4 parts water in your blender. Strain and spray the solution on the aphids. Repeat if necessary.

Make a spray using the aphids themselves, mixed with water in your blender. Strain and spray the solution on affected crops.

Make a solution of 4 ounces soap to 1 gallon water. Spray on affected plants, then hose off with clear water 15 minutes later. Repeat once or twice, on successive days, if necessary.

Mix a couple of cloves of garlic in water in your blender, strain, and spray on affected plants.

Rotenone or pyrethrum sprays are safe to plants and very effective against aphids.

• Aphids are repelled by a mulch of aluminized strips of film, which reflects light so that the insects apparently lose their sense of direction.

• Clear polyethylene plastic laid over the garden bed, with slits for the plants to grow through, is reported to deter aphids.

• Natural enemies of aphids

The larvae of many insects (lacewings and syrphid flies, for instance) feed voraciously on aphids. So do many insects themselves (ladybugs and praying mantises). You can purchase larval forms of these predators from many garden nurseries and supply houses. (Syrphid flies are attracted to plants of the daisy family—plant these in your garden beds to bring in the flies, which may well take care of your aphid problem.)

Wasps parasitize and thus eradicate aphids by injecting their eggs into them. Attract wasps to your garden with nearby plantings of any of the following: buckwheat, carrots, daisies, fava beans, goldenrod, Jerusalem artichokes, mint (all varieties), parsley, parsnips, and wild mustard.

Many birds—chickadees, house wrens, and titmice in particular—adore aphids for food. See if you can get them to set up housekeeping near your garden.

• Plant repellents or trap crops
Interplant any of the following, which act as repellents, among the plants you wish to protect: anise, basil, chives, and garlic.
Yellow and orange nasturtiums lure aphids away from other plants. Plant these throughout the garden, and, when they are well infested, pull them up and destroy them.

Armyworms

These larvae of a kind of night-flying moth are 1½- to 2-inch-long blackish green worms with yellow or white stripes. Somewhat similar to cutworms in habits, armyworms feed at night and hide just under the soil, or under stones and leaves, during the day. They attack mainly beets, corn, squashes, and tomatoes in gardens, as well as many grains in fields. Armyworms get their name from their habit of traveling in multitudes from field to field, although they rarely do so in gardens.

Manifestation
• You can see armyworms in the act of destruction if you go out at night with a flashlight and turn it on suddenly. They eat the leaves of their favorite garden vegetables, sometimes causing severe defoliation.

To Combat
• Trichogramma wasps lay their eggs inside the eggs of armyworms and feed on them. Wasp eggs can be purchased from many plant nurseries.
• A safe organic spray to combat armyworms is Bacillus thuringiensis (Bt).

Artichoke (Globe Artichoke)

See also *Jerusalem artichoke*

Tender perennials, not reliably hardy in northern regions, artichokes need a long, damp growing season and mild winters. In colder regions the plants can often be successfully wintered over if they're cut to the ground before frost and well protected over the winter (see "Garden Tips"). It's rare for first-rate heads to be produced in the North; however, you can take a chance.

Each plant, which grows from 3 to 5 feet tall and 3 to 5 feet wide, should give a good harvest for up to 5 years. Artichokes are sometimes grown as ornamental plants, producing lavender and purple flowers from the second summer on. The flowers can also be dried for indoor bouquets. Artichokes don't transplant well, so choose a permanent site for them.

When to Plant
• Plant artichokes when all danger of frost is past.

Where to Plant
• Artichokes like well-drained, rich or sandy loam (pH 6 to 7) and a steady supply of moisture, but the roots will rot if water is allowed to collect and remain around them for long periods. They'll take full sun or partial shade.

How to Plant
• Starting from seed isn't recommended—artichokes don't always breed true. Starting them from seed is also a nuisance, requiring a hotbed and later transfer to a cold frame. It's better to buy plants and put them directly into your garden.
• Dig separate holes or a long trench 8 inches deep and wide, then fill with 5 inches of high-nitrogen compost. Place the plants about 4 feet apart on the compost, then fill to the top with soil. Press the soil firmly but not too heavily around the roots.

Care During Growth
• In the North, artichokes like a deep mulch all summer long. Use dry grass clippings, aged manure, or a mixture of both. During bud production, apply a 6-inch layer of compost in a 1-foot radius around each plant.

Maturation Time
• Plants are mature 50 to 100 days after buds appear.

Harvesting
• The edible "head" of the artichoke is actually the immature flower bud, generally ready to pick in the early fall, when the weather is cool. The head should be firm and the scales around it tight. If you are in doubt about ripeness, pick one and cook it.
• You'll find artichokes easier to handle if you cut off about 1 inch of the stem with each head.
• Once you've harvested the head, cut the remainder of the plant stem that bore it down to the ground.

Diseases and Pests
• Botrytis blight.

Garden Tips
• Artichokes constantly send up suckers, from which new plants will grow. Remove these to plant elsewhere, taking care not to damage the roots.
• Artichoke plants can stand a few light frosts, but don't let fall advance

too far before mulching them for the winter. Cut the plants to the ground, then mound with about 1 foot of ashes, then another foot of dirt. Starting in early spring, remove this covering little by little, replacing with a light mulch as the plants resume growth.

Kitchen Tips

• Avoid pricking your fingers when handling artichokes by wearing rubber household gloves. Or snip off the ends of the sharp-pointed leaves with kitchen scissors.

• It's not necessary to remove the choke of an artichoke before cooking, but this can be done. Force open the center leaves from the top, and cut out the fine leaves and the choke with a curved grapefruit knife.

• Before cooking, let artichokes stand for 1 hour in a pot of cold water to which you've added 1 tablespoon of vinegar for every quart of water. This will prevent discoloration and make the flesh more succulent.

• Artichokes will turn grayish if cooked in aluminum or iron pots.

• Artichokes are much tastier if cooked in broth instead of water.

• Add to the cooking liquid the juice of a thick slice of lemon for each artichoke. Cover the pot, and cook for 30 to 40 minutes.

• An artichoke is done when the leaves come off easily with a slight pull.

• You can remove the choke from an artichoke very easily after it has been cooked. Spread the top leaves apart gently, pull out the fine prickly leaves in the center, then scoop out the hairy choke with a spoon.

• A nice way to serve cooked artichoke is to pour melted, salted butter into the "cup" that is left after the choke has been removed.

• It's traditional to dip cooked artichoke leaves in melted butter, but you can use dozens of other dips: mayonnaise or sour cream mixtures, or other sauces you dream up.

• Dice cooked artichoke hearts into very small bits and add to an omelet.

Arugula

See *Rocket*

Asparagus

Asparagus is an easy-to-grow perennial that, with proper care, will yield harvests for 2 months each spring for 10 to 15 years. Asparagus plants generally winter well.

You can plant asparagus from seed, but you won't be able to harvest any for 3 years, and even that first harvest will be meager. After 3 years you can make regular cuttings each spring. If you plant asparagus in the spring from 1-year-old roots (also called crowns), you can make a very light cutting, for perhaps 2 weeks, the second spring, with a full harvest each year thereafter. If you plant in the fall from 1-year-old roots, your first light cutting, which should last about 2 weeks, can be 1 year after the following spring.

When to Plant
• Since the thick-coated seeds of asparagus germinate slowly in cold soil, wait until the soil warms up a bit in the spring to plant seeds.
• Plant roots early in the spring, as soon as the soil is workable.
• Or plant roots late in the fall, shortly before the soil freezes.

Where to Plant
• Although asparagus will grow almost anywhere, to get the most tender stalks plant it in organically rich, well-drained soil, where it will get plenty of moisture without being waterlogged. It likes a slightly acid to neutral soil (pH 6 to 7) and plenty of sun.

How to Plant
• *Seeds:* Soak seeds overnight in warm water, then sow them ½ inch deep, 4 inches apart, in rows 4 inches apart. In a year they'll grow into crowns, which you can transplant, as described below, to their permanent bed.
• *Crowns:* Dig a trench 1 foot deep and 1 foot wide. If your trench can't be long, dig several 4 feet apart. Fill the whole length of each trench 6 inches deep with soil mixed with any or all of the following: well-rotted manure, bonemeal, compost, humus, peat moss. (Asparagus is a rich feeder.) Then place the roots 15 inches apart, crowns up, spreading the roots carefully so they don't break. Cover with 3 inches of rich compost mixed with soil, firming it down well. Leave the remaining 3 inches (to the top of the trench) until the plants start to sprout. As the shoots come up, gradually fill in the rest of the trench with soil, each time leaving the tips of the shoots exposed, until ground level is reached.

Germination Time
• Seeds germinate in 21 to 30 days.

Care During Growth
• Once seedlings are well up, cover the bed with a mulch of shredded leaves or well-rotted hay. In dry weather, feel beneath the mulch to see whether the bed needs watering: It's essential that asparagus get moisture throughout the growing season

to provide food storage for the next year's crop.

Maturation Time
• Asparagus is mature by late spring.

Harvesting
• After the 1- to 3-year waiting period, harvest asparagus spears when the stalks are 6 to 9 inches tall, and up to about ¾ inch in diameter, but before the tips start to open. Cut the stalks off with a knife at slightly below ground level. Leave any thin stalks for later harvest.

• Extend your asparagus harvest through much of the summer by harvesting first from only part of the bed, allowing the rest of the plants to grow into full leaf. In mid-June cut the ferny tops off some of the unharvested plants. By the end of June and into July, you can begin harvesting spears that have grown from the newly cut plants. You can do this with other unharvested parts of the bed at 4-week intervals until perhaps late September. The plants aren't harmed as long as you allow them to come to full leaf before you cut them.

• Continue watering even after harvesting: The plants need ample moisture until the end of the growing season.

• After the first very hard frost, cut the tops to the ground and cover the bed with well-rotted strawy manure or compost, or other organic mulch.

Storing
• Store asparagus without washing, in a cold place. Plan to use it within a couple of weeks.

Diseases and Pests
• Asparagus beetles, bacterial diseases, Botrytis blight, damping off, Japanese beetles.

Garden Tips
• If you like white asparagus, keep heaping soil around the spears as they grow, leaving only the tips exposed.

• Asparagus is a very strong feeder and needs lots of nitrogen, so add liberal amounts of well-rotted stable manure to the bed each year.

• Basil, parsley, and tomatoes are considered good companion plantings for asparagus. Tomatoes are said to deter asparagus beetles.

• Calendula is also said to deter asparagus beetles.

Kitchen Tips
• Asparagus continues to age and toughen after it has been cut, so the sooner you cook it, the better.

• Before refrigerating asparagus, trim the stem ends slightly (trim further just before using) and wrap the cut ends in wet paper towels.

• If you bend a fresh asparagus stalk carefully, it will snap at the point where it becomes tender—just where you want it to.

• It's possible to use much more of the asparagus spear than the part that snaps off from the bottom, but you have to peel rather deeply (use a potato peeler) to remove all the tough outer portion.

• When you've trimmed asparagus spears, stand them upright in the refrigerator in a small amount of cold water, covered with a plastic bag. You can also refresh limp asparagus this way. Let it stand in cold water for ½ hour before cooking.

• Asparagus can be cooked in a flat pan, but there's always the danger of overcooking the delicate tips. It's better to tie the spears together or wrap them in cheesecloth in bundles of 8 or 10. Stand them in gently boiling water, with the tips just above water level, for about 12 minutes. You can invert a deep saucepan as a cover. The tips will steam to softness while the tougher stems cook.

• Before serving, roll asparagus quickly in a dishtowel to remove all the water.

• Parboil fresh asparagus tips and pat them dry; then sauté lightly in butter and add to an omelet.

• Fresh young asparagus spears are delicious raw. Wash them and serve with a mayonnaise sauce. Or cut them up to use in salads.

• One pound of asparagus will usually serve three people.

. . .

Asparagus Beetles

Both the common blue-and-red asparagus beetle and the twelve-spotted asparagus beetle (tan with twelve spots) are about ¼ inch long. They winter over in cracks in wood and tree bark and in woody garden debris, emerging in early spring to attack asparagus plants and to lay their tiny black eggs on the new shoots. Shortly, orange or grayish sluglike larvae hatch to feed on the asparagus tips and on the green berries that form under the fernlike sprays of the plants. Later, the larvae burrow into the ground to pupate, emerging as beetles and repeating their life cycle. It's the adult beetles that chiefly damage the spears. There are two or more generations of beetles in a season, depending on weather. Wet weather holds them in check, and both eggs and larvae are killed by cold.

Manifestation

• Asparagus tips show evidence of gnawing, and spears often have black stains. Sometimes the plants lose their leaves.

To Combat

• Prevent beetles from wintering over by removing all debris from the asparagus bed at the end of the season.
• When harvesting asparagus, cut the shoots close to the ground.
• Remove and destroy the berries on the undersides of asparagus fronds, where the larvae of the twelve-spotted asparagus beetle chiefly feed.
• When you see beetles, hold a wide-mouthed jar of alcohol or an ammonia-water mixture under them and place your hand above the beetles. They will at once fall into the jar.
• Ladybugs and chalcid wasps are natural predators of asparagus beetles. You can buy larval forms of these at many garden nurseries and supply houses.
• Marigolds are said to deter asparagus beetles. Plant them here and there in your asparagus bed. The same is said of tomato plants.

Bacillus Thuringiensis ✦

Often referred to as Bt, this bacterium kills leaf-eating caterpillars, the larvae of moths and butterflies that cause much crop destruction. It comes in the form of a white powder that, when mixed with water, is sprayed on infested plants every 3 or 4 days. Specific for caterpillars, Bt is not harmful to pets or humans. It is especially valued for its lethal effect on cabbage loopers. (Bear in mind, however, that Bt can kill the larvae of many beautiful and beneficial butterflies.)

Bacterial Diseases ✦

See also *Cucumber beetles* (they carry bacterial diseases to many plants); *Flea beetles* (they carry bacterial wilt to corn)

Bacteria are microscopic organisms that can be recognized only by the destruction they cause in the garden. The chief bacterial diseases of garden plants are bacterial blight, bacterial wilt, and crown gall. Affected plants are asparagus, beans, beets, blackberries, blueberries, cabbage, celery, corn, cucumbers, eggplants, grapes, lettuce, melons, onions, parsnips, potatoes, pumpkins, raspberries, squashes, strawberries, sweet potatoes, tomatoes, and turnips.

The bacteria are carried chiefly in the digestive tracts of cucumber beetles, where they overwinter and are excreted on plants in the spring. They can also survive in the soil over the winter. Plants that are bruised or wounded in any way are particularly susceptible to these diseases.

Manifestation
• Bacterial blight and wilt can be recognized by spotting on young pods and drooping of leaves, which often show dull splotches and subsequently shrivel. Infected vines usually die.

• Crown gall can be recognized by the growth of hard or spongy knobs at the bases of many kinds of plants,

17

just above the soil or at soil level. The plants gradually weaken and may die.

To Combat
• Avoid careless handling of plants, which may result in injury.
• Remove and compost diseased plants wherever possible.
• Practice crop rotation, and avoid placing susceptible plants in any bed where bacterial disease has already struck. The disease organisms in the soil are likely to die out in 2 or 3 years.

• Avoid introducing crown gall to your garden by not buying any plants that show bumpy growths at the base. Wilt-resistant varieties of cucumbers, melons, and squashes are available.
• Cover plants with fine netting or cheesecloth to keep cucumber beetles off them.
• These bacteria don't like acid soil— if your plants can tolerate a fairly high acidity, add shredded oak leaves, aluminum sulfate, or pine needles to your garden soil.

Balm

See *Lemon balm*

Basil (Sweet Basil)

Basil is an easy-to-grow, heat-loving, annual herb whose aromatic leaves and flowers have a unique spicy odor and taste. Sweet basil is the most common type in culinary use, although other varieties—bush basil, lemon basil, lettuce-leaf basil, red basil, among others—are used in cooking, salads, and potpourris. You can grow basil from seeds or transplants; transplants are somewhat easier to manage.

When to Plant
• Transplants can go into the garden after the last frost. Seeds should be sown a little later, when the ground has warmed further; they tend to molder if the soil is cold and wet.

Where to Plant
• Basil will grow in any average, well-drained garden soil. It does best in slightly acid soil (pH 6.5) and can take full sun or partial shade.

How to Plant

• Sow seeds ¼ to ½ inch deep, 2 inches apart, in rows 12 inches apart. Place transplants 6 inches apart in rows 12 inches apart.

Germination Time

• Seeds usually germinate in 7 days, occasionally a little longer.

Care During Growth

• When seedlings are 2 inches high, thin them to stand 6 inches apart. After the second set of true leaves appears, pinch back the tips to increase bushiness.

• Keep pinching off flowers to get more leaf production.

• Be sure to water regularly—basil doesn't tolerate dryness.

Maturation Time

• Basil matures (produces seed-bearing flowers) in about 85 days.

Harvesting

• The best harvesting time for leaf flavor is when the flower buds just appear. The most aromatic part of the plant is the top 3 or 4 leaf nodes: Cut through the stem just below them. You can do this several times during the season.

• The final harvest, for using the leaves fresh or dried, should be cut just before full bloom.

Storing

• Keep basil in near-fresh condition by washing the leaves and stems, shaking them well or rolling them gently in a towel to remove as much moisture as possible, then putting them in a tightly closed glass jar in the refrigerator. Use within 3 or 4 days.

• To dry, put basil leaves in a paper bag, twist it closed, and hang it in your kitchen. Shake the bag now and then. Look into it after several days. Drying time depends on the amount of moisture in the air.

• For faster drying, remove the leaves from the stems and spread them on a screen or a clean porous cloth in a dark, well-ventilated place.

• Basil leaves also freeze well. Dip them in boiling water for a couple of seconds, then place them on paper towels, roll up, put in a plastic bag, and freeze.

Garden Tips

• If you're late in removing leaves, cut through the stems just below the leaves at the flower base, and in a week or so you'll have new leaves.

• The flavor of basil leaves degenerates as fall approaches. And once the plants set seed, the leaves are useless for flavoring.

• If you want basil seeds, wait until they've ripened on the plant. Then remove the flowers, separate out the seeds, and let them dry. Wrap them carefully in a paper towel, and store them over the winter in a corner of the refrigerator.

• Grow a few tomato plants in your basil bed: They're said to improve the growth and flavor of basil. Or plant basil with asparagus.

Kitchen Tips

• Use fresh basil leaves in salads.

• Dig up some of your basil plants in the fall and put them in pots in a sunny window. This way you can have fresh basil through much of the winter. (The flavor isn't quite as rich as that of garden-grown basil, however.)

• Pesto sauce is made principally from chopped fresh basil, olive oil, grated cheese, and crushed nuts (pine nuts, walnuts, or hazelnuts). The oil will rise to the top, and the sauce will keep very well in the refrigerator for weeks. There should be about ¾ inch of oil on top. For longer storage, freeze small quantities. Use pesto on everything: vegetables, potatoes, fish, and poultry, as well as pasta. Incidentally, if you're making pesto sauce to freeze, wait to mix in the grated cheese until after the sauce has thawed.

• Dried basil will bring more flavor to your food if you crush or crumble the leaves well between your palms as you add them.

• Make basil-flavored butter. Add 4 tablespoons chopped, fresh leaves to ½ cup butter at room temperature. Keep the butter in small glasses in the coldest part of the refrigerator, or store the glasses in the freezer. They'll always be on hand when you want a first-class sauce for a hot vegetable, fish, or meat.

• Make basil-flavored vinegar. Use a soft white wine or rice wine vinegar, add chopped fresh basil, and just bring to a simmer. Let cool, bottle, and store.

Bean

Growing beans is beneficial to garden soil—they add nitrogen.

All varieties of beans can be eaten fresh or left on the vines to dry for storing and later eating, or for planting the following season. Beans most commonly grown for eating fresh are snap beans (green garden beans), wax beans (yellow podded), Romano (Italian green) beans, lima beans, and fava (broad) beans. Beans most commonly grown for drying, often referred to as shell beans, are black-eyed peas, cowpeas, garbanzo beans (chick-peas), great northern beans, white (field) and red kidney beans, lentils, Mexican beans, mung beans, pinto beans, and soybeans. Again, these can also be eaten fresh. Most beans come in both pole and bush varieties.

Pole beans have trailing or climbing vines, from 5 to 10 feet or more in length. They bear later than bush beans but produce fruit over a longer period. They generally have larger pods and a greater yield. Since they're usually grown on fences, poles, or trellises, they take up less garden space than bush beans and are easier to harvest.

Bush beans bear pods earlier but stop growing at a certain point. They don't require the trouble of being tied or trained to supports, but they do take up more space in the garden.

When to Plant

• Beans are not vigorously hardy. With the exception of fava beans and soybeans, they like fairly hot weather. So delay planting until the soil is thoroughly warmed—well after the last frost, when night temperatures remain reliably above 50°F. You can sow additional beans up to a month later.

• For a fall crop, plant pole beans about 2 months before your first frost, bush beans a week or so later, and pole limas about 10 days before regular pole beans.

• Fava beans can be planted 2 weeks earlier than regular beans unless you have a very cold season.

• Lima beans and black-eyed peas like slightly warmer soil than other beans; you might want to start them indoors about 2 weeks before sowing green or wax beans outdoors. Or plant them outdoors about 2 weeks after the soil is warmed. Vining types of Fordhook limas, however, can be planted when you plant regular beans.

• If you want to take a chance on an early planting of bush beans, sow them in cool soil (though well after frost). Then make three successive plantings at 1-month intervals. This method will give you a continuous supply of beans until the end of the growing season.

Where to Plant

• Beans will grow in a wide range of soils if they are deep but not heavy, well drained but not too dry. Spade some compost or well-rotted manure into the soil before planting. Beans prefer a slightly acid soil (pH around 6) and partial shade.

How to Plant

• For quicker germination, soak bean seeds in warm water for a couple of days, or until you see them sprout. Then plant them.

- Pole beans

  Pole beans are best sown in rows and trained to grow up a trellis or high fence or on poles arranged tepee fashion (three 6- or 8-foot poles tied near the top with a cord or wire, forming a pyramid).

  For tepee or pole planting, poles should be rough so the vines don't slip. Plant 6 seeds in a circle around the bottom of each pole, about 2 inches deep, and cover them with loose soil, tamping down lightly. Tepees should be 3 to 4 feet apart.

  If you are using single poles, set them 2 feet apart, each in the center of a mound of soil, and plant 6 to 8 seeds equidistant around each pole.

  If you are planting beans in a row along a fence, sow them 2 inches deep and 2 to 3 inches apart. Or plant them 2 inches deep in hills that are 6 inches apart, 4 seeds to a hill. Cover with loose soil and tamp down.

  Pole limas are big plants; sow their seeds 1 inch deep, 2 feet apart. All lima beans should be planted with the "eyes" down.

- Bush beans

  Plant seeds 1 inch deep, 3 inches apart, in rows 2 feet apart.

Germination Time

- Seedlings emerge in 6 to 14 days.

Care During Growth

- Pole beans

  Thin beans sown in rows to 6 inches apart when the plants are 3 inches high. If you have planted in mounds or hills, thin to 2 plants per hill.

  Thin beans sown around single poles or the poles of tepees to 3 plants per pole before they begin to climb.

- Bush beans

  Thin seedlings to 14 inches apart when they're 3 inches high.

- Beans don't like hard surface soil. Cultivate now and then around the plants, but not too deeply—they have shallow roots.

- Beans don't need high-nitrogen fertilizers, which are likely to encourage foliage growth at the expense of fruits. But they do like phosphorus. Add some rock phosphate, dried fish meal, fish emulsion, poultry manure, or manure tea every 2 weeks after germination.

- Plenty of moisture is essential for bean growth, especially during the hot summer. Water early in the morning or early enough in the evening so the leaves will dry by nightfall. But try not to wet the foliage; doing so encourages mildew.

- Once the ground is very warm, you can use a straw mulch, which helps conserve water in the soil.

- Now and then throughout the season examine the undersides of leaves for insect eggs. Remove and destroy them.

• Pole beans will continue producing as long as you pick the fruit. Once both pole and bush beans begin to set seeds (when the pods start to become dry), they stop blossoming and producing new fruit.

Maturation Time

• Pole beans: 60 to 70 days after sowing seeds. Pole limas, around 80 days.

• Bush beans: about 53 days after sowing seeds.

Harvesting

• Bean plants produce more if you pick the beans promptly. Young beans not only have more flavor but can be eaten uncooked. If you let the early beans grow large, the vines will produce fewer pods. So pick regularly for a continuous crop. Pole beans yield fruit until frost; bush beans are usually through by the end of August.

• Pick beans late in the day, when the vines are dry.

• Beans that you intend to store dried can be left on the vines to dry at the end of the season, or the entire vines, with pods, can be pulled up and hung indoors in a dry place. The beans are ready to be shelled if the pods rattle when you shake them. The individual beans inside are thoroughly dry and ready for storing if you can't dent

them when you press them with your fingernail.

Storing

• Store fresh limas in their pods for as long as 3 weeks if the temperature is kept close to freezing. Shelled limas don't store as well as those kept in their pods.

• It's a good idea, before storing any dried beans, to heat them in a 150° oven for ½ hour—doing so will get rid of any bean weevils that may be present, which might otherwise continue to breed during storage.

• Store dried beans in large glass jugs where it's dry and the temperature is around 35°F.

Diseases and Pests

• Anthracnose, aphids, bacterial blight, Botrytis blight, borers (weevils), cabbage loopers, corn borers, corn earworms, cucumber beetles, damping off, flea beetles, fusarium rot, Japanese beetles, leafhoppers, leaf miners, mealybugs, Mexican bean beetles, mildew (lima beans, especially), mites, mosaic virus, nematodes (snap beans, especially), root rot, tarnished plant bugs, thrips, whiteflies.

Garden Tips

• Leave bean plants alone while they are wet with dew or rain or after watering. Any bruises made at such times open them to bacterial diseases.

• Don't plant all your beans at one time. Continuous sowings will give you a steady supply of beans and keep you from being inundated with a great number at one time.

• Don't plant beans near gladioli, which can harbor mosaic virus, which aphids can transmit to beans.

• Don't plant beans near onions, which will inhibit their growth.

• Interplanting potatoes between bean rows may repel Mexican bean beetles.

• Good companion plantings for beans are said to be cabbage, carrots, cauliflower, celery, corn, cucumbers, eggplants, lima beans, potatoes, radishes, rosemary, sage, and summer savory. Rosemary is said to deter Mexican bean beetles.

• Since beans like partial shade, try planting them among sunflowers. They'll also climb the stems.

• Plant pole beans in your corn patch. They'll enrich the soil, climb the cornstalks, and be easy to harvest.

• If you have a low tree or high shrub, try planting pole beans around it. With a little initial assistance, the vines will climb the branches and the beans will be very easy to pick.

• Don't let your trellised beans grow horizontally: The vines are likely to twist tightly around each other and hinder growth.

• Pole lima beans are better flavored than bush types.

• Fresh lima bean pods will open more easily if you let them stand a few hours after you've picked them.

• Fava beans don't do well in hot weather.

• Toward the end of the season, any garden beans you've left on the vines too long can be treated like shell beans.

• Soybeans thrive during a cool, wet season.

• At the end of the summer, pull up and dispose of, or compost, all bean vines, roots and all, to prevent bean beetles from overwintering in them.

Kitchen Tips

• One pound of cooked string beans will serve four people.

• Remove bean strings quickly by snapping off one end and pulling this down the side of the bean, drawing the string with it. Then do the same with the other end of the bean, pulling the string down the other side.

• Sauté string beans in a small amount of oil before you add liquid to them. The flavor will be enormously improved, and you will preserve vitamins by shortening the overall cooking time.

• The fewer string beans in a pan, the quicker they'll cook and the better they'll taste. If you cook more than a pound at a time, use two pans.

• One pound of fresh lima beans will

yield 1¼ cups shelled. For a vegetable course, this makes two slightly scant servings.

• If fresh lima beans are hard to shell, use scissors to cut a thin strip along the inner edge of the pod, where the beans are attached.

• Put a whole onion in the pan when you cook fresh lima beans. Doing so will give the beans fine flavor; they'll need little else but salt and butter.

• If you have dried your garden beans for future use, 1 cup of small beans will give about 2½ cups cooked; 1 cup of large beans, about 2 cups cooked.

• You needn't soak dried beans in cold water for hours to soften them. Instead, cover with boiling water and let stand for 1 hour before cooking.

• You can get rid of the gassiness produced by cooked dried beans if you soak them for 2 or 3 hours before cooking, then throw away the soaking water, cover with boiling water, and cook for ½ hour. Discard that water too. Cover with more boiling water, and cook till the beans are done.

• Simmer—don't boil—dried beans, or they're likely to stick to the pot as well as cause their water to foam up and overflow. Stir gently with a wooden spoon to avoid breaking the skins.

• Dried beans cooked without salt become tender sooner.

Bean Beetles

See *Mexican bean beetles*

Beet (Beetroot)

Hardy and easy to grow, beets do well under most conditions. Their eating quality depends on rapid, uninterrupted development. Some varieties have a medium red interior, others are a very dark red. If you're especially fond of beet greens, you might want to grow beets primarily for these, without waiting for the roots to reach maturity.

Beet seeds are notoriously slow to germinate and spotty at that. Many gardeners prefer to buy transplants.

When to Plant

• Although the general advice is to plant beet seeds as early in the spring as the soil can be worked, cold, wet soil inhibits germination. Plant about 2 weeks before the frost-free date in your area. Seeds will germinate at 50°F.

• You can plant beet seeds every 2 weeks until midsummer for harvesting all season. If you want large beets to harvest in the fall for winter storage, plant seeds in early July. You can also get a fall crop of "baby beets" by planting as late as mid-August.

Where to Plant

• Beets grow best in slightly alkaline soil (pH 7.0 to 7.5). Mix manure, potash, seaweed, wood ashes, or a little lime into the soil before planting. Beets also prefer a deep, fine soil, such as a rich, sandy, well-drained loam. They like sun, although they'll tolerate some shade.

How to Plant

• Beet seeds have hard shells. To help germination along, soak the seeds in water overnight. Or spread them on a hard surface and roll them with a rolling pin.

• Spade up the bed about 1 foot deep, smooth it, then scatter the seeds thinly, about 10 to a foot, in rows 15 inches apart. If you want to mark the rows, since the seeds germinate slowly and unevenly, mix beet seeds with radish seeds, which are fast germinators, before sowing. Cover with ½ inch soil, and press firmly. Water well.

• Or sow beet seeds by the broadcast method, scattering them more or less evenly over the bedding space. Cover with ½ inch soil, press firmly, and water well.

• Mist the bed daily, especially in hot weather.

• Space transplants 5 inches apart.

Germination Time

• Beet seeds take 1 to 2 weeks to germinate.

Care During Growth

• When the tops are about 6 inches high, thin the plants to 5 inches apart. (Use the thinnings in salads or for cooked greens.)

• Very dry weather (lack of water) makes beet roots turn woody, so be sure to water daily when necessary, preferably in the early morning. Mulching keeps the ground cool and conserves the water in the soil. Cool soil will give sweeter roots.

Maturation Time

• Maturation time is 30 to 35 days for greens, 50 to 70 days for roots.

Harvesting

• Harvest beet greens when the leaves are 4 to 6 inches long.

• Beet roots are tenderest and best tasting when young and are generally ready for pulling when they're 1½ to 2 inches in diameter. Harvest larger roots any time after this, but the larger they grow, the more woody they become.

• If you plan to store the roots, be sure to avoid cuts and bruises.

• The first hard frost improves the flavor of beets planted for fall harvesting.

• Remove the tops right after picking, since the stems and leaves will continue to draw moisture from the roots. Use the leaves in salads or for cooking.

Storing

• Beets for fall storage can be left in the ground until after the first light frost. Dig them up on a cold, dry day. Leave about 1 inch of stem. Never wash them, but allow the roots to dry before storing.

• Beets like cold and dampness. Keep them where it is as close to 32°F as possible, but with very high humidity. Pack them loosely in baskets, large cans, or similar containers, in moist sand, sawdust, leaves, or sphagnum moss. Check now and then to see that they don't dry out (dryness causes wrinkling of the skins).

Diseases and Pests

• Armyworms, bacterial diseases, cabbage loopers, cabbage maggots, corn borers, corn-root aphids, damping off, flea beetles, green peach aphids, leafhoppers, leaf miners, scab, tarnished plant bugs.

Garden Tips

• A beet seed is actually a fruit, containing one to six seeds. That's why some seeds will give rise to more than one plant.

• If beets don't do well, it's probably because the soil is too acid. Scratch in a little lime.

• Beets can often be left in the ground

over the winter if you protect them with a heavy layer of mulch.

• Beets grown in the cool temperatures of early spring will store more sugar in their roots.

• Don't overwater beets before warm weather comes—cold, wet soil is likely to cause them to bolt to seed.

• You can grow beets and onions together without either shading the other. Other good companion plants for beets are Brussels sprouts, cabbage, cauliflower, kale, kohlrabi, and turnips.

• You can also sow beets in a bed from which you've just harvested early vegetables, such as peas.

Kitchen Tips

• Two pounds of fresh beets will serve four to six people.

• You can cook beet greens in a little liquid, much as you cook spinach. (They taste better than spinach!)

• Beet greens, especially young, tender ones, are really delightful in salads. Before cooking beets to serve as a vegetable, cut off the greens, wash and chill them. Then shred them and mix with any salad greens.

• You can also cook beets with both the greens and the skins on, then plunge them into cold water. The skins will slip off easily, and the greens will be tender and delicious.

• Beets cooked with their skins on will remain very red if you leave about 2 inches of stem. A little vinegar

or cream of tartar added to the cooking water also keeps them very red.
• Baked beets are twice as good as boiled ones. Scrub but don't peel them. Bake at 325° for at least 1 hour or until the beets have totally shrunk away from the skins and the skins themselves are thoroughly wrinkled.

• If you are adding beets to a mixed dish, put them in just before serving—they stain everything.
• Beet stains on plastic or wooden bowls are difficult or impossible to remove. Remember this when preparing or storing.

Beetles 🪲

See also *Asparagus beetles*; *Blister beetles*; *Colorado potato beetles*; *Cucumber beetles*; *Flea beetles*; *Japanese beetles*; *Mexican bean beetles*

With some exceptions (see "To Combat"), beetles do harm to gardens in both their adult and their larval (grub or borer) stages. Most harmful adult beetles are brown or black and usually wingless. Those that injure plants are likely to have short, squarish-shaped jaws. Beetle larvae can be differentiated from the larvae of other insects because their head parts are distinct from their body portions and have antennae.

Manifestation
• Beetles devour leaves and flowers, including the blossoms of vegetable plants. The leaves are often eaten away, sometimes leaving only the ribs.

To Combat
• Remove garden debris at the end of the growing season: This is where many beetle eggs shelter over the winter.
• Cultivate the soil early in the spring, exposing beetle eggs and larvae to the air and to natural enemies.
• One of your best garden friends is

a beetle that eats other beetles: the large, fierce-looking, and swift-moving black ground beetle, often found under stones or matted leaves. In both its adult and its larval stages it eats the eggs and grubs of many plant-loving beetles.
• Set up bird feeders and high birdbaths, and leave nest-building materials (hair, rags, string, yarn) in bushes near your garden to entice birds. Bird enemies of garden beetles are Baltimore orioles, chickadees, cuckoos, house wrens, titmice, and towhees.
• Brew up some wormwood tea (see

Repellents for details), and spray the ground well with it in both spring and fall. Beetles hate this.

• Interplant susceptible crops with buckwheat, clover (all varieties), or soybeans—they make the soil inhospitable to beetle grubs. (They also enrich the soil.) Or use these as a cover crop for one season to cleanse the soil of beetle grubs.

Birds

Birds are one of nature's best means of combating garden insect pests. The diet of swallows, for example, consists almost entirely of insects and their larvae. Encourage birds by placing birdhouses, as well as birdbaths (make sure they're catproof) and bird feeders, in or near your garden. But go easy on feeding birds during the summer—let your garden insects provide their diet. Among birds that are the best insect predators are Baltimore orioles, black phoebes, bluebirds, bobolinks, chickadees, cuckoos, doves, house wrens, kingbirds, meadowlarks, purple martins, robins, sparrows, swallows, titmice, towhees, and woodpeckers.

Birds do little to harm most gardens (excluding orchards), but they do like blueberries, grapes, lettuce, peas, black and red raspberries, strawberries, sunflowers, and tomatoes, and occasionally they attack seedlings and transplants. The best way to protect your berry bushes from birds is to cover the bushes with birdproof netting as soon as the fruit begins to ripen, preferably on a frame that will hold the netting well above the fruit. The netting should reach the ground and can be anchored with bricks. Strawberry plants can also be covered with netting. Tie sunflower heads in old nylon stockings if you see birds beginning to do damage to them. Tomato plants grown in cages are easily covered with cheesecloth or plastic mesh or other netting to protect the fruit from birds.

Blackberry

Blackberries are quite winter hardy, though less so than raspberries. The early-ripening Darrow blackberry is exceptionally hardy. But with proper mulching (see "Garden Tips") most blackberries can survive very cold northern winters. The roots of blackberry plants are perennial, but the fruit-bearing canes are biennial: New ones grow each season that will bear fruit the next. Once they have fruited, the canes die. Blackberries are self-pollinating.

There are two kinds of blackberries: bush types, with erect canes that need no support; and vine or trailing types, also called dewberries, which should be tied to trellises or stakes. These are larger and milder than the standard bush blackberries and ripen about a week earlier. Dewberries include the boysenberries, loganberries (vigorous growers but susceptible to winterkill), and youngberries. The trailing varieties send out new roots from the tips of their canes; erect varieties propagate by producing suckers from their roots. There are also thornless blackberries. These are slightly less hardy than the usual blackberry plants, but they'll get through most northern winters if well protected with a mulch.

When to Plant
• Plant blackberries in early spring, as soon as the soil can be easily worked.

Where to Plant
• A fairly high spot in the garden is preferable, but make sure the plants will be shielded from strong winds. An inclined northern slope is ideal. The soil should be moderately fertile and moderately acid (pH 5.00 to 5.75). Although not heavy feeders, blackberries like plenty of organic matter in the soil, which is good for moisture retention. The soil should also be well drained. Blackberries do well in partial shade, but they like morning sun.

How to Plant
• Work a little humus into the soil before planting. Plant bush-type rooted canes 4 feet apart, in rows 6 feet apart. Plant trailing types 6 feet apart, and train them on trellises or tie them to stakes as they grow.
• Immediately after planting, cut the plants to 6 inches in height and see that the center crowns are covered by no more than 2 inches of soil. Press the soil down around and over the roots. Water well.

Care During Growth
• Pruning and watering are the two most important things for good blackberry growth.
• The new fruiting canes, which start growing each spring and will bear berries the following year, should have about 2 inches of their tips nipped off early to encourage lateral growth and more berries.
• Keep plants on the low side—prune them to about 3 feet each June.
• Blackberry plants have shallow roots. Don't cultivate too deeply after planting—only enough to remove weeds.

• When the summer sun gets hot, mulch the plants with grass clippings, old hay, or straw to conserve soil moisture. And water frequently, especially when the berries begin to form.

• Pull up any suckers that emerge far from the main plants.

Maturation Time

• Most blackberries begin to ripen in early midsummer (some early varieties ripen 2 weeks earlier) and continue until early fall.

Harvesting

• Don't pick blackberries when they first turn black—they're still sour. Wait for them to lose their shininess. They should pull easily off the stems, taking their cores with them.

• Berries picked in the early morning are sweeter than those picked in the afternoon.

• Keep picking every few days over the entire harvest period. Continue watering after the harvest, well into September.

Storing

• Blackberries should be kept cool and dry.

• Don't wash blackberries before storing.

Diseases and Pests

• Anthracnose, bacterial diseases, borers, Botrytis blight, mites, rust, sterile-plant virus (also called nubbins).

Garden Tips

• Some garden plants harbor fungi that can attack blackberries, so don't plant berry bushes or vines where eggplants, peppers, potatoes, or tomatoes were grown during the 3 previous years.

• After each harvest, cut out, close to the ground, the canes that have fruited. These should be burned or removed from the garden. Don't compost them.

• You can also thin out some of the new canes after the harvest. The sturdier ones will produce the most fruit the next year.

• After pruning and thinning erect types of blackberries, cut all remaining canes to a height at which they stand stiff and upright.

• Mulch all blackberry plants well for the winter, especially if you expect little snow cover. Use grass clippings, leaves, salt-marsh hay, or straw.

Kitchen Tips

• Well-chilled blackberries are less likely to become mushy when you wash them.

• If you have washed berries and must store them, spread them on a towel to dry before refrigerating.

• All berries are highly crushable. Don't let them stand too long in tall, narrow containers.

• You'll need 4 cups of fresh berries for a 9-inch pie.

• For an unusual dessert, freeze washed and drained blackberries in a flat serving dish; then, at serving time, remove them from the freezer and pour cream over them. The cream will freeze slightly to the berries.

• A great way to freeze blackberries for storage is to lay them out flat in plastic bags (you can sprinkle a little sugar over them if you like) and set the bags in the freezer. When you want to defrost some, just break off a piece of the frozen sheet of berries.

• Try pouring wine over blackberries instead of cream.

• Fresh blackberries that are frozen and then thawed release much of their juice. So if you're making fruit sauce, jelly, or jam, freeze the berries first; the result will be much richer.

Black-eyed Pea (really a bean)

See *Bean*

Blackheart 🐞

Blackheart is a disease of celery plants, caused by too little calcium in the soil, alternating periods of overwetness and prolonged overdryness, and too much salt in the soil. Prolonged extremely hot weather can also bring on blackheart.

Manifestation

• The newly emerging inner leaves of developing celery plants turn dark brown or black.

To Combat

• Add lime to the soil, thus raising the calcium level.

• Plant celery so that it matures when the hottest days of summer are past.

• Water regularly, and don't allow the soil to dry out completely.

• Avoid too much potassium in the soil.

. . .

Blackleg, Black Rot 🐞

Blackleg or black rot is caused by fungi normally present in most garden soils that multiply rapidly when the soil is very wet, the temperature is high, and susceptible plants (cabbage, cauliflower, and other brassicas) are grown in the same spot for several seasons. The fungi can also be transmitted by seeds and by cabbage maggots.

Manifestation
• Plant stems turn black, starting at the surface of the soil.

To Combat
• Practice crop rotation, avoiding for 2 to 3 years planting brassicas in a bed where any grew before.
• Use rotted rather than fresh manure for fertilizing, since fresh manure may carry many of these disease organisms. The same is true of kitchen garbage, especially potato peelings, so use only composted garbage.
• Brassica seeds that you suspect of carrying blackleg fungi can be soaked in 112°F water for ½ hour. Drain and dry them immediately, and store in a cool, dry place until you plant them.

Black Spot

Black spot is a fungus disease that attacks primarily roses, although it also strikes parsnips. It occurs in many soils, and, if a host plant is present, will grow swiftly in wet heat.

Manifestation
• Leaves develop speckled black, circular spots, then turn yellow and drop off.

To Combat
• Plant parsnips in a different bed each year, not returning them to any one bed until 2 or 3 years have passed.
• Don't leave garden debris over the winter.
• Avoid wetting the leaves when watering parsnips.
• Interplant chives with parsnips—they're said to inhibit the growth of the black spot fungus.

• • •

Blister Beetles

There are many varieties of blister beetles, all of which contain a chemical that will raise blisters on the skin if you crush them. Only the adult beetles damage plants—the larvae are actually beneficial, since they eat quantities of grasshopper eggs. Blister beetles appear in early to midsummer, swarming over the leaves and blossoms of many vegetables, especially potatoes and tomatoes. The beetles are ½ to ¾ inch long and come in many colors: black, brown, gray, or striped.

Manifestation

• Beetle-damaged leaves are full of small holes, as are the blossoms of the ravaged plants, so fruit often fails to form. Many of the leaves blister beetles feed on end up looking like lace.

To Combat

• Probably the best way to control these beetles is hand picking: Knock them off into a wide-mouthed jar of soapy water, alcohol, or an ammonia-water solution. Wear gloves if there's any danger of your crushing the beetles.

• Pyrethrum and rotenone sprays are helpful.

• Cover plants loosely wiith cheese-cloth.

• A dusting of flour on the leaves of attacked plants often deters blister beetles.

Blossom Drop

Blossom drop is seen chiefly in peppers and is usually caused by night temperatures that are too low or alternating periods of extreme dryness and extreme moisture.

Manifestation

• The small white flowers that would normally develop into peppers drop to the ground.

To Combat

• Don't set peppers out too early in the season.

• If a sudden cold spell sets in, cover peppers with cans, buckets, or other protective devices, especially at night.

• • •

Blossom-End Rot

Blossom-end rot is thought to result mainly from calcium deficiency: Either there is not enough calcium in the soil or there isn't enough water in the soil to dissolve the calcium and make it available to the plants. As with blossom drop (see *Blossom Drop* for details), blossom-end rot can also occur when there are alternating periods of extreme dryness and extreme moisture. The chief plants affected by blossom-end rot are eggplants, melons, peppers, summer squashes, and tomatoes.

Manifestation
• Leaves turn yellow and drop off. Plants are stunted. Black, leathery patches develop on the bottoms of the fruit. Bacteria and fungi may also develop on these spots, causing mold or rot.

To Combat
• Mulching helps keep the soil around the plants evenly moist. Or see that there is plenty of organic matter in the soil.
• If the soil is deficient in calcium, add dolomitic limestone.
• If only leaves seem affected, try misting them during the day when the sun is out; doing so can reduce moisture stress on the leaves, and it allows time for evaporation so that mildew won't develop.

Blueberry

Blueberry bushes are easy to grow and are practically free from disease and insect pests. (The wild forms are called billberry or whortleberry.) They grow 4 to 6 feet high and, besides being grown for their fruit, make beautiful shrubs for ornamental plantings and hedges: The foliage is glossy green and turns a brilliant crimson in the fall.

The highbush blueberry is best for the North and grows well up to southern Maine and down to South Carolina. The hardiest varieties are Bluecrop, Blueray, and Northland. There are early-bearing, midsummer-bearing, and late-bearing varieties (see "Maturation"). Although blueberry bushes are self-fruitful to some degree, two or even three varieties should be planted together: Cross-pollination gives larger berries and much heavier production. Or plant an early, a midseason, and a late variety together for better fruiting as well as a longer harvesting season.

The best blueberry shrubs to plant are 2 to 3 years old, and, if possible, have their roots wrapped in a ball of soil covered with burlap. A planting will last 30 years or more.

When to Plant

• Blueberry bushes must be planted when they're dormant: from early to midspring or in late fall, up to the time the ground freezes.

Where to Plant

• The soil should be loose textured, moist but well drained, rich in humus or other organic matter—such as peat moss, pine or oak sawdust, or wood shavings—and very acid (pH 4.0 to 5.5). You can increase soil acidity by adding aluminum sulphate (½ cup mixed with soil and mulched around each plant), or adding a mulch of peat moss, pine needles, shredded or composted oak or mountain laurel leaves, or straw. Plant blueberry bushes in full sun.

How to Plant

• Blueberry bushes should be planted 5 feet apart on all sides. Dig holes wide and deep enough to allow the roots full spread; this is especially important if the plants are bare rooted. Set each bush with its uppermost roots 1 or 2 inches below the surface. If you set them too deeply, the stems may rot; too shallowly, the roots may dry out. Fill in with soil, and tamp down well. An acidic mulch (see "Where to Plant") is good at this time. Then water well. Some growers leave a slight circular depression around each plant to hold water.

Care During Growth

• Don't cultivate around the plants; you may disturb their shallow roots. Instead, keep an acid-rich mulch (see "Where to Plant") replenished each year, around the plants; doing so will control weeds and help conserve soil moisture.

• Apply some well-rotted manure each May.

• Blueberries need lots of water. Feel under the mulch: If the soil seems dry, it's time to water. Water is especially important during the first year after planting and also in the spring, when fruit is developing. Blueberries need a couple of inches of water every 10 days or so, more frequently during hot weather. Continue watering throughout the fall if there's a dry spell.

• A sawdust mulch in midfall will protect the bushes against possible winter injury.

• Pruning: Pruning isn't necessary until blueberry bushes are 4 to 5 years old. Even then, in the Northeast it should be kept to a minimum. Prune while the plants are dormant— in late fall, winter, or early spring. Cut out the older, unproductive stems and branches or any wood that seems diseased. (Burn it or cart it away— don't compost it.)

Maturation Time

• Blueberry plants will start to bear the year after transplanting. They generally fruit during July and August, but some early varieties start ripening in late June, and some late varieties produce berries in September. Most bushes produce fruit for about a month.

Harvesting
• In its prime, when a blueberry bush is 6 to 8 years old, it will yield 4 to 6 quarts of berries in a season.
• Don't pick the berries when they first turn blue—they have to hang for about a week to reach full sweetness. A ripe berry will fall easily into your hand at the lightest pull. Picking sessions should be about a week apart, preferably early in the day, and never immediately after a rain (wet berries decay quickly).

Storing
• Blueberries will keep well for 2 weeks or more if you spread them shallowly on a platter or cookie sheet in the refrigerator and keep them dry.
• They can also be frozen and will remain flavorful for 6 months or more. But they become mushy when thawed.

Diseases and Pests
• Bacterial diseases, birds, Botrytis blight, flea beetles, mealybugs, mummy berry, powdery mildew, scale, thrips.

Garden Tips
• It never hurts to add 3 or 4 inches of peat moss or old sawdust and 1 cup or so of cottonseed meal around each plant each year. Other good mulches are bark chips and shredded newspaper.
• If you want extra-big berries each year, cut off some of the shoot tips so there are no more than 4 or 5 buds to a branch.
• Don't fertilize after June 1—doing so stimulates production of new shoots that won't have time to develop the strength to withstand the winter.
• If blueberries are undeveloped, the soil may be too alkaline. A blue hydrangea bush growing among your blueberry plants will help you keep tabs on the acidity of the soil: If it blooms pinkish, the soil needs more acidity. Add ferrous sulphate and peat moss.
• Pick up and remove all dropped, shriveled-looking berries; these may harbor mummy berry fungus, which can spread to the other berries.
• When it's very cold and windy, pile snow around each blueberry bush to protect it. Or form a low, round wire fence around each bush, and fill the enclosed area with snow.

Kitchen Tips
• Don't wash blueberries until you need them. Wet berries don't keep as long as dry ones. If you have washed

the berries and must store them, spread them on a towel to dry before you refrigerate them.

• Well-chilled blueberries are less likely to become mushy when you wash them.

• For an unusual dessert, freeze washed and drained blueberries in a flat serving dish; then, at serving time, remove from the freezer and pour cream over them. The cream will freeze slightly to the berries.

• You'll need 4 cups of fresh berries for a 9-inch pie.

• For an exceptional blueberry pie, bake the bottom crust first; then cook the berry filling on top of the stove but use only half the berries. When the filling is cooked and thickened, gently blend in the uncooked berries. Fill the baked piecrust and chill.

• Fresh blueberries that are frozen and then thawed release much of their juice. If you're making a fruit sauce, jelly, or jam, freeze the berries first; the result will be much richer.

• A great way to freeze blueberries for storage is to lay them out flat in plastic bags and set the bags in the freezer. When you want to defrost some, just break off a piece of the frozen sheet of berries.

• Pour a little dry or sweet white wine over blueberries instead of cream.

Borage

Sometimes called bee bread, borage is a hardy, annual, summer-blooming herb with attractive blue, star-shaped flowers that appeal to bees and hummingbirds. Its edible blossoms and leaves have a cucumberlike flavor and are used in salads, as garnishes, and as a flavoring for cold summer drinks. Unlike many edible herbs, borage isn't usually dried but is used fresh from the garden.

The plants grow up to 2 feet high. If you let some of the flowers go to seed, borage generally seeds itself year after year. It does not transplant well.

When to Plant

• Plant borage seeds as soon as the ground can be worked.

Where to Plant

• Borage tolerates poor soil; in fact, too-rich soil produces leggy plants. The soil (pH 6 to 7) should be friable and well drained, slightly on the dry side. Plant in a sunny spot.

How to Plant

• Sow the seeds about 1 inch apart. Don't bury them, but strew soil lightly over them, then press down with a board. Water afterward, using a fine spray.

Germination Time
• Seedlings emerge in 7 to 14 days.

Care During Growth
• Once seedlings are up, they don't require much watering. When they are about 2 inches tall, thin them to 10 inches apart.
• Surround the plants with a fine-grained mulch over the summer, and enough moisture will usually be conserved in the soil to keep them going well.

Maturation Time
• Borage takes about 80 days to produce seed, but the young leaves (and blossoms) can be picked at any time.

Harvesting
• Choose the tenderest leaves for use in salad, picking them from the tops of the plants. Older leaves (see "Kitchen Tips") can be used in cooked dishes.
• Borage leaves are not often picked for drying, though the dried leaves can be used in making tea. Pick them late on a sunny, dry day and spread them evenly in a nonhumid atmosphere.

Storing
• Store dried leaves in airtight bottles.

Garden Tips
• Since borage is very attractive to bees, plant it where you want sure pollination of other plants.
• Borage seems to repel tomato worms. Use it as a companion planting among your tomatoes. Other good companion plants are squashes and strawberries.

Kitchen Tips
• Use young borage leaves or thin slices of the peeled fleshy part of borage stalks to give a cucumber flavor to salads.
• Borage blossoms are fine added to salads.
• Add a little water to fresh borage leaves, cook them like spinach, then shred and serve them with a butter or cream sauce.

Borors

See also *Corn borers*

There are many kinds of borers, but they generally fall into two groups:

Vine borers (also known as squash vine borers and stem borers) are usually the larvae of an orange-and-black moth that lays its eggs on the stems and at the soil-stem line of the vines of cucumbers, eggplants, gourds, melons, pumpkins, summer and winter squashes, and tomatoes.

Cane borers, the larvae of beetles and sawflies, infest woody plants such as blackberries, currants, elderberries, and raspberries, as well as many ornamental bushes.

Manifestation

• *Vine borers*: In spring, rows or clusters of tiny red or orange eggs may be seen at the bases of plant stems, where they emerge from the soil or just below the soil surface. About midsummer, vines may show little holes, with a greenish froth around them. Plants may suddenly wilt. Look for a tiny pile of "sawdust" (frass) near the stems—this is larval excrement, a sure sign that a grub is at work.

• *Cane borers*: Eggs are laid near the tips of berry canes. If the tips seem to droop around midsummer, look for borer holes. Later the tips will wilt and fall over.

To Combat

• Vine borers

Don't leave vegetation to decompose and overwinter in the garden. Pull up vines, and burn them or bag and dispose of them.

Wood ashes well sprinkled over the ground often prevent borers from entering plants. You can also shake fine wood ashes over vines and leaves when they're wet to repel borer larvae.

A mulch of heavy aluminum foil has been reported to be a successful deterrent to vine borers. The reflected light seems to confuse the moths.

Remove and destroy borer eggs wherever you see them.

Dust the bases of plants, if the infestation is heavy, with rotenone. Dust every 2 days for about a week.

Liquid Bt (Bacillus thuringiensis) injected into vine stems at about the time the first blossoms appear will kill vine borers. If you see holes in the stems, inject into these holes, as well as 1 inch above them. Repeat the treatment in about 10 days.

Once you see evidence of a borer in your plant stem, take a sharp knife and make a longitudinal slit in the stem near the entrance hole, probing carefully until you locate the white grub. Remove and dispose of it. Then press the stem down against the soil and cover the wound—as well as 1 foot on each side of it—with soil. Water well. The vine will produce new roots. You can encourage further rooting if you cover several nodes of the vine with soil.

Make a second planting of summer squash seeds in mid-July. By the time these seedlings are well up, the moths that lay vine borer eggs are gone.

Cover plants with netting or screening attached to stakes and anchored to the ground with bricks or stones until midsummer,

when the egg-laying moths are gone.

• Cane borers

Wherever you see evidence of cane borers, cut off the affected cane about 1 foot below the wilted portion, or below the borer's entrance hole. Burn this pruning.

Since borers overwinter in prunings and in old, nonproducing canes, be sure to remove and burn these.

Botrytis Blight

Also known as Botrytis bulb rot, Botrytis leaf mold, gray mold, and neck rot (in onions), Botrytis blight is one of the most common fungus diseases of flowers, fruits, and vegetables. It can affect artichokes, asparagus, beans (especially kidney, lima, and snap beans), berries of all kinds, cabbage, endive, lettuce, onions, and tomatoes. Botrytis blight thrives under prolonged cool, wet conditions, both in the garden and during storage. In storage it most commonly attacks berries, cabbage, and onions, and tomatoes if they're bruised.

Manifestation

• Brown, orange, or yellow patches appear on leaves, flowers, and fruit, gradually turning into a furry gray mold that becomes slimy.

• Soft-coated berries, such as raspberries and strawberries, can develop a gray mold on their surfaces.

• Onions, especially thick-necked ones, show a brown streak growing down the center of the neck into the interior, turning the inner section a slimy brown that gradually expands

outward. Onions that have been bruised can develop the blight at the bruised spot.

• Cabbage, especially in the cold damp of storage, can develop Botrytis blight in the vicinity of any bruises.

To Combat

• Good air circulation is important. Take care that foliage isn't overcrowded, particularly in low areas that are cool and damp. Raised beds are helpful, as well as a location that gets full sun.

• Water plants early in the day so moisture on the foliage will evaporate before evening. Try not to wet the leaves.

• Destroy all affected fruits and leaves.

• Remove matted, damp leaves from the garden in the fall to prevent the fungus spores from overwintering there.

• When harvesting onions, take care not to bruise them. Be sure the tops and necks, especially those of thick-necked onions, have thoroughly dried before you bunch or tie them together for storage. Or store them in a single layer in a cold, dry, well-ventilated place.

• The same is true for cabbage heads. Avoid bruising them during harvest, and be sure they have good ventilation during storage.

Boysenberry

Boysenberries are relatives of blackberries and loganberries, with much the same cultivation. Some varieties are thornless. Boysenberries are moderately hardy, requiring heavy winter mulching in areas where temperatures go much below 0°F. Boysenberry shrubs are vigorous, easily grown, and very productive. They can grow to 5 feet in width. The shrubs bear fruit the first year after planting.

When to Plant

• Plant rooted boysenberry canes in early spring, as soon as the soil can be easily worked. In the fall, you can layer the tips of new canes that have grown during the summer (bend them to the ground and cover them with soil); they will root in the spring and can be cut from the mother plant.

Where to Plant

• Boysenberries grow best in moist, well-drained soil, enriched with not too much peat moss or manure

(overrich soil produces excessive growth at the expense of fruit).

• Choose a site near a trellis or fence so the plants can be tied vertically as they grow.

How to Plant

• Stand the roots of the shrub in a pail of water, and let them soak for a few hours before planting.

• Space the plants 6 to 8 feet apart.

• • •

Care During Growth

• Boysenberries need very little care (see *Blackberry* for details on maturation time, harvesting, and storing).

Garden Tips

• Boysenberry shrubs can also be grown close to the ground, by letting the plants sprawl instead of training them to vertical growth—but they'll give considerably fewer berries. In areas with very low winter temperatures, however, sprawling plants are more easily mulched with large amounts of straw.

• At the end of summer, prune out the old canes, cutting them clear to the ground. (The next season's berries will be borne on the new canes.)

Kitchen Tips

• All berries are highly crushable. Don't let them stand too long in tall, narrow containers.

• Never wash boysenberries before storing them in the refrigerator. They'll stay fresh much longer

• Well-chilled boysenberries are less likely to become mushy when you wash them.

• For an unusual dessert, freeze washed and drained boysenberries in a flat serving dish; then, at serving time, remove from the freezer and pour cream over them. The cream will freeze slightly to the berries.

• A great way to freeze boysenberries for storage is to lay them out flat in plastic bags (you can sprinkle a little sugar over them if you like) and set the bags in the freezer. When you want to defrost some, just break off a piece of the frozen sheet of berries.

• Fresh boysenberries that are frozen and then thawed release much of their juice. So if you're making fruit sauce, jelly, or jam, freeze the berries first; the result will be much richer.

• If you're making a boysenberry pie or pudding using frozen berries, use less liquid and a little more thickener, because frozen boysenberries are much juicier when thawed than fresh ones.

• Try pouring wine over boysenberries instead of cream.

Braconid Flies 🐝

Also called braconid wasps, braconid flies parasitize the larvae and pupae of many garden pests, including cutworms, gypsy moth larvae, and hornworms, by laying their eggs in these hosts. The braconid larvae feed on the hosts until and sometimes after they emerge.

Brassicas

See *Broccoli; Brussels sprouts; Cabbage; Cauliflower; Collards; Horseradish; Kale; Kohlrabi; Mustard greens; Radish; Rutabaga; Turnip*

Broccoli

Many varieties of broccoli are now available. Broccoli is easily grown, for either a spring or a fall crop, and can be grown from seeds or transplants. If your season is long enough to grow corn, you can grow broccoli from seed. The quality of broccoli is best when it matures in cool weather. Though not vigorously hardy, it can stand light frost in the fall.

When to Plant

• For a spring crop

Plant broccoli seeds indoors in mid-February, or 6 to 8 weeks before setting out. Seedlings should be about 4 weeks old before being transplanted to the garden 2 weeks before the last spring frost.

Or sow seeds outdoors in very early spring for an early crop. If frost threatens, cover the seedlings with gallon plastic jugs that have had their bottoms removed.

• For a fall crop

Sow seeds outdoors from late spring to early summer, or set out broccoli plants from early to midsummer (plants set out in midsummer have fewer pests problems.

• • •

Where to Plant

• Broccoli likes well-drained, average garden soil that's rich in nitrogen and is neutral to alkaline (pH 6.5 to 7.5). It likes sun but not too much heat.

How to Plant

• For maximum head size and an abundant crop of side shoots, don't crowd broccoli plants. If you are sowing seeds, plant them ¼ to ½ inch deep, 2 feet apart, in rows 2 feet apart. If you are setting out plants, remove the lowest leaves first, then space the plants 2 feet apart on all sides. If your soil is very rich, you can space plants somewhat closer—16 inches apart, in rows 16 inches apart.

Germination Time

• Broccoli seeds take 1 to 2½ weeks to sprout, depending on the warmth of the soil: the cooler the soil, the longer the sprouting time.

Care During Growth

• Broccoli is fairly slow growing. It does best when daytime temperatures are around 70°F and nighttime temperatures 60° to 65°F.

• Once the plants are up, mulch to keep the soil cool. Use aluminized plastic film, old leaves, grass clippings, or hay.

• Be sure the plants get ample water, especially if the season is dry. With plenty of water, broccoli can be made to produce all season.

• Hoe some well-rotted manure into the soil in late spring.

• For broccoli that is to be harvested in the fall, keep watering well into early fall, and add more well-rotted manure.

• When autumn frosts begin, bunch hay or straw loosely around the plants.

Maturation Time

• Broccoli is ready to harvest 55 to 75 days from the date of transplanting to the garden, depending on the variety. If seeds are planted outdoors, the time to maturity from day of planting is 80 to 100 days.

Harvesting

• Harvest the large center broccoli head before the buds open and start to yellow; buds should be tight and green. Cut the stem 6 to 7 inches below the head, at an angle (to discourage stem rot). After this first cutting, side shoots will develop, from which small clusters of tasty heads will grow. A second cutting of the new growth can stimulate still another growth of side shoots, well into the fall. Broccoli will continue growing until the first hard frost.

Storing

• Broccoli should be kept cold, at about refrigerator temperature. Don't wash it before storing.

Diseases and Pests

• Aphids, blackleg, cabbage loopers, cabbage maggots, cabbageworms, cutworms, flea beetles.

Garden Tips

• Avoid planting broccoli in a spot where you've grown other cole crops (Brussels sprouts, cabbage, cauliflower, collards, horseradish, kale, kohlrabi, mustard, radishes, rutabagas, turnips) the year before. Better yet, allow 2 years between such plantings.

• When you harvest broccoli, don't discard the small, tender leaves that grow up the stem and around the head. Cook them up—they're delicious and nutritious!

• If young broccoli plants are exposed to too much cold, they may produce small buttons instead of normal flower stalks.

• Broccoli stalks should be chopped or ground up before being added to the compost pile; otherwise they'll take too long to degrade.

• A good companion planting for broccoli is onions.

Kitchen Tips

• Divide broccoli into 3-inch-long flowerets so it will cook more quickly and stay greener. Cook the stalks too, but peel off the thick skin.

• If broccoli stalks are *very* thick, either split them lengthwise or cut them into cubes and cook them with the buds.

• To cook and serve broccoli whole, try steaming it covered, standing up, like asparagus. The water should come just up to the buds—the steam will cook them. Lift the cover now and then to keep the buds green. They taste best when slightly crackly, so don't worry about their being undercooked: 10 to 12 minutes is usually all it takes.

• If you're going to use broccoli in a mixed dish, parboil it first for 5 minutes. But beware of overcooking—it should still be bright green and crisp.

Broccoli Raab

See *Turnip*

Brussels Sprouts

This "thousand-headed cabbage," called also miniature cabbages, or simply sprouts, is a moisture-loving plant that is best grown for fall harvesting, since very few varieties mature properly in hot weather. Brussels sprouts can, as a matter of fact, withstand frost well, and the sprouts themselves are much tastier after one sharp frost.

When to Plant

• *For early (summer) harvesting:* Start seeds indoors for transplanting to the garden 4 to 6 weeks later, or as soon as the outdoor soil can be worked. Early spring transplanting does no harm, since cold doesn't stop the plants' development. Seeds can also be sown directly in the garden in late spring.

For fall harvesting (preferable): Start seeds indoors in middle to late spring, and transplant seedlings to the garden in midsummer. Some gardeners, where location allows, transplant to the outdoors in late summer for a late harvest. Plants that mature after early frosts produce sprouts of much finer flavor.

Where to Plant

• Plant in cool, moist soil. Choose an area where the soil has plenty of nitrogen (add well-rotted manure). Brussels sprouts like a neutral to alkaline soil (pH 7.0 to 7.5) and like full sun but can tolerate partial shade.

• Do *not* plant where any cole crops (Brussels sprouts themselves, broccoli, cabbage, cauliflower, collards, horseradish, kale, kohlrabi, mustard, radishes, rutabagas, or turnips) grew the year before.

How to Plant

• Seeds

Indoors, plant 3 seeds to each small container of potting soil, ¼ inch deep, and water well. For better drainage, put a thin layer of crushed eggshells in the bottom of each container before adding soil.

Outdoors, add compost and some crushed eggshells to the soil before planting (Brussels sprouts need calcium). Then sow seeds ¼ inch deep in rows 2 feet apart.

• Transplants

Prepare the soil as described for seeds. Pick a cool day for transplanting, and space the plants 2 feet apart on all sides. Tamp the soil down firmly around each transplant. Water immediately, and water daily for the first week. Some gardeners believe that removing the lower leaves from each transplant puts less strain on the roots so that they adapt more quickly to their new location.

Germination Time

• Seeds germinate in 4 to 10 days.

Care During Growth

• Indoors, when the seedlings are well up, thin them to the sturdiest plant per pot.

• If you sow seeds outdoors early in August for October harvesting, be sure to keep the beds moist to aid germination during the hot weather. Continue this until the seedlings are well established. When they are well up, thin them to stand about 2 feet apart. You can surround each plant with a narrow plastic cup with its bottom removed to protect against cutworms.

• If the days are hot and dry, a rotted oak-leaf mulch will help keep the soil moist and cool.

• Fertilize once a month with a couple of tablespoons per plant of 1 part each bonemeal and wood ashes and 2 parts cottonseed meal.

• Be sure to continue watering, especially during dry periods.

• As soon as the sprouts start to form, remove all leaves from the sides (trunk) of each plant, preserving leaves only at the top.

• Toward the end of the season, when the plants are about 1 foot tall, pinch off the small top leaves to make the remaining sprouts larger.

• In early September, add more high-nitrogen fertilizer and continue watering. The cooler weather of early fall will stimulate new growth.

• About mid-September you can pinch back all growth at the top so the plants will put their energy into further development of the remaining sprouts.

• Even after the first frosts, the plants will continue to grow. If you mulch them in late November with straw, leaves, or other organic material, they'll often produce for several more weeks.

Maturation Time

• Depending on the variety, Brussels sprouts will be ready to harvest 85 to 100 days after transplanting.

Harvesting

• There's generally a 3-week period for summer harvesting; fall harvesting can be extended further, into the late fall or even early winter (see "Care During Growth").

• The sweetest-tasting and best-flavored sprouts are those harvested after a few light frosts.

• Snap or twist off the sprouts, starting at the bottom of the stalks, when the buds feel solid. Work upward as they mature. Don't strip the leaves—the plant needs them for further growth. After picking from the bottom, if the plants look leggy, you can mound some soil around each one to give it more support.

• Brussels sprouts can endure extreme cold. Should there be a really hard freeze, remove the sprouts and cook them before they thaw.

Storing

• Don't wash Brussels sprouts before you store them.

• They'll keep for about 3 weeks in a cold place.

Diseases and Pests

• Aphids, blackleg, cabbage loopers, cabbage maggots, cabbageworms, clubroot, cutworms, flea beetles.

Garden Tips

• Since Brussels sprouts love nitrogen and peas, beans, and clover add nitrogen to soil, plant these among the sprouts.

• A ring of garlic cloves planted close around each Brussels sprouts plant is said to help fend off aphids.

• Nasturtiums can be planted among the sprouts plants to lure aphids away.

• Good companion plantings for Brussels sprouts are beets, celery, dill, lavender, mint, onions, potatoes, sage, and thyme.

Kitchen Tips
• Wash Brussels sprouts under cold running water and drain them. Pull off the loose leaves. Cut a little cross at the bottom of each stem end.
• Before you cook the sprouts in any manner, blanch them: Drop them into rapidly boiling, salted water, bring it quickly to a boil again, then drain and spread the sprouts out on a towel to cool. From here on cook as you like—but don't overcook. After blanching, Brussels sprouts should rarely be cooked more than 7 to 10 minutes. They should retain their greenness and be slightly crisp.
• Nutmeg and grated cheese are excellent additions to Brussels sprouts dishes.

Bt
See *Bacillus thuringiensis*

Budworms
See *Corn earworms*

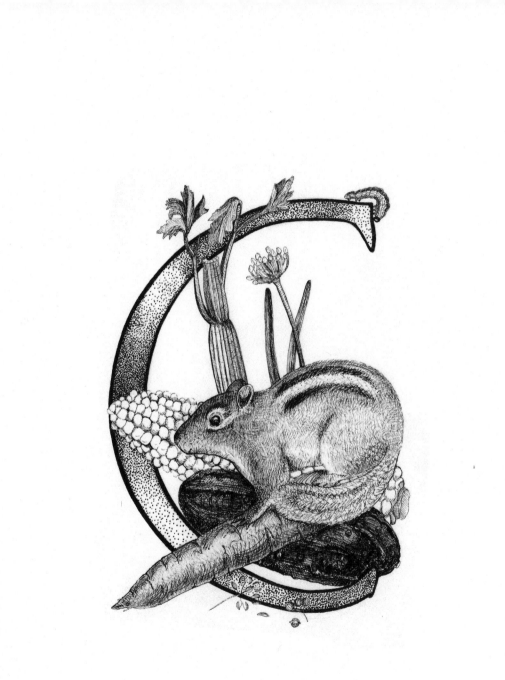

Cabbage

Cabbage, a hardy crop, is sensitive to heat and generally requires cool soil and cool weather. The possible exception is savoy cabbage (a variety with textured leaves), which bears up well during hot weather and can be grown as a spring, summer, or fall crop. Most cabbages thrive in cool, sunny weather and are grown as spring or fall crops. They can take light frost. There are rapid-growing early varieties of cabbage and later ones for winter storing. Later ones can easily be grown from seed, but for early cabbage it's best to purchase plants.

Chinese cabbage, similar to other types in its growing requirements, falls into two main groups: the head varieties, often called Chinese cabbage, Chinese celery, or celery cabbage, and the loose-leaf varieties, the most popular of which is pakchoi, also called bok choy, with long green leaves that resemble Swiss chard. Pakchoi particularly needs cool weather to mature properly. It is tenderer and has a milder flavor than regular cabbage. It's easy to grow and fast to mature, but where summers are warm it is best grown as an early spring or, preferably, a fall crop.

When to Plant

• Head cabbage (all varieties)

Space out your harvest by choosing plants or seeds with different maturity dates. Or plant any variety at 2-week intervals until about 2 months before the first expected fall frost.

For an early crop: Whether you are planting early, midseason, or regular varieties, sow seeds outdoors every 2 weeks from mid- to late spring (the seeds germinate best at 70° to 75°F). Or, better, set out transplants when they're 4 to 6 weeks old, between early and late spring.

For a late crop: Generally, fall varieties do best when they're direct-seeded in the garden in late spring to early summer. Set out transplants between early and midsummer.

• Chinese cabbage (all varieties)

Chinese cabbage tends to bolt (go to seed) during long, hot summer days. For this reason most gardeners treat these varieties as a fall crop, sowing the seeds directly in the garden in midsummer or setting out transplants in late summer.

For spring harvesting, sow seeds directly in the garden as soon as the ground can be worked, or set out transplants in midspring.

Where to Plant

• Plant where the soil is deep, loamy, high in nitrogen, and full of humus to hold moisture. Cabbage likes full sun but can tolerate partial shade. The soil should be neutral to alkaline (pH 7.0 to 7.5).

How to Plant

• Two weeks before planting, it's a good idea to work fresh manure into the soil.

• Cabbage plants have shallow roots, which spread laterally, so they need plenty of space. The more space between plants, the larger the heads.

• Plant seeds ½ inch deep, 2 inches apart (for later thinning), or 15 to 18 inches apart (without need for thinning), in rows 24 to 30 inches apart. Firm the soil lightly over them. Late

varieties need more space: Plant them 24 inches apart with 36 inches between rows.

• If you are setting out plants, be sure the roots are well buried, and remove the lower leaves so the roots will adjust more easily to their new location.

Germination Time

• Head cabbage: Seeds germinate in 7 to 10 days.

• Chinese cabbage: Seeds sprout at around 45°F. You can speed up germination by misting the newly sown seeds daily. Plants emerge 10 to 21 days after sowing, depending on soil and weather.

Care During Growth

• Head cabbage

If you haven't permanently spaced the seeds at planting time, thin them—when seedlings reach 2 inches in height—to at least 15 inches apart.

Cabbage requires abundant moisture: Water regularly, except in hot weather.

It is also a heavy feeder and needs ample nitrogen. Apply manure tea regularly around the roots. Or side-dress occasionally with well-rotted manure, scraping it lightly into the soil so the roots aren't disturbed.

Use mulches to keep the soil cool: aluminized plastic film, grass clippings, hair, or leaves.

Continue fertilizing and watering even into September. Cabbage gets a new spurt of growth when the weather turns cool and continues even when the temperature hits freezing.
- Chinese cabbage
Thin seedlings to 8 to 12 inches apart when they are 1 to 2 inches high.

Maturation Time
- Head cabbage generally matures in 50 to 100 days, depending on variety and weather, after seedlings emerge; or 65 to 120 days from day of sowing seed.
- Chinese cabbage matures in 60 to 70 days. Some early varieties are ready in 50 days.

Harvesting
- The harvest period for individual head cabbage plants can be extended over 3 weeks. Harvest when the heads are round and hard, usually— for fall harvesting—from September to October. Heads should be picked before a hard freeze sets in. If you intend to store them, pick heads while they're still bright green and hard. You may want to remove the entire plant from the soil (see "Storing"). Or you can cut off the head (at a sharp angle to prevent rain-caused stalk rot) but leave the rest of the plant, which will often continue to produce small heads.

- Individual leaves of Chinese cabbage can be cut over a long period, or the entire plant can be harvested in spring or fall, when it is 10 to 14 inches high.

Storing
- Properly stored, cabbage will keep 2 to 3 months, sometimes longer. Choose a cellar, barn, or shed where the temperature stays between 32° and 40°F and the humidity remains high.
- Handle with care all cabbages that you intend to store. Any nicked or bruised heads may become susceptible to Botrytis leaf mold or alternaria leaf spot, fungal diseases that thrive under the cold, damp storage conditions cabbage needs.
- There are several ways to store cabbages:
Hang them head down, leaving on the stems and roots.
Remove roots and damaged outer leaves, wrap the heads in newspaper, and pack loosely in boxes.
Cover the heads with sand and store in a cold, moist, well-ventilated place.
- Check on your stored cabbage from time to time, removing any heads that show signs of spoilage.
- Chinese cabbage can't be stored for as long as head varieties. Harvest loose-leaf cabbage after a hard freeze, but don't remove the roots. Stand the plants upright, burying the roots in

boxes of moist sand or soil, and store them at close to freezing temperature. They should keep for up to 2 months.

Diseases and Pests

• Alternaria disease, aphids, bacterial diseases, blackleg, Botrytis blight, cabbage loopers, cabbage maggots, cabbageworms, clubroot, cucumber beetles, cutworms, damping off, earwigs, flea beetles, green peach aphids, nematodes, slugs, tarnished plant bugs, thrips, whiteflies.

Garden Tips

• Allow 2 years or more between plantings of cabbage on the same piece of ground to avoid offering breeding places for its disease and insect pests.

• Grow beans, clover, or peas in your cabbage patch during off years to restore to the soil the nitrogen that cabbage needs.

• Since cabbage roots grow close to the surface, avoid cultivation if possible.

• Chinese cabbage is prone to bolt to seed during alternating cold and warm periods.

• Some cabbage heads, when they grow large, show signs of cracking. If you see this, carefully expose and cut away about half of the root. Cover with soil again, and water well. You may need to repeat this procedure after a prolonged rain (2 days or more).

• If space is a problem, try interplanting early cabbage between well-spaced tomato plants. The cabbage will be ready to harvest before the tomato plants need the space.

• Wild mustard plants carry clubroot—don't let any of them grow in or near your cabbage patch.

• Plant dill or hyssop with cabbage as an insect deterrent.

• Plant a ring of garlic cloves around each cabbage plant to help keep it free from aphids.

• Nasturtiums are often used as a trap crop to lure aphids away from cabbage.

• Interplanting cabbage with other nonbrassica vegetables is said to lessen the assaults of aphids and cabbage root flies. Alternate rows.

• If cabbage maggots are a problem, make tar-paper collars to lay flat around young cabbage plants.

• Grow clover or other low-growing grasses around and between your cabbage plants—these lessen flea beetle damage. Or make a mulch of chopped green clover.

• A sprinkling of wood ashes over cabbage plants after each rain helps control cabbage loopers.

• Good companion plantings for cabbage are said to be beans, beets, celery, corn, dill, lavender, mint, onions, potatoes, radishes, rosemary, sage, thyme, and tomatoes.

Kitchen Tips

• Don't shred cabbage too fine if you're going to cook it.

• If you want cabbage to be less gassy, parboil it for 5 minutes, rinse in cold water, then cook it again in fresh water or in any manner you want, to the consistency you like.

• To counter the odor of cooking cabbage, put a couple of slices of stale bread in the cooking water, then fish them out with a small strainer when the cabbage is done.

• For most dishes, cook cabbage uncovered for no more than 6 to 8 minutes, depending on how thin you've cut it. It should be slightly crackly.

• Try steaming cabbage. Steam shredded cabbage for about 10 minutes; steam large chunks for a bit longer.

• Red cabbage will keep its color while cooking if you add 1 tablespoon vinegar or lemon juice or ¼ cup wine to each 2 cups of cooking water.

• If you want whole cabbage leaves for stuffing, here's how to remove them: Bring water to a boil in a deep pan, stick a fork into the base of the cabbage, and submerge the head in the boiling water for 1 minute. Remove, drain, and carefully pull off the leaves that have softened. Return the rest of the head to the boiling water, and repeat the process until you've removed all the leaves you need.

• You can also separate cabbage leaves if you wash, dry, core, and freeze the cabbage head. Defrost it, and the leaves will come off easily.

• To stuff cabbage leaves, place the stuffing in the center of each leaf, then either fold the leaf over on all sides to form an envelope or roll the leaf up, tucking in the open sides. Use long green scallions cut lengthwise into strings to tie the cabbage rolls or envelopes. Cook as your recipe directs.

• To serve cabbage in some kinds of salad, you may want to blanch the cabbage by a quick parboiling. Then rinse in cold water, drain, and chill it well before cutting.

• For a very crunchy salad, cut a cabbage head in half, and soak it in salted ice water for 1 hour or so. Chilling also makes it easier to slice the cabbage in thin strips.

Cabbage Butterflies

See *Cabbageworms*

Cabbage Loopers 🐛

Sometimes called measuring worms or inchworms, cabbage loopers are greenish, 1½-inch-long, thin caterpillars that move by arching up in the middle and creeping forward. They are the larvae of a silver-spotted brown and gray moth that lays small, white eggs, usually on the upper surfaces of leaves.

Cabbage loopers attack beans, beets, broccoli, Brussels sprouts, cabbage, cauliflower, celery, collards, kale, kohlrabi, lettuce, nasturtiums, parsley, peas, potatoes, radishes, rutabagas, spinach, tomatoes, and turnips, as well as many ornamental plants.

Manifestation

• The leaves of affected plants show holes of all shapes and sizes, gradually extending into the interiors of the plants. The loopers themselves are often evident.

To Combat

• Look for and crush the small, white eggs on both surfaces of leaves, starting when the plants are young.
• Handpick the loopers when you see them.
• Hose down affected plants, or wait until after a rain, then sprinkle fine wood ashes over them.
• Spray with Bacillus thuringiensis (Bt) once a week when you see evidence of the worms.

• Nasturtiums can be used as a trap crop. You can easily see the loopers on nasturtium leaves, pick them off, and destroy them.
• Trichogramma wasps lay their eggs in the eggs of cabbage loopers and thus destroy them. These wasps are attracted to sweet fennel, so plant the fennel near your cole and other plants. You can buy trichogramma wasp eggs from many nurseries.
• In infested areas, be sure to destroy all plant debris after harvesting. Cabbage looper pupae winter over in cocoons attached to the plants on which they feed. These cocoons are so delicate that you can see the outlines of the pupae inside. Destroy them.

Cabbage Maggots 🐛

Cabbage maggots, also known as cabbage root maggots and root maggots, are the larvae of the cabbage root fly. This ¼-inch-long fly is bristly haired and dark gray with black stripes, flying close to the ground to lay tiny, white eggs at the bases of seedling stems or in the soil close to them. The eggs hatch into wedge-shaped larvae with no discernible heads, which burrow into the lower stems and roots of host plants, chiefly beets, broccoli, Brussels sprouts, cabbage, cauliflower, celery, collards, garden cress, kohlrabi, radishes, and turnips. These maggots can transmit spores of blackleg. They thrive in cool, moist weather.

Manifestation

• Plants attacked by cabbage maggots become stunted and pale green. The roots are ruined by the slimy tunnels the maggots leave.

To Combat

• Interplanting brassica beds with nonbrassica vegetables results in smaller infestations of cabbage maggots.

• Marigolds interplanted throughout the beds are also reported as being very effective against the maggots.

• Radishes, because they're especially attractive to cabbage maggots, can be used as a trap crop among your other brassicas.

• Cut 4-inch collars—squares or disks—of tar paper or flypaper, and fasten them snugly around seedlings at soil level to reduce significantly egg laying at the bases of the plants.

• Surround the seedlings with wood ashes as an egg-laying deterrent.

• Cover plants with tents of fine gauze or netting tacked to stakes and held to the ground with stones.

• You can purchase from some nurseries a microscopic nematode that destroys cabbage maggots within a day or two. It is obtainable under the name Seek and can be used as a mulch (it arrives mixed with cedar shavings) or mixed with water, strained, and sprayed on infested soil.

• At the end of every harvest period, pull up and discard infested plants.

. . .

Cabbage Moths

See *Cabbageworms*

Cabbage Root Flies

See *Cabbage maggots*

Cabbageworms 🐛

Cabbageworms, also called imported cabbageworms, are the green larvae of white cabbage butterflies. They are extremely destructive in the garden, attacking mainly broccoli, Brussels sprouts, cabbage, cauliflower, collards, kale, kohlrabi, lettuce, nasturtiums, radishes, rutabagas, and turnips. The white cabbage butterfly, with black spots on its white wings, emerges in early spring to lay its eggs, mainly on the undersides of leaves. These hatch into green caterpillars, which, after their destructive eating, pupate in cocoons suspended by silken threads from twigs, plants, and nearby objects. From these pupae a new generation of cabbage butterflies emerges. The process is repeated several times during a season.

Manifestation

• The green caterpillars are clearly visible on the plants they attack. They eat large holes in the leaves and tunnel inside the vegetables, where they are sometimes—and sometimes not—visible.

To Combat

• Starting early in the spring, examine both surfaces of leaves for numerous cabbageworm eggs, and either crush them or remove them with cotton swabs dipped in alcohol.
• Handpick and destroy the worms wherever you see them.
• Destroy the cocoons of pupating larvae wherever you see them.
• Many aromatic plants deter cabbage butterflies from laying their eggs in the immediate vicinity. Interplant vegetables with any of the following: dill, hyssop, lavender, marigolds, mint, onions, pennyroyal, rosemary, sage, tansy, or thyme.

• Make a water solution of thyme or sage in your blender, strain it, and spray on plants periodically.
• Both buckwheat and nasturtiums can be interplanted as trap crops for cabbageworms, which seem to prefer them to the vegetables. You can handpick the worms from these.
• Fine wood ashes sprinkled over the plants after they've been lightly hosed or after a rain are also a deterrent to cabbageworms.
• Some gardeners sprinkle plants with salt or with a saltwater solution at the first sign of cabbageworms.
• Bacillus thuringiensis (Bt) is effective against cabbageworms. Start spraying in the spring, and continue about twice a week throughout the season.
• Rotenone spray is also an excellent control. Use this when you see the first larvae.
• Trichogramma wasps are a natural enemy of cabbageworms. You can

buy the wasp eggs from many nurseries.
• In infested areas, be sure to collect

and destroy all plant remains, including weeds, after harvesting.

Cane Blight

Cane blight is a fungal disease, primarily of raspberries, the spores of which overwinter in diseased canes. The manifestation and treatment of cane blight are similar to those of Botrytis blight (see *Botrytis blight* for details).

Cane Borers

See *Borers*

Cantaloupe

See *Melon*

Caraway

Caraway is a 2- to 3-foot hardy biennial (some unimportant varieties are annuals), well adapted to northern culture. The parsnip-shaped roots of caraway can be cooked and eaten as a vegetable; the licorice-flavored leaves can be used in salads, soups, stews, and as a garnish; and the crescent-shaped seeds can be used to flavor cheese and in candies, cakes, cookies, puddings, and breads. The liqueur kümmel is made from caraway seeds.

Caraway doesn't tolerate transplanting well, so it is usually grown straight from seed. The leaves of the biennial plants stay green throughout the first winter. Although the plants die at the end of the second season, they generally reseed themselves and will carry on indefinitely. Feathery, carrotlike greens appear during the first year. The plants flower early in the second season, and the seeds are ready for harvesting by midsummer.

When to Plant

• Caraway is generally planted early in the spring, but seeds of the biennials can also be sown in late summer for early maturing the following year.

Where to Plant

• Plant in medium-heavy but well-drained soil, mildly acid to neutral (pH 6 to 7), in full or partial sun.

How to Plant

• Sow seeds ½ inch deep, about 1 inch apart, in rows 2 feet apart.

Germination Time

• Germination and early growth are quite slow, taking 10 to 14 days.

Care During Growth

• Be sure to weed well.
• When the plants are 2 inches high, thin them to about 6 inches apart.
• Caraway needs only occasional watering during a prolonged dry season.

Maturation Time

• The annual forms flower at the end of the first summer, the biennial early in the second season. Both mature their seeds in midsummer or early fall. Roots of the biennial can be dug for eating about the time the seeds are ripe.

Harvesting

• The umbels (flower clusters) turn brown at the end of the second summer after planting. Cut them from the plant carefully to keep the dark seeds from scattering. You can dry the umbels, then shake the seeds loose. Any that escape into the garden will come up the next season.

Storing

• Let the seeds dry in the sun or in a warm, dry place, then store them in a dark container. They'll keep their fragrant flavoring for a year or more.

Diseases and Pests

• Carrot rust flies.

Garden Tips

• If you want a steady supply of seeds or roots from the biennial form, see that a new crop gets planted each year.
• Caraway seeds are often planted to loosen and aerate heavy soils.
• Peas are a good companion plant for caraway.
• Don't plant caraway near fennel.

Kitchen Tips

• Caraway leaves add a lovely flavor to salads or soups.
• Cook and serve the thick, fleshy caraway root as a vegetable.
• Crush caraway seeds by pounding them with a hammer covered with a

dishtowel or by putting them in a blender. Add these to a meat or vegetable sauce for a nice new flavor.
• Caraway seeds are marvelous in creamed soups. Simmer 1 to 2 tablespoons of seeds in a clear soup stock for about 15 minutes, then strain out and discard the seeds before adding milk, cream, or other ingredients. Don't cook the soup for too long after this, or you'll lose the subtle caraway flavor.

Carrot

Carrots are generally considered a cool-weather crop. They're hardy and can stand light frosts in the spring or fall.

When to Plant
• For a spring crop, sow seeds as soon as you can work the soil, about 2 weeks before the probable last frost.
• For a continuous harvest well into the fall, keep sowing seeds at 3-week intervals until 3 months before the first expected frost.
• If you want to gamble a little, plant some carrot seeds in the very late fall, just before freezing weather. Cover lightly with soil, and mulch well. Remove the mulch in very early spring—you may get an extra-early crop.

Where to Plant
• Although carrots can tolerate partial shade, it's best to plant them in a sunny spot. The shorter varieties do fairly well in shallow, somewhat heavy soil, but all other types like deeply worked, stone-free, sandy, loamy soil (pH 6 to 7), which will not easily compact. They won't grow very big if the soil is hard. For this reason, carrots do particularly well in raised beds.
• Before planting, it's best to prepare the seedbed by spading 1 foot deep, then digging in any or all of the following: well-rotted compost, peat, rotted sawdust, or aged manure.

How to Plant
• Carrot seeds take a long time to germinate. They'll sprout faster if you soak them overnight, then roll them lightly between layers of damp paper towels and put them in a plastic bag. Examine daily—as soon as any begin to sprout, plant them in the garden.
• Make long, shallow furrows 15 inches apart, ¼ inch deep, and place the seeds about 2 inches apart. You can also scatter the seeds evenly in the furrows, for thinning later (see "Care During Growth"). Cover with light soil or a mixture of soil, sand, and a little fine peat moss. Water well,

and mist every morning, especially in hot weather.

• Or you can plant carrot seeds by the broadcast method, strewing them evenly over the carrot patch, then covering them with a ¼-inch layer of soil. Water and keep moist until seedlings appear.

Germination Time
• It may take 2 weeks or more before seedlings emerge.

Care During Growth
• When seedlings emerge, continue misting—carrot seedlings are delicate. Never let the soil become dry or crusty.

• When the seedlings are about 2 inches high, thin them so they're at least 3 inches apart on all sides. (The wider the spacing between carrots, the faster they'll grow and the bigger the roots will be.) If you give the carrot patch a good soaking first, you'll find thinning easier.

• Repeat: Always keep the soil moist while carrots are in their early stages of growth. Even later, lack of moisture will produce bitter carrots.

• If you see the crowns pushing above the soil line, cover them with soil or their orange color will turn green.

• Use a mulch of leaves or grass clippings if the weather turns hot and dry.

• Keep weeding until carrot leaves are big enough to shade the soil.

Maturation Time
• Depending on the variety, carrots take 60 to 90 days from seed to harvest. The small, shorter varieties mature earlier than the long-rooted ones.

Harvesting
• Carrots continue growing until cold weather chills the soil. But they should be harvested when the tops of the roots are orange and about ¾ inch to 1 inch in diameter. Too-young carrots aren't very sweet. Too-old ones develop woody centers and become tough and bitter.

• You'll find pulling carrots easier after a rain or after using the spray from a hose to loosen the soil around them. Avoid cutting or bruising any you intend to store.

• Once you have picked carrots, remove most of the leafy tops. The stems and leaves pull moisture out of the roots.

Storing
• Never wash carrots before storing. Cut off all but 1 inch of the tops, allow the roots to dry, and store them where it's dark, in containers of lightly moist sphagnum moss, sand, or sawdust. High humidity is necessary to keep carrots from shriveling.

• Or carrots can often be left in the garden and "ground stored" over the winter. Once heavy frost hits, cut back the tops to 1 inch and mulch well—at least 8 inches deep—with straw, shredded leaves, or hay. You'll be able to harvest carrots all winter long. (Mark the rows with stakes so you can find them under the snow.)

Diseases and Pests
• Carrot rust flies, corn-root aphids, damping off, scab, thrips.

Garden Tips
• Always avoid fresh manure or un-rotted compost in a carrot bed.
• Carrots thrive on potash: Wood ashes, seaweed, dried fish scraps, and well-rotted manure supply this sub-stance.
• Some people plant radish seeds along with carrot seeds—the rad-ishes will sprout first and break the crust of the soil for the delicate carrot seedlings. Once the seedlings are well up, remove the radishes care-fully.
• Carrots that mature in hot weather are usually shorter and less tender.
• The first hard frost improves the fla-vor of carrots.
• If carrots have forked roots, the soil was too hard. Soil in which carrots grow must always be kept loose.
• Carrots are good "second tenants" in your pea patch: Plant them as soon as you've picked your last peas in early summer.
• Good companion plantings for car-rots are said to be beans, chives, leeks, lettuce, onions, peas, rosemary, sage, and tomatoes.

Kitchen Tips
• To serve as a vegetable, use young, slender carrots. They're sweeter. The thicker, tougher, older ones (often deeper in color) are best for soups and stews.
• If you *do* cook old carrots, cut them in quarters lengthwise and remove the long, woody middle sections. Add a little sugar or honey to the cooking water.
• Instead of peeling carrots before cooking, you can scrub them and boil them whole, then rinse in cold water. The skins will rub off easily, but if the carrots are young, leave the skins on—they make the whole carrots more tasty.
• Small cooked carrots—or larger ones cut into 2- to 3-inch lengths and whittled a little to round the edges—make a lovely garnish. Butter them lightly, and dust them with very finely chopped parsley or other leafy herbs.
• Cooked mashed carrots can be used interchangeably with pumpkins or winter squashes in any recipe.
• Use a potato peeler to shave carrots to serve with greens in a tossed salad or to add to coleslaw.

• To make carrot curls, slice carrots lengthwise into several thin strips to within ½ inch of the small end. Soak them in ice water until they curl. Drain and refrigerate until time to serve.

Carrot Rust Flies 🐞

These shiny green insects with yellow heads look like tiny houseflies. They emerge from below-ground hibernation around May, to lay eggs near the crowns of caraway, carrots, celery, coriander, dill, fennel, parsley, and parsnips. The eggs hatch into yellowish maggots, which bore down into the plant roots, where they feed and grow larger. Their entire life span is only a few weeks, so there are about three generations of carrot rust flies in a season.

Manifestation
• Leaves wilt, turn yellow, and fall off. In the roots, carrot rust fly maggots leave rust-colored tunnels. Entire roots can be destroyed.

To Combat
• Grow susceptible plants in beds where other host plants were not grown the previous season.
• Carrot rust flies are known to breed in stinging nettles. Remove these plants if you see them in the vicinity of your garden.
• Black salsify, chives, and sage, interplanted among vulnerable vegetables, often help repel carrot rust flies.
• Make tents of cheesecloth, gauze, or wire-mesh screen over susceptible vegetables.
• Spray a water solution of ground wormwood, strained, on the soil around plants to deter the flies from laying eggs there.

Caterpillars 🐞

See also *Cabbage loopers*; *Cabbageworms*; *Gypsy moth caterpillars*

Caterpillars are the larvae of moths and butterflies and are covered individually in this book. There is almost no garden plant that isn't palatable to some kind of caterpillar.

Manifestation

• For the most part, caterpillars defoliate plants. If you see leaves with large portions eaten out of them, you can be pretty sure caterpillars of some kind have been at work.

To Combat

• Birds are great caterpillar eaters. Encourage their nesting near your garden. Particularly good birds to attract are Baltimore orioles, chickadees, cuckoos, robins, swallows, titmice, and wrens.

• Praying mantises likewise consume enormous amounts of caterpillars.
• Many wasps, particularly trichogramma and paper wasps, parasitize moth and butterfly eggs so they never hatch. You can attract wasps to your garden by planting black-eyed Susans, goldenrod, oxeye daisies, and sweet fennel.
• Rotenone is a good control for caterpillars.

. . .

Cats and Dogs

Apart from building a fence around your garden, a possible method of keeping cats and dogs out is to sprinkle freshly ground sharp pepper over and around your plants frequently. (But keep in mind that cats do a lot of good in the garden, controlling mice, moles, and rabbits.)

Cauliflower

Cauliflower is a cool-weather crop that requires warm temperatures in the early part of its development but needs cool weather to develop large white heads. For this reason, it's best sown as a fall crop. Although it can't stand as much cold as cabbage, once it matures cauliflower takes light frosts well. In fact, a mild frost gives it a sweeter flavor.

Each variety of cauliflower reacts differently to a particular environment: Try planting more than one kind to see which grows best for you. Purple cauliflower (sometimes called purple broccoli or broccoli cauliflower) generally produces larger heads than most white varieties. (It turns bright green when cooked!) Never grow cauliflower in the same bed two years running (even three years, if possible) or where any brassicas grew the year before.

When to Plant

• Early cauliflower

Sow seeds indoors in rich potting soil approximately 4 to 6 weeks before the last expected frost.

Transplant the hardened seedlings to the outdoors about the time of the last frost.

Or plant seeds outdoors about 6 weeks before the last expected frost.

• Late cauliflower

Plant seeds from midspring to early summer. Or set out plants in midsummer, or about 3 months before the first expected frost.

Make several weekly seed plantings throughout June to ensure that some will hit the right weather at the right time for proper development.

Where to Plant

• Cauliflower needs rich soil, high in nitrogen and on the alkaline side (pH 7.0 to 7.5). A very little lime mixed into the soil when you transplant is generally a good idea. Cauliflower likes sun but not too much heat.

How to Plant

• Cover seeds planted indoors with light potting soil ¼ to ½ inch deep. Use peat pots or other biodegradable growing containers, which can be placed directly in the garden without disturbing the roots or plants.

• Or sow seeds directly in the garden ½ inch deep if the soil is light and won't crust over. Otherwise cover them with ½ inch of fine sand. Water with a light spray.

• Thin the seedlings, or set out 4- to 5-week-old plants, to 18 inches apart (self-blanching varieties and all late cauliflower should be planted 24 inches apart) in rows 30 inches apart.

• Choose a cool, cloudy day for transplanting. And try to handle the entire plant—root, stem, and leaves—as gently as possible. Pat the dirt firmly around each plant. Some gardeners trim off about half the leaves when transplanting, to minimize wilting.

Germination Time

• Seeds germinate in 3 to 10 days, depending on soil temperature.

Care During Growth

• After thinning or transplanting, water seedlings every day for 1 week and whenever the weather is dry. Cauliflower likes plenty of moisture.

• Once the plants have become established, use mulches to keep the soil cool—aluminized plastic film, grass clippings, hay, or leaves.

• Hoe well-rotted manure or aged compost into the soil around the plants in May. Continue to keep them well watered.

• If you see cabbageworms or cabbage loopers at any time, pick them off the plants and destroy them.

• The head (called the curd) of cauliflower will turn yellow, green, or purple when grown exposed to sunlight. If you wish to keep it white, take the longest leaves that grow around the head and tie them gently over the curd, fastening loosely with soft string or yarn, strips of cloth, or clothespins. This is called blanching, and it improves the flavor. Some varieties of cauliflower are self-blanching because their inner leaves naturally grow over the curd. Purple cauliflower doesn't need blanching.

• Late cauliflower will benefit from the application of additional well-rotted manure and watering in early September. Cool weather will give it a new spurt of growth.

• Even if you haven't blanched the heads, you may want to tie the leaves over the curds in late fall to protect them from frost.

Maturation Time

• Cauliflower is usually ready to harvest 50 to 80 days from the day of transplanting, depending on the variety. Purple cauliflower takes somewhat longer—80 to 100 days, depending on the variety.

• Direct-seeded cauliflower reaches maturity about 14 days sooner than transplants.

Harvesting

• The harvest period for cauliflower generally covers 2 weeks for early types, 3 weeks for late.

• Harvest as soon as the heads fill out; otherwise they'll deteriorate. Cut off the main head on a slant, but don't disturb the rest of the plant, which will in most cases produce little side heads for later harvesting. A protective mulch around the plants at this time will often spur them to produce new heads late in the season.

Storing

• Cauliflower doesn't store for very long. Never wash it before storing. Keep in a cool, dark place. Late varieties will store longer.

Diseases and Pests

• Aphids, blackleg, cabbage loopers, cabbage maggots, cabbageworms, cutworms, flea beetles, tarnished plant bugs, thrips.

Garden Tips

• You can sow cauliflower seeds earlier outdoors if you plant under cloches, which warm the soil.

• A ring of garlic cloves buried around each plant is said to help keep cauliflower free from aphids and cabbageworms. (The garlic will send up protective aromatic shoots.)

• Nasturtiums are often planted as a trap crop to lure aphids away from cauliflower.

• Some gardeners tie a nylon stocking over each cauliflower head when it is about 2 inches in diameter, to protect the head from cabbageworms.

• Purple cauliflower is a heavier feeder than white.

• Don't use fresh manure or fresh compost in the cauliflower patch.

• Interplant cauliflower in alternate rows with other nonbrassica vegetables. Good companion plantings are said to be beans, beets, celery, corn, dill, lavender, mint, onions, rosemary, sage, and thyme.

Kitchen Tips

• An average cauliflower (about 1½ pounds), served as a vegetable, will feed three to four people.

• If you're going to cook cauliflower whole, trim it at the stem end and make a crosscut there with a sharp knife so this harder portion will cook more quickly.

• Don't cook cauliflower in an aluminum pot; doing so will darken the vegetable.

• Cauliflower will stay white if you add a little sugar, lemon peel, or white vinegar to the cooking water.

• Parboil a whole cauliflower for 8 minutes in boiling, salted water, then drain and cool quickly in a pot of cold water. For further cooking, simmer it in fresh water or steam it. If you're going to bake it or use it in another fashion, do the 8-minute parboiling first.

• Cauliflower will stay white and taste sweeter if you cook it in half milk and half water, without a cover. Or you can cook it in milk alone (use the milk later for a sauce or as the base for a cream soup).

• For more even cooking, divide the head into small flowerets. Peel the stalk to expose its center, then slice. Firm young leaves can be cut up and cooked with the rest of the head.

• The bright green leaves themselves make fine eating. Blanch them lightly and serve with butter, or stuff them just as you would cabbage leaves.

• Cauliflower should be barely tender when served—don't overcook it!

• Don't discard cauliflower stalks when you cook the head. Trim off the dry, fibrous parts, blanch, and cut up to serve cold in salads. Or cut the stems into strips or slices and serve with a white or hollandaise sauce.

Celeriac

Also called celery knob, celery root, and turnip-rooted celery, celeriac is grown exactly like celery, although it is less sensitive to summer heat. (See *Celery* for details.) It is grown for its celery-flavored, turniplike roots and not, as is celery, for its stalk. It is also less subject to diseases than celery.

Celeriac takes from 100 to 120 days to mature from seed. Although when fully grown the roots can average 4 inches across, you can begin harvesting when they're about 2 inches in diameter. Store at temperatures close to freezing, or even a bit below, to avoid root rot.

Celery

Celery, although it is not vigorously hardy, is resistant to most plant enemies. It can be grown in the garden from seed or transplants. If it is grown for its stalks (for eating), celery can be considered an annual. If grown for its seeds, it is a biennial, since the seeds are produced on long flower stalks in the second season.

When to Plant
• For early celery, start seeds indoors in flats about 2 months before setting out seedlings. Generally, celery seedlings are set out in the garden after all danger of frost is past and, to be safe, about a week after tomato plants are set out.
• Or sow seeds directly in the garden from mid- to late spring.
• For late (fall) celery, plant seeds indoors in flats any time during midspring, and set out transplants in midsummer. Or you can plant seeds outdoors in early summer.

Where to Plant
• Because it is a heavy feeder and has short roots, celery needs rich, moist soil, preferably neutral to alkaline (pH 7.0 to 7.5). It likes a little shade but should get at least 6 hours of sun a day.

How to Plant
• If you plant seeds indoors in flats, cover them with ¼ inch of soil, keep moist, and try to maintain a temperature of 65° to 75°F until seedlings appear. It's best to cover the flats until the sprouts come up, then expose them to sunlight—although if possible keep them on the cool side.
• One method of planting seeds outdoors is to dig trenches 10 inches deep and 30 inches apart, filling the first 6 inches with compost or well-rotted manure. Cover this with 3 inches of soil, then strew the seeds sparingly the length of the trenches. Cover with another ¼ inch of soil, and keep the surface moist. Once seedlings appear, thin them to 8 inches apart.
• Or seeds can be strewn over rich soil in rows 24 to 30 inches apart, then covered with ¼ inch of soil, and

the seedlings thinned later to 8 inches apart. The soil should be kept moist.

• If you are setting out transplants, space them 8 inches apart in rows or trenches (see above) 30 inches apart.

Germination Time

• Celery seeds are slow to sprout—germination may take 14 to 21 days.

Care During Growth

• For steady growth, apply manure tea once a month after transplanting to the outdoors, or when the seedlings are about 3 inches tall.

• Be sure the soil never dries out: Try a heavy mulch, which helps keep down weeds and retain moisture.

• If you're growing the plants in trenches, add more soil around them when they're about 8 inches tall.

• Celery stalks may be blanched to allow less light to reach the plants and make them white and tender (although nowadays many people prefer celery unblanched). If you want only the inner stalks and heart to be white, slip a rubber band around the stalks to hold them together. To get white outer stalks as well, make sleeves of wrapping paper or several layers of newspaper and tie them around the stalks, using string or rubber bands, so that only the leaves are exposed. Blanching generally takes about 3 weeks.

Maturation Time

• Although you can cut off outside stalks throughout the growing season, celery usually reaches its full maturity in 90 to 95 days. Pascal celery, a more robust, vigorous late-season variety, takes around 120 days.

Harvesting

• You can pick celery from the time the plants are half grown until they're fully mature. Cut separate stalks from different plants, leaving the bulk of each plant to continue growing. Use a sharp knife to cut each stalk at the base.

• The final harvest should be when the first hard freeze is expected (mature celery can tolerate light frosts). If you are harvesting for storage, remove the plants with their roots.

Storing

• You can keep celery fresh for as long as 2 months if you stand plants upright with their roots in buckets or boxes of moist sand or soil. Store them in a cellar or root cellar, as close to 32°F as possible.

• Keep all stored celery very cold.

Diseases and Pests

• Aphids, bacterial diseases, blackheart, cabbage loopers, cabbage maggots, carrot rust flies, corn borers, damping off, green peach aphids, leafhoppers, mildew, root rot, tarnished plant bugs, thrips.

Garden Tips

• If you're growing celery for its seeds, mulch the plants well over the winter with straw, shredded leaves, grass clippings, or other materials.

• Celery seeds are very small. To help distribute them when planting, mix them with a little fine soil, sand, or coffee grounds—about ½ cup of added material to a package of seeds.

• Celery seeds remain viable for about 5 years.

• Indoor seedlings that become leggy are getting either too little light or too much heat. Seedlings should be kept on the cool side—but not too cold. A temperature as low as 55°F for a week or more may make the plants bolt to seed.

• If you want extra-thick stems, cut off the top inch of the celery plant when it's about 4 inches high.

• Good companion plantings for celery are said to be Brussels sprouts, bush beans, cabbage, cauliflower, kale, kohlrabi, leeks, tomatoes, and turnips.

• At the end of the season, you can remove whole celery plants from the garden and pot them with fresh soil. Keep watering, and they'll continue to grow in a sunny window for weeks; as you remove stalks for use, new ones will grow.

Kitchen Tips

• Pascal (green) celery contains more vitamin A than white.

• The quickest, most thorough way to rid a celery stalk of strings is to scrape it from top to bottom with a short-bladed knife.

• Stuff celery with any sandwich spread or cracker dip.

• To make celery crisp, stand it up to its leaves in a pitcher of cold, salted water in the refrigerator. Add some lemon juice to keep it white.

• To make celery curls, cut cleaned celery into 4-inch pieces. Then cut each piece into narrow strips down to about 1 inch from the end. Soak in ice water for ½ hour or so, and the strips will curl.

• Use a small amount of water and low heat when cooking celery. Boiling too fast makes celery tough.

• Save celery leaves to use in soups and stews. If they're fresh and green, cut them into tossed salads.

• Dry celery leaves, then rub them through a sieve. Save the resulting powder for flavoring soups, stews, and salad dressings. Use this powder also to make celery salt at a fraction of what you'd pay to buy it.

• Maybe you've never heard of celery fritters, but try them. Cut up those tough outside stalks that you might not otherwise use, and add them to any fritter recipe. Celery fritters are a great accompaniment to meats and chicken.

Celery Cabbage

See *Cabbage*

Celery Knob, Celery Root

See *Celeriac*

Celtuce

Celtuce belongs to the lettuce family but differs from other lettuces in having both an edible separate stalk and leaves, which resemble romaine lettuce. Although the celtuce stem somewhat suggests celery in appearance, there is no connection between the two. Celtuce leaves are used in salads or cooked like spinach. The central stem can be eaten raw when young or cooked like broccoli when more fully developed.

Celtuce is grown just like lettuce. (See *Lettuce* for details.) Plants should be thinned to about 10 inches apart in rows 18 inches apart. The seedstalk is ready to eat about 85 days after seeds have been sown in the garden. It's at its best when the stalk is 6 to 8 inches long and 1 inch in diameter at its base. It's generally best to peel away the outer, stringy layer before eating or cooking.

Chalcid Wasps

Tiny chalcid wasps (¹⁄₁₆ to ⅛ inch long) are very beneficial in any garden. They lay their eggs on the larvae and inside the bodies of many injurious insects. They have an 8-day life cycle, with generations continuing as long as host materials are available. (See *Trichogramma wasps* for details.)

Chard

See *Swiss chard*

Chervil

There are two plants called chervil. One, known as bulbous, tuberous-rooted, or turnip-rooted chervil, is a biennial cultivated for its fleshy, edible root and eaten as a vegetable, much like carrots. It is not, however, very commonly grown in the United States. The second is the annual herb that we know as salad chervil. This is the type discussed here. It is one of the few cool-weather herbs, resembling parsley in its leaves (which have a tarragonlike flavor) and growth habits. It can grow up to 20 inches in height.

When to Plant
• Plant seeds early in the spring, after the last frost.

Where to Plant
• Plant in moist but well-drained, friable soil (pH 6 to 7) that's not too rich. Salad chervil likes partial shade.

How to Plant
• Scatter seeds about 1 inch apart in rows about 4 inches apart, and cover them lightly with soil.

Germination Time
• Seeds germinate in 14 days.

Care During Growth
• When seedlings appear, thin them to about 4 inches apart.
• Cultivate as you would for carrots or parsley. Pull weeds by hand, bearing in mind that chervil seedlings are delicate.

Maturation Time
• Chervil reaches maturity 75 days from the planting of the seeds.

Harvesting
• Pick a few chervil leaves from each plant at any time they seem big enough for use. Remove leaves often to discourage plants from flowering and thus going to seed.

Storing
• To dry, place stems with their leaves on a screen or stretched thin cloth in a dry, dark place. When dry, strip the leaves from the stems and store them in airtight bottles away from light.
• To freeze, see "Kitchen Tips."

Garden Tips
• Too-rich soil makes chervil seedlings leggy.
• Some gardeners plant radishes with chervil, claiming that the radishes stimulate the chervil to sturdier growth and improve its flavor.
• Dill is a good companion plant for chervil.

Kitchen Tips
• Fresh chervil is wonderful mixed with salad greens, as a garnish, or in

a sauce for chicken or fish. It also goes well with any vegetable soup.

• Keep chervil in near-fresh condition by washing it, shaking well, and putting it in a tightly closed glass jar in the refrigerator.

• To freeze chervil, wash and gently roll dry in a dishtowel, then store it in an airtight container in the freezer. It will keep its fresh, green color if you use it without thawing.

Chick-pea

See *Bean*

Chicory

See *Endive*

Chinese Broccoli

See *Kale*

Chinese Cabbage

See *Cabbage*

Chinese Chives, Chinese Leek

See *Chives*

Chipmunks

Also known as ground squirrels, chipmunks rarely do much damage to a garden. Indeed, they eat slugs and insects, so if you have them, make your peace with them.

Chives

Chives, in the onion family, are an easy-to-grow, hardy perennial, come up each spring, and will yield harvests for 10 years or more. Their round or cone-shaped lavender flowers look pretty in the garden and make an attractive garnish for salads. If grown from seed, chives usually do best from the second year on. They spread quickly, forming clumps 8 to 12 inches high. You can further divide the clumps every few years. Chives can also be grown indoors in pots for culinary use. (See "Garden Tips.")

A variety called garlic chives is also known as Chinese chives, Oriental garlic, or Chinese leek. These bloom later, are somewhat taller, and have white, star-shaped flowers that smell faintly like roses. The leaves (stems) are flat and have a light flavor of garlic.

When to Plant

• Chives may be started indoors, from seed, at the end of winter. Keep moist. Set plants (or sow seeds) outdoors in early spring, after the heaviest frosts are over.

Where to Plant

• Chives like a slightly acid to neutral soil (pH 6.5 to 7.0) but grow almost anywhere, provided there is good drainage. They like sun but will grow in partial shade.

How to Plant

• Plant chive seeds in small clusters (about 10 to a cluster), ½ inch deep and 12 inches apart. If you are planting in rows, keep the rows 12 inches apart.
• Space small clumps or transplants 12 inches apart.

Germination Time

• Seedlings appear 15 to 20 days after seeds are sown.

Care During Growth

• Transplant seedlings in clumps of 4 or 5 when they're about 3 inches high.
• If the plants appear straggly in mid-season, cut them down to a few inches (use the cuttings in your kitchen); they'll grow up again.

Maturation Time

• Chives reach their full growth 60 to 70 days after seeds are planted.

Harvesting

• Chives can be clipped at will any time during the growing season. Picking encourages fresh growth.
• When you harvest garlic chives, it's best to clip only the outer leaves.

Continued growth will occur from the center.

Storing

• Chives lose most of their flavor when dried. Instead of cutting them for drying, see "Garden Tips" for how to grow them indoors.

• To freeze chives, wash the stems well and shake vigorously. Then put them in waxed paper, plastic wrap, or a tightly capped jar. They'll keep their green color if you use them without defrosting.

Diseases and Pests

• Onion fly maggots.

Garden Tips

• Chives make a nice border for a flower bed.

• If onion-fly maggots attack chives, move your chive patch every second year (transplant in the fall or spring).

• For fresh chives in winter, plant seeds indoors in pots in early September. You'll have chives by Thanksgiving.

• Or pot a few clumps from the garden in late fall and keep them indoors for winter use.

• Or transfer some of your garden chives to sunken pots very late in the fall, before the ground freezes, mulching them lightly. Take up the pots during the January or February thaw, and bring them indoors. The chives will think it's spring and start to grow, and you'll be eating them in late winter or very early spring.

• When clumps of chives become too thick, divide them in the fall or spring, planting the divisions in smaller clumps.

• Garlic chives self-sow freely. If you don't want an ever-expanding patch, cut off the flower heads before seeds form.

• Chives planted with roses are said to combat black spot; planted with carrots, they are said to repel carrot rust flies.

Kitchen Tips

• The best way to cut chives is with a small pair of kitchen scissors. Cut them off at the top, and the chives will keep growing.

• Sprinkle very finely cut chives liberally over plates of hot or cold soup.

• Add plenty of finely cut chives to mayonnaise or any creamy salad dressing.

Cilantro

See *Coriander*

Clubroot 🪲

Clubroot is a usually fatal plant disease caused by a slime mold that attacks roots and below-soil stems of plants, mainly brassicas, such as broccoli, Brussels sprouts, cabbage, cauliflower, collards, garden cress, horseradish, kale, kohlrabi, mustard, radishes, rutabagas, and turnips, especially when these are grown in quite acid soil.

Manifestation
• Leaves become yellow and roots exhibit knobby swellings.

To Combat
• Rotate crops, avoiding planting any brassicas in a bed where other brassicas have been grown for the past 2 years.
• Increase the alkalinity of your soil if the pH is below 6.5.
• Pull up and burn all affected plants. Bag and discard them if you can't burn them.

Cole Crops (Brassicas)

See *Broccoli; Brussels sprouts; Cabbage; Cauliflower; Collards; Horseradish; Kale; Kohlrabi; Mustard; Radish; Rutabaga; Turnip*

Collards

A variety of kale, collards are an easily grown cool-weather crop. Their blue-green leaves have a cabbagelike flavor. Collards are fairly winter hardy and will withstand light freezing—in fact, their flavor improves after a frost. Unlike kale, collards also withstand summer heat well.

When to Plant
• Plant seeds or set out transplants early in the spring, as soon as the ground can be worked. You can also make a second planting in early to midsummer for a fall-winter crop.

Where to Plant
• Collards like cool, moist soil that is rich in nitrogen (well-rotted manure is excellent mixed into the soil) and slightly acid to neutral (pH 6 to 7). Plant collards in the sun.

How to Plant
• Sprinkle seeds lightly in a line, or in lines 24 inches apart, and cover them with ½ inch of fine soil.
• Or space transplants 18 to 24 inches apart in rows 24 to 30 inches apart.

Germination Time
• Seeds germinate in 10 days.

Care During Growth
• When the seedlings are about 2 inches high, thin them to 18 to 24 inches apart.
• Collards don't need much attention aside from occasional weeding and watering whenever the ground seems dry.

Maturation Time
• Collards reach maturity 75 to 80 days from planting of the seeds.

Harvesting
• Collards are harvested like kale: You can use the whole young plant, or you can cut the tender lower leaves, leaving the inner portion to continue to grow and produce.

Storing
• Collards are one of the few vegetables that should be washed before storing. After washing, shake them well and store at about 35°F—just short of freezing.

Diseases and Pests
• Collards have the same enemies as cabbage. (See *Cabbage* for details.)

Garden Tips
• The outer leaves of collards, because they are exposed to more sunlight, are richer in vitamin C than the inner ones.
• If you remove only single outer leaves, the plant replaces them rapidly.
• Nasturtiums are often planted as a trap core to lure aphids away from collards.

Kitchen Tip
• Use the leaves of collard greens for stuffing and rolling just as you would cabbage. You don't have to blanch them first; just wash, fill, and roll. They'll soften nicely while they cook.

Colorado Potato Beetles

These black-striped and black-spotted yellow beetles winter in the ground, emerging in the spring to lay eggs on the undersides of the leaves of eggplants, peppers, potatoes, and tomatoes. The eggs hatch in about a week into red larvae with black spots along their sides. Both adults and larvae feed on plants, often doing great damage.

Manifestation
• The orange-yellow eggs can be seen on the undersides of leaves. Both the larvae and the adult beetles strip leaves and shoots from the plants.

To Combat
• Look for clusters of orange eggs by holding a mirror under plant leaves. Remove and crush the eggs, or remove the infected leaves.
• Handpick the beetles and larvae and dispose of them.
• Interplant beans, catnip, coriander, horseradish, nasturtiums, or tansy among susceptible plants—these are reported to repel Colorado potato beetles.
• Keep your soil rich in compost or manure. Or wet the soil (not the plants) with manure tea. Boil pieces of cedar bark or wood until the water turns tan. Sprinkle affected plants with this solution—beetles and their larvae hate it.
• Put 1 cup or so of the beetles themselves in your blender with some garlic and hot peppers and a little water, purée them, then strain and spray affected plants with the liquid once a week.
• A special strain of Bacillus thuringiensis known as Bt kills both Colorado potato beetles and their larvae. You can order these bacteria from many plant nurseries.
• Ladybugs go after potato beetles. So do wasps and yellow jackets.
• Rotenone is effective against these beetles. Spray in June, and again in August to catch the second generation.
• Don't leave decomposing vegetation around in the fall. Beetles overwinter in this material.

Compost Pile 🌱

Compost is broken-down organic material that is the soul of good garden soil. It is dark brown, compacts loosely when pressed together, and has a pleasant, earthy smell. It gives nutriment to plants, conserves moisture in the soil, and improves drainage and aeration.

A well-layered compost pile will quickly produce rich nourishment for your soil. To set one up, make the first layer of chopped or shredded green manure (soft stems and leaves, grass clippings, weeds, and so on); then add a thin layer of animal manure (you can buy this packaged if necessary); then a couple of inches of soil; and last a very light sprinkling of lime or wood ashes. After that, add chopped kitchen wastes (vegetable only), as they accumulate, each time covering lightly with soil.

A too-small compost pile won't heat up properly. If you don't use a bin, make the pile approximately 5 feet square. You can make a good compost bin out of a 40-gallon plastic rubbish barrel with a cover. Remove the entire bottom. Then cut out a 5-inch strip along the bottom of the barrel, about a third of the way around. This provides the space through which you will shovel out compost as it sinks. Drill holes about the size of a quarter, in rows or at random, all over the sides of the barrel. Each time you deposit material for composting in the top, cover the barrel to keep the heat in and the rain out.

Kitchen wastes that are best for a compost pile include chopped fruit and vegetable peelings and leftovers, coffee grounds, crushed eggshells, stale bread, and tea leaves. Include also hair and animal brushings, old flowers, discarded plants, and wood ashes. Leaf mold is high in carbon and valuable in the compost pile. Manure—fresh or aged—is an excellent addition. Don't neglect the addition of soil from time to time. It provides necessary organisms and absorbs excess nitrogen and moisture as well as odors.

The heat in a compost pile (necessary to kill seeds and decompose organic matter) will build up more evenly (through the uniform distribution of oxygen) if you turn the pile occasionally with a spading fork. Mixing materials of different textures in the compost pile helps form air pockets, aiding in the breakdown of organic matter. If you don't use a bin, cover the outside of your compost pile with black plastic to help it heat up faster. Doing this also prevents the nutrients from leaching out when it rains. If your compost pile smells of garbage, it needs more oxygen and may contain too much moisture. Turn the contents with a spading fork to expose them to the air.

A compost pile is largely inert during a freezing winter, but you can continue adding shredded kitchen wastes with a little soil (keep a bag of soil in your cellar or garage for this purpose). With the coming of spring, the pile will return to action. You can also store kitchen scraps in an outdoor container over the freezing winter, then compost them in the spring.

You can easily make bags of compost, storing them in your cellar or garage until you wish to use them: Take a large plastic trash bag and add the following, more or less in layers, as they come to hand: (1) Garden leaves, fresh or dried, and soft-stemmed plants, such as weeds, houseplant prunings, and so on. (2) All kitchen garbage, with the exception of meat or fowl. Fish is excellent, all vegetable leavings and trimmings, tea leaves, coffee grounds, and so on. You can keep a covered receptacle in your kitchen to receive this garbage, then periodically add it to your compost bag. (3) An occasional trowelful of soil of any kind. (4) A little liquid now and then if the contents of the bag seem dry. Compost won't form unless there is some moisture in the mixture. (But it mustn't be soggy.) Many of the food and plant residues you put in the bag already contain moisture. (5) Ground-up eggshells (you grind them in your blender or food processor). (6) An occasional trowelful of wood ashes.

When each bag is three-quarters full, twist the top closed, tie it with a twist tie, and set it where it can remain undisturbed for several months. Keep putting the newest bags in the back, and use the front ones as you need them. By following this process, you can have a never-ending supply of rich compost.

Most diseased plants shouldn't be composted. Bag and discard them, or burn them.

Coriander

Also known as Chinese parsley and cilantro, coriander is an annual herb easy to grow from seed and valued for its pungent leaves and seeds. It needs no special care and, once established, normally reseeds itself year after year. It can reach a height of 1½ feet.

When to Plant
• Plant seeds directly in the garden early in spring, after all danger of frost is past.

Where to Plant
• Plant in light, well-drained soil (pH 6 to 7), in full sun.

How to Plant
• Coriander is difficult to transplant, so seeds should be sown directly in a permanent bed. Sow seeds thinly, in rows 1 foot apart, covering them with ¼ inch of fine soil. Firm the soil lightly, and keep the bed moist.

Germination Time
• Plants emerge in 2 to 3 weeks.

Care During Growth
• Thin seedlings to about 8 inches apart when they're 2 inches high.
• Coriander needs little other care.

Maturation
• Seeds mature in about 90 days.

Harvesting
• You can harvest fresh leaves throughout the season, leaving the rest of the plant to continue producing.

• Keep an eye on the fruits in late summer when they begin to turn brown, before the weight of the seeds causes shattering.

• The best time to cut the ripe stalks is early in the morning.

Storing

• Dry both leaves and seeds on a screen or tray in a warm place out of the sun. Separate the dried seeds from the dried leaves, and store each in tightly covered containers.

Diseases and Pests

• Carrot rust flies.

Garden Tips

• Hot summer sun may cause coriander to bolt to seed too early. If you want the fresh leaves, plant coriander in midsummer, so that the cooler fall months will stimulate it to put out leaves for a much longer period than will result from early plantings.

• Dill is a good companion plant for coriander.

Kitchen Tips

• Use fresh coriander leaves, coarsely chopped, the next time you make a curry. They're also wonderful, used sparingly, in salads or mixed in with most cookie doughs.

• For freezing, wash and drain fresh coriander leaves well and roll them gently in a dishtowel to remove as much water as possible. Freeze them in small jars or well wrapped in waxed paper or plastic wrap. They keep their flavor admirably. Use them straight from the freezer in soups, especially creamed soups.

• Coriander butter is particularly delicious. Chop the leaves quite fine, then mix 4 tablespoons of leaves with ½ cup of soft butter. Keep in a small jar in the refrigerator, and use on rice, vegetables, or broiled fish.

Corn

You can prolong your harvest of sweet corn by planting varieties that have different maturing dates: There are early, midsummer, and late varieties. Or make periodic plantings, one or two weeks apart, of any one variety. If you have a short growing season, choose early-maturing types, some of which are ready to harvest 60 days from the day of sowing (some long-season varieties may take up to 100 days to mature). Generally, there is less choice among early types, although early corn is somewhat hardier.

Corn is a heavy feeder that takes a lot of nutrients out of the soil. See "Care During Growth" for how to handle this.

If you're growing popcorn, keep it separated from sweet corn by at least 50 feet. Cross-pollination can ruin both crops. However, if the two types of corn produce their pollen at different times, there's little danger of cross-pollination. You can count on collecting about a pound of popping corn for every four plants you sow.

When to Plant
• Corn isn't vigorously hardy and should be planted when all danger of frost is past—when (according to the Pilgrims) the leaves of the white oak are as large as a mouse's ear. Some gardeners wait to plant their corn until tulips bloom. The sweeter the variety of corn, the warmer the soil should be—well above 50°F.

• Sow corn every 2 weeks until midsummer, using early-maturing varieties for your last planting. Corn planted late in the season (early to midsummer) is less likely to fall prey to corn borers.

Where to Plant
• Plant corn in full sun—a southern slope is ideal—in very fertile, well-drained soil. Always enrich the soil well first: Dig in composted manure, bonemeal and cottonseed meal, and wood ashes. Corn especially likes a soil rich in nitrogen and slightly acid to neutral (pH 6 to 7).

How to Plant
• Since corn is largely wind pollinated, it is now thought that for proper pollination to occur it should be closely planted in blocks rather than in widely separated rows. Sow the seeds at random, or in at least 4 rows within the block, with ultimately no more than 15 inches on all sides between plants.

• Popcorn, because its plants are smaller than those of sweet corn, can be planted 10 inches apart.

• You can speed germination by soaking the seeds in tepid water for about 24 hours. Or roll them up in a moist paper towel and keep them damp until the kernels just being to sprout. Be careful not to damage the sprouts when you plant.

• You can also speed germination as well as growth by using a clear plastic mulch over the entire corn bed.

• Sow seeds 1 inch deep, 15 inches apart, in blocks, as previously described. Or plant in rows within the block, 4 inches apart, thinning to about 15 inches apart when the seedlings are 3 inches high.

Germination Time
• Seeds germinate in 7 to 10 days, depending on the weather.

Care During Growth
• Every now and then throughout the growing period give the corn a boost

with any of the following: fresh or rotted manure, manure tea, fish emulsion, compost, shredded leaf mulch, or humus.

• Be sure the plants get plenty of water, especially during dry spells. Moisture is particularly important before silking and during the entire time the ears are filling out. If you water when the corn is tasseling, try to irrigate from below so the tassels don't get wet—it's hard for the wind to carry wet pollen.

• Corn is shallow rooted—hill the plants firmly with soil when they're about 2 feet high to strengthen the stems against windstorms and keep them from bending over. Or place a brick or a small rock firmly against the base of each stalk in the direction it's leaning. Soil or wood ashes are very good heaped up around the stones.

• Don't remove the bottom shoots (tillers, or suckers). The plant needs these for nourishment.

• Mulching conserves moisture and keeps down weeds.

Maturation Time

• Corn matures in 60 to 100 days, depending on variety. Midget corn ripens in 58 to 66 days.

Harvesting

• The time to pick the ears is when the tassels have become brown and dry and the tips (upper ends) of the ears feel fully formed. You can also pull back a strip of the husk and have a look at the teeth. Press one of the kernels with your fingernail: If the liquid is watery and clear, leave the ear to ripen for possibly another week. The corn is ready for picking when the liquid looks milky.

• Corn begins to lose its sweetness immediately after picking. Husk the ears right away, and keep them cool until you cook them, preferably the same day.

• *Popcorn:* Wait until the stalks and leaves are completely dry and rustly before harvesting. Before removing the kernels, keep the ears in a dry place for a couple of weeks. They're ready for shelling when a sharp twist of the ear (use both hands) makes the kernels drop off.

• Harvest time for ripe corn lasts 5 to 10 days.

Storing

• If you have to store corn for a while, don't remove the husks. Keep the ears cold.

• Here's a tip for keeping corn relatively fresh for several days: Cut the stalk itself, diagonally, well above and below the ear. Stand stalks in a pail in a few inches of water and keep cool.

• *Popcorn:* Keep the kernels in closed jars for a couple of weeks so that whatever moisture is left in them will be distributed evenly. Then you can pop them.

Diseases and Pests
• Armyworms, bacterial diseases, corn borers, corn earworms, corn-root aphids, cucumber beetles, cutworms, earwigs, flea beetles, Japanese beetles, leafhoppers, raccoons, squirrels, thrips, verticillium wilt.

Garden Tips
• Every strand of corn silk at the top of a developing ear results in a potential kernel. For good ear fill it's important that each strand get fertilized: This is the chief reason for planting corn close together.
• The pollen of yellow sweet corn is dominant over that of white. If you plant both white and yellow varieties, your white corn may show some yellow kernels. This doesn't affect eating quality.
• Hybrid sweet corn doesn't breed true: You won't get the same variety if you plant seeds from hybrid ears.
• Don't water popcorn too much while the ears are filling out—overwatering may cause the kernels to split.
• If you have trouble with birds getting at your corn, try slipping a large-size paper cup over each ear of corn as it begins to develop.
• A few rows of sunflowers planted between beds of different varieties of corn can act as pollen traps and lessen or prevent cross-pollination.
• Soak ground-up citrus rinds and seeds overnight, then strain and spray this solution on your corn if it's bothered by corn earworms.
• Fish and fish waste are one of the best sources of nitrogen for corn. Bury them 6 inches deep throughout your corn bed.
• Try planting cosmos among your corn. They are said to repel earworms.
• Interplant lettuce (which can't take hot summer sun) among your corn. The corn will shade it.
• Peas, beans, and other legumes, interplanted among corn, add nitrogen to the soil. Pole beans, planted in early July, will climb the corn.
• Other plants that flourish among corn are cabbage, cauliflower, cucumbers, lamb's-quarters, lettuce, melons, potatoes, pumpkins, spinach, and squashes. The thick vines of pumpkins and squashes choke out many weeds.
• You can also plant clover between corn rows; it inhibits weeds as well as contributing nitrogen to the soil.
• Once you've harvested your corn, cut down the stalks. Chop or shred them and spread them over the bed. Or bend them down, stamp on them, and spread compost, loam, or peat moss over them. They'll partially decompose over the winter, and you'll have a rich bed for your spring planting.

Kitchen Tips

• If you can't use corn the day you pick it, stand it—with the husks still on—in a little water in the refrigerator, stem side down. It will keep its flavor well for a day or two.

• Use a stiff vegetable brush to remove the silk from shucked corn.

• Salt added to the water in which you cook corn toughens it.

• Put the tenderer green husks from inside the corn into the cooking water. They add beautifully to the flavor.

• To boil corn, put it in a large pot, cover with boiling water, put a lid on the pot, then turn on the heat. As soon as the water returns to a boil, remove the pot from the heat, still covered, and let it stand about 8 minutes. Test, drain, and serve. Cooked this way, the corn can stand in the hot water for as long as 20 minutes and still have fine flavor.

• Corn becomes tough from overcooking. Test an ear from the pot occasionally.

• Here's a way to cook corn that uses very little water. Take the tender inner husks, wet them, and use them to line the sides and bottom of a heavy pot. Put the shucked corn in, and cover with more husks. Cover the pot tightly, and set over low to medium heat. When the lid feels hot, turn the heat as low as possible and cook for about 12 minutes longer.

• If you have to cook corn a little ahead of time, bring the water to a boil, add the corn, cover, and turn off the heat. Let it stand until you're ready to serve. It will rarely need more cooking.

• Try roasting corn in your oven. Pull out the silk, but leave the husks on. Roast at 325° for about 50 minutes. Remove the husks (wear rubber household gloves—the husks are *hot*) and serve. This method gives much better flavor than boiling.

. . .

Corn Borers

Also known as the European corn borer, this larva of a European nocturnal moth attacks mainly corn but can also damage beans, beets, celery, peppers, and potatoes, as well as many garden flowers. The female moth lays small masses of pale yellow eggs on the undersides of leaves and on stalks of corn and other plants. From these hatch pale yellow larvae with rows of brown spots. These caterpillars, which may grow to 1 inch in length, start to eat holes in the leaves and then bore into the stems and into the ears of corn. The larvae overwinter in the stems of the plants they attack, pupate in the spring, and then emerge as egg-laying moths during the summer.

Manifestation

• Small holes in the stalks, with sawdustlike castings around them, are generally the first signs of corn borer damage. The stalks may bend, and corn tassels look damaged. Borers get into the ear tips and may reach the cobs as well.

To Combat

• It is sometimes possible, when you see a hole in a stem that you suspect is a borer hole, to slit the stem open below the hole and remove and destroy the borer.

• Since the larvae spend the winter inside plant stalks, chop up all stalks, as well as all other plant debris, right after harvesting, and either add them to your compost pile or burn them.

• Rotenone is useful against corn borers.

• The larvae of trichogramma wasps parasitize corn borer eggs. A New England species of this wasp, called *Trichogramma ostrinia*, is especially well adapted to this task. You can buy the eggs of this wasp from some garden supply houses.

Corn Earworms

These green to brown 2-inch caterpillars with lengthwise light and dark stripes are also known as tobacco budworms and tomato fruitworms. The caterpillars spend the winter mainly inside cornstalks, emerging in the spring to attack corn primarily, but also beans, lettuce, peas, peppers, potatoes, squashes, and tomatoes. They then burrow into the ground to pupate, emerging in about 2 weeks as green-and-brown moths, which lay eggs, producing new caterpillars. There can be two, three, or even more generations in a season, depending on the length of the summer.

Corn earworm larvae generally start eating the leaves and then proceed to eat into the fruit. On corn, earworms also attack the silks and then bore into the ears, feeding on the kernels and sometimes the cobs themselves.

Manifestation

• The leaves of attacked plants wilt and brown. Examination of the fruit easily reveals the caterpillars. Frequently only the tips of the corn ears are affected; pulling back the husks will uncover the earworms. (In such cases, if the corn is ripe, just cut off the tips.)

To Combat

• Pick off and destroy any caterpillars you find.

• Citrus rinds and seeds contain a chemical that discourages corn earworms. Grind these rinds and seeds up in warm water, let the solution stand for about 8 hours, then strain it and spray directly on affected plants.

• A drop of mineral oil applied to the very tips of corn ears as soon as the silks brown is an effective deterrent.

• A little lime dusted on the outside husks of corn as soon as the silks have wilted also deters earworms.

• Corn earworm eggs are destroyed by trichogramma wasps, which lay their own eggs inside them, killing them before they hatch. You can buy these eggs from many nurseries.

Corn-Root Aphids

See also *Aphids*

These tiny blue-green aphids differ from other aphids in that they attack only the roots of plants—corn especially, but also beets, carrots, strawberries, and many ornamental plants. Like other aphids, corn-root aphids are nurtured and protected by ants (cornfield ants), which feed on the honeydew secreted by the aphids and store the aphid eggs in their own nests over the winter, introducing the newly hatched young in the spring and throughout the summer to the plant roots they eventually devastate.

Manifestation

• If you dig up plants you suspect are infested, you may see the pinpoint-sized aphids at work. You may also discover cornfield ants and their tunnels, which they build close to the plants. Since the aphids suck juices from roots, the plants eventually wither and die.

To Combat

• Destruction of the ants' nests and tunnels will rid the area of corn-root aphids. Before planting in the spring, dig the garden bed down to at least 8 inches, exposing the dirt thoroughly to the elements. Do this every other day for about a week.

• Rotate corn and other attacked vegetable crops each year to noninfested plots.

. . .

Corn Salad

Also called field salad, Italian corn salad, lamb's lettuce, or mâche, corn salad is easy to grow and attacked by few pests. There are broad-leaved and round-leaved varieties. The leaves are dark green, slightly resembling leaf lettuce, and are eaten raw in salads as well as cooked. The flowers are also edible. Corn salad reseeds itself readily.

When to Plant
• For a late-spring or early-summer crop, plant seeds in the spring, as soon as the ground can be worked. Seeds can also be sown through the end of July. Later plantings should be shaded.
• You can also plant seeds in the late fall, before hard frost sets in. Well mulched over the winter, they often sprout successfully very early the next spring.

Where to Plant
• Although corn salad has no special soil requirements, it does best in a medium-fertile soil (pH 6.5 to 7.5) that is well drained. Corn salad likes sun with a little shade, particularly during the hottest part of the day. Since it doesn't tolerate heat well, try interplanting with taller plants that will shade it: broccoli, Brussels sprouts, onions, tomatoes, turnips, and others.

How to Plant
• Scatter the small, round seeds in the garden bed, covering them ¼ to ½ inch with fine soil. Or dribble the seeds along narrow furrows that are 12 inches apart, covering the seeds ¼ to ½ inch deep. Keep the bed moist.

Germination Time
• Seeds germinate in 7 to 14 days.

Care During Growth
• Continue to keep the bed moist as the seedlings grow and provide shade if necessary during hot, dry weather. Thin plants to about 5 inches apart when they reach a height of about 1½ inches.
• If plants are grown in the fall, just mulch them well before hard winter sets in—you'll get extra-early edible plants in the spring.

Harvesting
• Cut the leaves throughout the season as needed, allowing the plants to continue growing, or pull up and use the entire plant when it reaches the size you want.

Garden Tips
• Leave a few plants here and there, undisturbed, allowing them to go to seed. Corn salad generally comes up year after year, reseeding itself.

• It doesn't hurt to provide some mulch over hard winter periods.

. . .

Cowpea

See *Bean*

Cress

See *Garden Cress*; see also *Watercress*

Crop Rotation

Don't plant the same vegetable in the same bed two years in a row. The nutrients required by that plant may become depleted from the soil; also, insects and disease pathogens that attack that particular crop can increase to very harmful levels if the crop is continually planted in the same place.

Every 4 years or so, plant a leguminous crop (beans, lentils, peas) in each of your garden areas by turn. This practice not only maintains but even increases soil fertility. You might also plant nonedible legumes, such as alfalfa and clover, in each bed now and then, then plow them under in late summer.

Crown Gall

See *Bacterial diseases*

Crucifers

See *Broccoli; Brussels sprouts; Cabbage; Cauliflower; Garden cress; Horseradish; Kohlrabi; Mustard; Nasturtium; Radish; Rocket; Rutabaga; Turnip; Watercress*

Cucumber

Cucumbers are a tender, frost-sensitive crop. They are rapid growers and need plenty of water, nourishment, and hot weather. They come in vining and bush varieties.

Vining varieties keep growing through the summer and into the autumn, as long as the weather permits. An individual vining cucumber plant will outproduce a bush plant. Vining varieties, although they'll grow on the ground, will produce more if supported on a trellis or a fence. You can also squeeze more into less space if you trellis the plants.

Bush varieties are generally more compact than nontrellised vining types. Their producing period is somewhat shorter than that of vining cucumbers. But if grown closer together, the ultimate yield of bush varieties may not be much less than that of the vining types in a comparable sized space. More and more new bush cucumber varieties are becoming available.

Standard varieties of cucumber (called monoecious) produce male and female flowers, with the fruit forming behind the female flowers. But some new gynoecious (producing female flowers only) varieties outproduce standard cucumbers (see "How to Plant"). Some new cucumber varieties have built-in disease resistance. Oriental long cucumbers can grow to 15 inches in length and are referred to as "burpless" (nonbitter).

When to Plant

• Sow cucumber seeds indoors in early to midspring, or about 4 weeks before the last expected frost. Transplant outdoors when the soil has warmed to about 65°F, or at about the time iris blooms.

• Or plant seeds outdoors when all danger of frost is past, in middle to late spring or even at the very beginning of summer. You can make later sowings any time up to midsummer.

Where to Plant

• Plant cucumbers in full sun. Although they'll grow in average gar-den soil, you'll get a better crop if you dig well-rotted manure or other organic matter into the garden bed first. Cucumbers need lots of nitrogen and appreciate fertile, light, warm, moist, well-drained soil that is near neutral to slightly alkaline (pH 6.5 to 7.5).

How to Plant

• If you are starting seeds indoors, plant 2 seeds ½ inch deep per small peat pot or other container. When the seedlings are ready to go to the garden, cut the weaker of the plants at soil level, leaving the vigorous one for transplanting. Place them in the garden, covering the roots ½ to ¾ inch deep. Space bush varieties 3 feet apart on all sides. Vining types that are to be trained up a trellis or fence should be 1 foot apart. Vining plants that are not to be tied up need a great deal more room—space them 4 to 5 feet apart on all sides.

• Seeds sown directly in the garden should be planted ½ inch deep, about 6 seeds to the foot, in rows 3 to 4 feet apart. Thin the plants when they are about 4 inches high, selecting the most vigorous ones and spacing them about 3 feet apart for bush varieties, 1 foot apart for those to be trained up a trellis, and 4 to 5 feet apart on all sides for vining types allowed to wander at will.

• If you're planting seeds of the gynoecious (female) type, to get better fruit you will need 1 seed of a standard pollinator variety for about every 6 of the female type in the row. The two kinds of seeds come color-coded in the seed packets. (Bear in mind which are the standard type plants when you thin. You might want to mark them.)

Germination Time

• Seeds germinate in 7 to 10 days, depending on soil temperature and weather.

Care During Growth

• As the seedlings emerge, break the crust gently around them every few days to speed their growth.
• Cultivate to remove weeds.
• It's very important to keep the soil moist throughout the growing period. Cucumbers need about 1 inch of water weekly—more if the weather becomes hot and dry.
• Because cucumbers are heavy feeders requiring extra-rich soil, apply manure tea, leaf mulch tea, or fish emulsion regularly around the roots. Keep applying compost.
• Vining cucumbers are pretty fair climbers up a trellis. You may need to help them occasionally with plant ties.

Maturation Time

• Cucumbers mature in 50 to 80 days, depending on variety, from when seeds are sown.

Harvesting

• Cucumbers can be harvested over a 4-week period at least. The plants produce more when the fruits are picked regularly—don't let the early ones grow too large or the vines will bear fewer. Cucumber plants continue producing to the end of the season if their fruits are picked regularly.
• Pulling a cucumber off the vine may damage the plant. Instead, use your thumb to push the stem off.

Storing

• The best temperature for cucumber storage is between 45° and 55°F. But cucumbers don't store well for long periods—they should be used within 7 to 10 days after picking. Otherwise pickle them. They don't freeze well either.

Diseases and Pests

• Bacterial diseases, borers, cucumber beetles, cutworms, damping off, flea beetles, mildew, green peach aphids, leafhoppers, mosaic virus, nematodes, squash bugs, tarnished plant bugs, thrips, whiteflies.

Garden Tips

• Don't grow cucumbers in the same place 2 years in a row.
• Improve the pollination of your cukes by planting them close to bee-attracting flower beds.
• Cucumbers planted in the spring produce much more fruit than summer-planted cucumbers.
• Seeds planted horizontally, edgewise, germinate better than those planted flat or upright.
• Take special care when transplanting not to disturb the roots.
• Bush cucumbers don't bear fruit for as long as vining types. Plant bush varieties in succession, 1 or 2 weeks apart, to get a longer harvest.
• You can grow vining cukes in 6-foot-tall mesh cages—the vines will grow up the mesh, making the fruits easy to pick. This practice saves space, too.
• Or train cucumber vines to grow on a 6-foot-high trellis, arbor, or fence, or on groups of three poles fastened together at the top, tepee fashion. Use twist ties to anchor the vines. This practice exposes more leaves to the sun and makes harvesting easier. If necessary, you can fasten nylon or cloth slings to help hold the larger fruits to the support.
• If nights are cool after you've planted cucumber seedlings outdoors, cover the plants with paper or plastic tents, or large inverted cans.
• Don't water too heavily in early spring, and avoid handling the plants at any time while they're wet with dew or rain.
• Some gardeners hand-pollinate their cucumber flowers. The female flower has a slight bulge at the base. Use a small, pointed paintbrush to transfer the pollen from the male flower to the female. This is best done at a cool time of day.
• Some gardeners remove the female flowers during the first 2 or 3 weeks of their appearance. This gives a slightly later but more numerous yield.
• Vining cukes left to grow on the ground will be better off if you put a straw mulch under them.
• Young cukes often develop spines from the "warts" on their skins. This is natural.

• Cucumbers may turn bitter if they don't receive enough water or if the fruits are exposed to too much sun. It's best to shade them slightly if possible.

• Remove cukes from the vines as soon as they're ready for picking—leaving them unpicked will cut your yields drastically.

• You can plant cucumber vines in your asparagus bed. By the time they're ready for climbing, the asparagus harvest is past, and asparagus stems and foliage make excellent stakes.

• Remove and destroy all wilted vines in September; they may harbor mosaic virus and borer eggs.

• Some gardeners maintain that interplanting cucumbers with broccoli, catnip, corn, or tansy significantly reduces the attacks of cucumber beetles.

• Other good companion plantings for cucumbers are beans, corn, lettuce, nasturtiums, peas, radishes, and sunflowers.

Kitchen Tips

• For most uses, pick cucumbers while they're small, thin, and very green. Those left to grow larger and thicker and starting to show yellow on the surface tend to be pulpy, tough, and full of large seeds.

• For a professional look to cucumber slices, take a sharp-tined fork and score a cucumber from top to bottom (pressing in at the top and drawing the fork toward the bottom, making sharp lines). Do this all the way around the cucumber, then slice it crosswise.

• To make peeled, diced cucumbers very crisp for salad, sprinkle them with salt and refrigerate in a bowl for a couple of hours. Drain them—they will have released quite a bit of water—and dry with paper towels or a dishtowel. Then refrigerate again until you're ready to use them.

• Here's how to prepare cucumbers for cooking so they won't be mushy: Peel, slice down the middle, and remove the seeds. Then salt them well and let stand for 1 hour or more to draw out excessive water. Wipe off the salt, and dry with a dishtowel.

• Cook cucumbers as you would eggplants. You can stuff and bake them; or boil and drain them, then cover with a sauce or cream, and put them under the broiler.

Cucumber Beetles 🪲

Some of these greenish-yellow beetles are called striped cucumber beetles (they have black stripes); others are known as spotted cucumber beetles (with black spots). They are ¼ inch long and spend the winter at the bases of or in the lower stems of plants. As the weather warms, the beetles lay eggs at these spots and then, with the newly hatched larvae (known also as southern corn rootworms), begin feeding on seedlings and other plants.

They attack beans, cabbage, corn, cucumbers, melons, peas, potatoes, pumpkins, and squashes, as well as many ornamental plants. The adults usually feed on the leaves, the larvae on the roots and stems of young seedlings. The larvae then pupate underground, to emerge later as adult beetles. Besides the havoc they wreak directly on plants, both adults and larvae transmit bacterial wilt. Mature plants can withstand cucumber beetle attacks better than seedlings can.

Manifestation
• Plants whose roots have been tunneled by larvae turn yellow and die. More mature plants show beetle infestation by large, irregular holes in their leaves. Adult beetles also attack new shoots as they appear on established plants.

To Combat
• Cultivate the soil thoroughly before planting to expose any dormant beetles. Destroy them.
• Rotate plantings—try not to plant vegetables that have already been attacked by cucumber beetles in the bed where you grew them before. And don't grow other susceptible plants in that bed either. Wait 2 to 3 years before beginning again with plants in the old bed.
• Look for wilt-resistant varieties of cucumbers, melons, and squashes.
• Plant susceptible vegetables as late as possible, after the first potential onslaught of beetle infestation is over.
• Handpick beetles as soon as you see any—the earlier the better—to reduce the larval population.
• Interplanting susceptible vegetables with beetle-deterrent plants has been shown to be effective: Plant alternating rows of broccoli, catnip, radishes, or tansy.
• Cucumber beetles prefer goldenrod to most other plants. Consider planting these near your vegetables to act as a trap crop, then pick off the beetles by hand.
• Physical barriers also work well: Cut out the bottoms of plastic milk jugs, and set these over young seedlings until they get established in the garden. Or make a frame of stakes around the bed, covering them with cheesecloth or netting, held at the bottom with stones. You can also make a wall of boxes around the garden bed and cover it with screens.
• Beetles don't like the resin in

freshly cut pine. Make tepee trellises for climbing beans using freshly cut pine poles—this will greatly lessen beetle attacks. Fine wood ashes dusted over the plants after a rain or a watering are a deterrent. Or make a spray of ½ cup each wood ashes and hydrated lime to 2 gallons of water.

• Rotenone spray is also excellent against both the beetles and their larvae.

• Always remove garden debris, particularly of affected plants, at the end of the season to prevent beetles from wintering over in it.

. . .

Cucumber Mosaic

See *Mosaic virus*

Cucurbits

See *Cucumber; Melon; Pumpkin; Squash*

Cumin

A delicate, quick-growing, annual herb, cumin is a member of the parsley family. It grows to about 6 inches tall. Originally a native of a hot, dry climate, it requires very little watering. Cumin is grown chiefly for its seeds for flavoring foods and, ground, as an ingredient in curry powder.

When to Plant
• Plant cumin seeds out of doors in late spring.

Where to Plant
• Plant in full sun in any ordinary garden soil (pH 6.5 to 7.5). Avoid too-rich soil, which is likely to produce leggy plants.

How to Plant
• Sprinkle the seeds lightly over the bed, covering them with no more than ¼ inch of soil, then press down with a board.

Germination Time
• Seeds germinate in 10 days.

Care During Growth
• Very little watering is needed. Remove weeds by hand, taking care not to damage the delicate seedlings.
• If the plants seem too thick, thin them to about 2 inches apart.
• As the summer advances, mulch plants lightly with fine soil to preserve the moisture in the ground.

Maturation Time
• White flowers appear in June; they produce small fruits 2 to 3 months after the seeds were planted. These fruits contain the seeds.

Harvesting
• Take care to collect the ripened seeds before they fall to the ground, in late August or early September.

Storing
• Wash the seeds, and let them dry thoroughly in a well-ventilated place on wire-mesh trays. They can then be bottled. If you want them ground, to make your own curry powder, pulverize them in the blender, then store the powder in jars or bottles.

Kitchen Tips
• Besides using ground cumin seeds as an ingredient in homemade curry powder (much better than bought!), mix some whole cumin seeds into cream cheese, add to bread and cookie dough, and use in many kinds of meat, fish, and vegetable sauces.
• Add some ground cumin to ordinary ketchup to give it zip.

Currant

Currants, both black and red varieties, are very hardy and easy to grow, and require only moderate care. Because currants are host plants for a fungal disease that is fatal to white pine (five-needled pine) trees, they should never be planted within 1,000 feet of white pines. In some states the growing of currants is prohibited in certain areas—consult the Cooperative Extension Service of the U.S. Department of Agriculture in your state before planting.

When to Plant
• Place the plants in the ground in the fall, since they bloom very early in the spring, often before the ground can be worked.

Where to Plant
• Currants prefer northern exposure and a cool, heavy, moist, but well-drained soil that is slightly acid (pH 5.75 to 6.50). They can take a moderate amount of shade.

How to Plant
• Set the plants about 4 feet apart and 2 to 3 inches deeper in the soil than they were in the nursery. Prune off about half the tops as soon as the plants are set in the ground. Water well after planting.

Care During Growth
• A permanent mulch is very beneficial to currant bushes. Use grass, hay, leaves, peat, sawdust, or straw, replacing whenever necessary. An application of well-rotted manure in the middle of the winter is also recommended. No further fertilizer is needed.
• Since currants bear their fruit at the base of year-old canes (and on some slightly older), each year remove all the branches that are more than 3 years old and any that seem too crowded. This can be done in early spring or early winter.
• Remove suckers that grow outside the plant rows and any branches that sprawl on the ground.
• Check for borers in August: Cut off and burn any wilted branches.

Maturation Time
• Currants begin to bear fruit 2 years after planting.

Harvesting
• Most currant varieties have long stems that make picking easy. Pick whole stem clusters rather than separate berries. Pick the berries when they're dry.
• The harvesting period lasts several weeks. If you're using the berries for jelly, harvest them just before they're fully ripe.

Storing
• Refrigerate currants as you would any other berries, taking care to keep them dry. Wash only before using.

Diseases and Pests
• Anthracnose, borers, mildew, root rot, and rust.

Garden Tips
• Avoid overuse of manure with currant plants; it often causes excess woody growth.
• An occasional fertilizing with wood ashes doesn't hurt.
• Most currant diseases can be controlled by spraying with rotenone. Cut out and burn any canes that seem sickly or infested.

Kitchen Tips
• Because currants are highly crushable, don't leave them piled on top of one another for long periods.
• If you're making currant jelly, don't double the recipe—it will come out better made in small amounts.
• Currant jelly has boiled enough if it drops thickly from a cold metal spoon or jells on a cool plate. Remove

jelly from the heat while you're testing it.

• Before you pour the jelly into sterilized glasses, set the glasses in a pan containing a little boiling water. They'll be less likely to crack.

• Here's a swift and easy way to make currant "jam." After you've washed the currants and removed all the stems, mash the berries and add honey until they're as sweet as you like them. Mix well and refrigerate. Use within 3 weeks.

• Here's a great dessert topping: Sweeten whipped cream, then gently fold in washed and refrigerated currants to taste. The resulting sweet-and-sour concoction is excellent on bread puddings, rice puddings, and other such desserts.

Cutworms

These 1- to 1½-inch-long, smooth caterpillars, the larvae of various species of noctuid moths, are often found coiled in the soil. They are usually pale, although some are gray or black. If you touch one, it immediately curls itself into a ball.

Cutworms stay coiled in the soil during the day but come out at night to attack tender seedlings, shearing them off at the soil line. Some climb stems to eat buds and leaves, but most of the damage is at ground level. They'll eat any succulent-stemmed young plants, generally favoring beans, all the brassicas, corn, cucumbers, lettuce, peppers, and tomatoes, as well as many garden flower seedlings. They don't generally do much damage to mature plants.

Manifestation

• The damage of cutworms is unmistakable: young seedlings sheared off at ground level.

To Combat

• Plow as early in the spring as the ground can be worked. Doing this will destroy early weed seedlings, which cutworms live on in the first stage of their development. Dispose of any worms you see. Do your planting about 2 weeks after this plowing.

• A heavy watering will bring cutworms to the surface of the soil, where you can pick them up and drop them into a can of water and ammonia, or water and soap or detergent.

• Trap cutworms by laying boards here and there in your garden. Lift the boards during the day, and pick up and destroy the coiled cutworms.

• The best protection against cutworm damage is to make collars for young seedlings: Use plastic cups or small milk or juice cartons or cans, all with the bottoms and tops cut out. Set one around each seedling, pressing it a couple of inches into the soil and extending a few inches above. Cutworms cannot get past these.

• Plastic soda straws also make effective barriers—cut them to the desired length, slit them, then slip one around the stem of each seedling, 1 inch into the soil and a couple of inches above.

• Trichogramma wasps lay their eggs inside the eggs and larvae of cutworms, demolishing them. You can buy the eggs of these wasps from many nurseries. Or you can use plants as lures to attract these wasps to your garden: buckwheat, carrots, all varieties of daisies, dill, goldenrod, Jerusalem artichokes, parsley, and parsnips.

• Interplant tansy among your seedlings to deter cutworms.

• Rotenone can also be used as a control against cutworms.

Damping Off

Damping off is a disease caused by a variety of soil fungi that invade seeds or the tissues of newly emerging seedlings, causing them to rot. It's more likely to strike when seeds have been planted in soil that is wet and cold. It can also attack seedlings in hot, wet weather, particularly if they are overcrowded. Plants especially susceptible to damping off are asparagus, beans, beets, cabbage, carrots, celery, cucumbers, eggplants, lettuce, melons, onions, peas, peppers, pumpkins, radishes, spinach, squashes, and tomatoes.

Manifestation

• Seeds rot and don't germinate. The stems of afflicted seedlings show rotting at the point where they emerge from the soil. They wilt, fall over, and die.

To Combat

• Seeds started indoors should be planted in sterile sandy soil, perlite, sphagnum moss, or vermiculite.
• Don't plant seeds outdoors too soon if the weather is very wet.
• Don't overwater the soil in which seedlings are growing. And don't overcrowd seedlings.
• At the first appearance of seedlings, begin gently loosening the soil around them every day. This both hastens growth and inhibits damping off.
• Remove diseased plants and a good portion of the soil immediately surrounding them.
• Gardeners report that a water-garlic or water–garlic powder solution sprayed on the ground near seedlings inhibits damping off.
• At the first sign of damping off in seedlings, water them daily with chamomile tea (3 teaspoons of chamomile leaves steeped in 1½ pints of boiling water until cool, then strained), until all signs of the disease have disappeared.

Deer 🐞

Deer can be a problem in some areas. You won't know that nibbled vegetables and other destruction are deer caused, however, unless you actually see deer in the vicinity or in your garden.

To Combat
• Deer dislike blood meal—use it as a fertilizer throughout the garden.
• Baby powder also seems to be offensive to deer—sprinkle it around the border of your garden bed and at the beginnings and ends of the rows.
• Make a spray of 1 egg to 1 quart of water for any of your plants that attract deer. Although you won't be able to detect the sulfur odor of the deteriorating egg, the deer will, and it offends them.
• Make borders, or interplantings among your vegetables, of any of the following: creeping barberry, daffodils, holly, rosemary, and zinnias.

Dewberry

See *Blackberry*

Dill

Also called dillweed, dill is an annual, aromatic herb that is very easy to grow and in good soil may reach a height of 3 feet. It is easily started from seed and generally self-sows year after year. The feathery leaves and stems of dill are used fresh in salads and as a food flavoring. The seeds and flower parts, dried, are mainly used in pickling. The seeds are also used in breads, soups, stews, and salad dressings. Dill seed will remain viable for 3 years.

When to Plant
• Sow seeds as early in the spring as the ground can be worked, but after all danger of heavy frost is past. For a continuous supply, make successive sowings every 2 weeks, to the end of late spring.

Where to Plant
• Average garden soil (pH 6 to 7) is fine, although it should be well drained. Dill likes full sunshine.

How to Plant
• Sow the seeds thickly, as many as 15 or 20 to the foot, in rows 18 inches

apart. Cover them with ¼ inch of fine soil, and firm it down lightly. Keep the ground slightly moist until germination.

Germination Time
• Plants emerge in 1 to 3 weeks, depending on soil and weather conditions.

Care During Growth
• When the seedlings are about 3 inches high, thin them to 6 inches apart.
• Dill requires no special watering as it grows unless the season is especially dry.

Maturation Time
• Foliage is ready to use 60 to 70 days from planting of seeds, seeds ready for collection in 100 days.

Harvesting
• The feathery leaves can be snipped throughout the growing season, but don't remove too many at a time from any one plant.
• Harvest the flower heads at the end of the season when they begin to ripen but have not yet turned brown; otherwise they will shatter and the seeds will fall.

Storing
• Dry the seeds and flower heads separately, on screens, in an airy, shady place. They can be stored in bottles and jars. The leaves tend to lose flavor when they're dried.

Diseases and Pests
• Carrot rust flies.

Garden Tips
• Since the stems of dill plants are fragile, they often tend to fall over. For this reason many gardeners prefer to plant dill in patches rather than rows.
• If you need to transplant dill seedlings, wait until they're 4 inches tall. And do the transplanting in the evening.
• Don't plant dill near carrots. But it is said to grow well among Brussels sprouts, cabbages (guarding them against cabbageworms), cauliflower, kale, kohlrabi, and turnips.

Kitchen Tips
• Scandinavians use a great deal of fresh dill in their cooking. Take a tip from them: Add several sprigs (lots of them!) of fresh dill to the water in which you cook shrimp or lobster.
• Cut the feathery tips from a sprig or two of fresh dill and mix into potato salad (hot or cold). Wonderful.
• Sprinkle lots of fresh dill tips over cream soups, hot or cold, just before serving.

• • •

Dogs

See *Cats and dogs*

Downy Mildew

See *Mildew*

Early Blight

See *Alternaria disease*

Earwigs

These slender, black, ½-inch-long, beetlelike insects are easily recognized by the pair of forcepslike appendages at the rear ends of their bodies (the use of which is unknown). They hide in cool, moist, dark places during the day and are active at night. They chiefly infest loose heads of Chinese cabbage and lettuce, as well as the leaves and ears of corn.

Manifestation
• Earwigs feed on the edges and stem ends of edible leaves, leaving brownish edges around the holes they make, as well as brownish excreta. They also gnaw the tassels of corn, leaving stumpy bristles where the long silks were, interfering with the fertilization necessary for kernel formation. Thus the cobs show uneven kernel distribution, often with large empty areas.

To Combat
• Remove from your garden shaded, cool, damp debris and pieces of rotting wood, where earwigs congregate during the day.
• Make beer traps for earwigs: Put about ½ inch of beer in glass jars, then lay the jars on their sides in shallow hollows in the garden bed so that the jar openings are at about soil level. You'll find plenty of drowned earwigs in the morning. You can strain them out and use the beer again. Or keep a single bottle of beer in the refrigerator for this purpose—it will last for weeks.
• Because earwigs like to congregate in dark, hidden places, you can collect them late in the day or even very early in the morning under boards, in pieces of damp corrugated cardboard, or in dampened rolls of newspaper that you have set out. Shake the insects into a pail of water-detergent solution.

Earworms

See *Corn earworms*

Eggplant

Eggplant is a tender, frost-sensitive, hot-weather crop requiring a long growing season. For this reason, it's often hard to grow in the northern part of the United States. However, if you start eggplants early indoors, and the summer is a long one, you can often be successful with them. Or buy seedlings at planting time.

When to Plant
• Sow seeds indoors in very early spring (approximately 7 weeks before transplanting to the garden).
• Set out transplants in late spring, or even early summer, after danger of even a light frost is past and night temperatures can be depended on to stay about 50°F.

Where to Plant
• Eggplants need a rich, warm, well-drained soil that is slightly acid to neutral (pH 6 to 7). They also need full sun.

How to Plant
• Sow seeds in flats indoors, ¼ to ½ inch deep. Try to keep the temperature quite warm—72° to 80°F if possible—until the seeds germinate.
• Set out seedlings or transplants in the garden 30 inches apart in rows 3 feet apart.

Germination Time
• Eggplant seeds usually germinate in 7 to 12 days.

Care During Growth
• Be sure the plants get plenty of moisture—not just during the hot, dry days of summer but until the very end of the growing season.
• If there are any cool periods (temperatures near 50°F) during the growing season, especially in September, cover the plants with plastic or newspapers, especially at night.
• Fertilize every 2 weeks with cow manure tea.
• Too many fruits on one plant will diminish their size. If you want larger eggplants, remove all but 4 or 5 blossoms from each plant.

Maturation Time
• Eggplants are ready to harvest 100 to 140 days from the time seeds are

planted; or 61 to 82 days from the date of transplanting to the garden.

Harvesting

• Early eggplants taste best—they can be eaten from the time the fruits appear to when the skins become dark purple, glossy, and smooth, usually when the largest diameter of the fruit is no more than 4 inches. The fruit should be firm and heavy for its size, and the seeds should be pale, not brown.

• If eggplants are left too long on the vine, the skin becomes dull, the seeds become brown and hardened, and the flesh turns bitter.

• Cut an eggplant to remove it from the vine, and leave a short piece of stem attached to avoid water loss.

• Keep the fruits picked for continuous production up until frost.

Storing

• Eggplant stores best at 50° to 60°F.

Diseases and Pests

• Bacterial diseases, blossom-end rot, Colorado potato beetles, damping off, flea beetles, fusarium wilt, green peach aphids, hornworms, Japanese beetles, leafhoppers, mosaic virus, powdery mildew, verticillium wilt, vine borers, whiteflies.

Garden Tips

• If indoor seedlings become leggy, either they're not getting enough light or the temperature is too high.

• Eggplant blossoms pollinate themselves (each blossom contains both male and female elements).

• Sulfur acidifies the soil—if your soil needs a little acidifying, bury a few paper matches at the bottom of each transplant hole when setting seedlings or transplants in the garden.

• Banana peels provide phosphorus and potash, which are good for eggplants. Cut a few peels into small pieces, and bury them near your plants.

• Mulching greatly increases the yields of eggplant vines. One of the best methods is to spread raw leaves over the eggplant bed and around the plants, cover these with gravel or sheets of black plastic, then place a layer of clear plastic on top. Do this when the first fruits appear. Such mulching conserves moisture, keeps the soil warm, and controls weeds.

• Wormwood tea (see *Repellents* for how to make) sprayed on the leaves of eggplants repels most insects.

• When several fruits are developing on the same vine, they'll mature faster if you pinch off any new blossoms.

• When the skin of an eggplant becomes dull looking, it's too old to be of use. Another test is to press the skin: If it stays indented, the fruit is past its prime.

• Beans, lamb's-quarters, and potatoes are said to be good companion plants for eggplants.

Kitchen Tips
• Try to use eggplants within a couple of days of picking. If they are refrigerated for more than 3 or 4 days, they lose flavor.
• Use a potato peeler to pare an eggplant. If you're slicing it, it's sometimes easier to peel the slices.
• Drop eggplant pieces into salted water as you peel or cut them and they won't discolor. When you drain them, press the pieces well with absorbent toweling.
• But it's not necessary to peel eggplant. You can often bake and eat it, skin and all. It tastes much better this way and is very nutritious.

• Young eggplants are sweet. But older ones often have a slightly bitter flavor. Slice these thick, sprinkle with salt, and let them stand under a weight for an hour or so to pull out the bitterness with the excess water. Wipe them dry, and use less salt when you cook them. One way to weight slices down is to spread them flat, covered by a tray, with some bottles of water on top.
• Sliced eggplant absorbs fat easily. To counteract this blotter effect, dip the slices in batter (or in egg, then in seasoned flour or crumbs) and cook quickly in *very* hot, but not smoking, fat or oil.

Elderberry

Cultivated elderberries are larger and juicier than the wild varieties. Their purplish black or red berries are used in wine, pies, jellies, and tea.

The elderberry is a fast grower and vigorous producer, hardy, and relatively disease free. It has handsome, large, white flowers in June and is often grown as an attractive shrub. It can be propagated by cuttings, seeds, and suckers but is most commonly brought into the garden as 1-year-old plants, some of which start bearing the first fall after spring planting. Plentiful harvests begin with the second year. The plants grow 6 to 8 feet in height. Always plant two varieties of elderberry bushes: Cross-pollination is necessary to ensure a good set of fruit.

When to Plant
• Plant elderberry bushes in early spring, as soon as the ground can be easily worked.

Where to Plant
• Elderberry will grow almost anywhere, but it does particularly well in a rich, very moist soil (pH 6 to 7), in the sun or partial shade.

How to Plant
• Space the plants 7 to 8 feet apart if you're growing them mainly for their berries, 3 feet apart for ornamental hedges. Dig the holes deep and wide enough to accommodate the roots easily, cover with soil, and water well.

Care During Growth
• Elderberry bushes need no care to speak of. Since they spread by means of suckers from the roots, watch for these and cut them off to keep the plants from growing rampant.

Maturation Time
• The purple (red in some varieties) berries ripen in mid- to late summer.

Harvesting
• Be sure to pick the berries before they fall off. Cut off the clusters. If you hold them under cold running water, you can easily strip the berries from the stems with a fork.

Storing
• As with other berries, fresh elderberries have a limited storage time. They are best kept refrigerated, then washed before use. If you've used the running-water method to strip them from their stems, let them dry before storing.
• Elderberries freeze very well.
• They can also be dried, for use in tea. To dry, lay them out on a screen in a hot, dry place.

Diseases and Pests
• The only thing that may attack elderberries is the same type of borer that attacks currant bushes.

Kitchen Tips
• Elderberries contain more vitamin C than oranges or grapefruit.
• Elderberries, red or black, make excellent jams, especially when mixed with apples.
• Crush well-washed and drained elderberries, and let them stand in vodka for a few days, then strain very well and use as a fine fruit liqueur.

Endive

Endive is an annual or biennial herb of the chicory family, three types of which are often called endive: Curly endive, sometimes called chicory, has loose and fringed or curly leaves; Batavian or broad-leaf endive, often called escarole, has thicker leaves with a white midriff; and French endive, also called Belgian endive, witloof, or witloof chicory, is generally tied and blanched as it grows, producing a very tender, pale salad green. There is also another tasty form of endive, closely related to escarole, called radicchio. Very slightly bitter, it resembles a small red cabbage, and is becoming popular as a salad ingredient.

All endives can stand summer heat and fall frosts, although a long stretch of hot weather tends to make them bitter.

When to Plant
• For an extra-early harvest, start seeds indoors in flats in February, or 6 to 8 weeks before outdoor planting time.
• Outdoors, sow seeds or plant seedlings as early as the ground can be worked, usually from the middle of April on. For succession harvesting, sow seeds every 2 weeks until the end of July. The later sowing will give you a fall crop.

Where to Plant
• All the endives like a slightly acid to near-neutral soil (pH 6 to 7), high in potash, but not too high in nitrogen. They like sun and lots of moisture but need excellent drainage.

How to Plant
• If you are planting indoors, sow seeds ¼ inch deep, and keep the soil moist until seedlings appear. Endive seeds are very small: You can mix them with a little sand and broadcast them lightly over flats, then thin to about 2 inches apart when seedlings emerge.
• If you are planting seeds outdoors, mix the seeds with sand to aid in strewing in rows, keeping the rows about 20 inches apart. Cover with ¼ inch of soil.
• Plant roots or seedlings 12 inches apart in rows 20 inches apart.

Germination Time
• Under moist conditions, seeds will germinate in 5 to 14 days.

Care During Growth
• Hay and straw strewn over the seedbed will aid in germination.
• When seedlings show their first two sets of leaves, thin them to 12 inches apart for escarole and chicory, 6 inches apart for witloof.
• For witloof, add wood ashes from time to time throughout the growing season. Curly endive and escarole like a little humus and well-rotted manure every 3 weeks or so.
• Once well established, endive is somewhat tolerant of low soil moisture, although it doesn't prefer this condition. But good drainage is very important, because the roots rot easily.
• It isn't necessary to blanch endive (blanching lowers vitamin A and vitamin C content), but doing so does produce milder-tasting leaves. The time to blanch is about 60 days after

planting, or when the plants are two-thirds grown.

• To blanch: Choose a time of day when the plants are dry, and tie the outer leaves upright loosely, using string or rubber bands. This method will blanch the inner leaves. For more complete blanching, place pails or flowerpots with their drain holes plugged over the plants. Untie the plants after a rain to let them dry; otherwise rot may set in. Then retie them. Blanching takes 2 to 3 weeks, depending on the temperature.

Maturation Time

• Curly endive and escarole are ready to harvest 35 to 98 days after seeds are sown. Witloof is slower to mature: generally 140 days after seeds are planted.

Harvesting

• Endive can be harvested any time the leaves look mature enough for eating. (Don't wait too long—the leaves grow tough, especially in warm weather.) You can remove separate leaves from the plants or cut the entire heads.

• Escarole and curly endive will produce secondary growth if you leave 1 to 2 inches of the stem when removing the head, without damaging the roots.

Storing

• All the endives store well in a very cool place—close to but not freezing.

They can be washed, shaken out, wrapped in plastic wrap, and stored in the coldest part of the refrigerator.

Diseases and Pests

• Endive is rarely prone to disease. But occasionally: aphids, Botrytis blight, cutworms, slugs and snails (in mild, damp areas).

Garden Tips

• For a fall crop, endive seeds don't germinate well when the ground is too warm. Try chilling them, planting indoors in a cool place until they sprout, then transplanting to the garden.

• Try growing endive among your tomato plants: The tomatoes will shade them from the hot summer sun.

• Grass clippings, hay, leaves, and straw provide protection to endive plants when the weather turns cold in late fall.

• Autumn crops of endive are milder and less bitter than summer ones.

• Water endive plants from below—overhead sprinkling promotes leaf rot. And for this reason never let water stand in the crowns of the plants.

• Dig up witloof plants in the late fall, roots and all, and store them in a cool cellar. You can force them at any time during the winter: Plant them close together in sand 4 inches deep, and keep them at 65°F, in very high humidity and total darkness. In 3 to 4 weeks you'll have witloof to eat. Second and third cuttings are possible if you don't disturb the roots.

• You can also get an early outdoor crop of any of the endives if you remove the plants from the garden in the late fall, with a ball of earth surrounding the roots, and keep them in a cold place through the winter. Put them back in the garden in very early spring, and you'll have endive to eat before most seeds sprout!

Kitchen Tips

• Although all the endives are most commonly used fresh—in salads or also, in the case of witloof, stuffed as appetizers—they can be cooked and served as a green leafy vegetable, like spinach. Don't overcook them. They can be braised, with a little butter, or served with a light cream, mushroom, or tomato sauce.

. . .

Escarole

See *Endive*

European Corn Borers

See *Corn Borers*

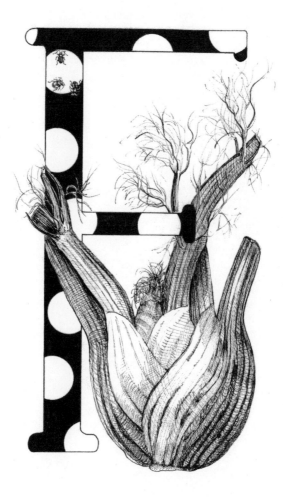

Fennel

A perennial herb of the carrot family somewhat resembling celery, fennel is usually grown in the North as an annual (for its leaves and stems) or a biennial (for its seeds). If you are growing fennel for the seeds, it's safest to dig up the plants after the first season and store them over the winter (see "Care During Growth") for replanting the next spring, when they'll bloom and produce seeds. The leaves, stems, and seeds of fennel resemble licorice or anise in flavor and aroma.

The common garden species (*Foeniculum officinale*, also called *F. vulgare*) is grown for its seeds and leaves, which are used in sauces, salad dressings, fish dishes, stews, and cakes and pastries. The variety known as Florence fennel, Italian fennel, sweet fennel, or finocchio is grown for its thick, celerylike stalks and the bulblike structure at its base, and used in salads and as a cooked vegetable.

Fennel grows quickly from seed, often reaching 3 feet in height, with blue-green stems that are usually blanched to a near-white (see "Care During Growth").

When to Plant
• Plant seeds outdoors in late spring.

Where to Plant
• Plant in light, well-drained soil. Fennel has a wide pH tolerance range of 5.0 to 7.5. If possible, add fresh straw and fresh manure to the soil 1 or 2 weeks before planting. Fennel likes full sun.

How to Plant
• Sow seeds ½ inch deep, about 1 inch apart.

Germination Time
• Seeds germinate in about 2 weeks.

Care During Growth
• When seedlings are 2 inches tall, thin them to stand about 12 inches apart.
• Fennel needs no special care during growth except light watering when there's a run of dry weather.
• If you want to blanch the stems of Florence fennel (toward the end of the first season), about 10 days before harvesting make paper collars

around the bulb and lower stem portions of the plants, holding them in place with string or rubber bands. Or mound dirt well up the stems, covering the bulbs.

• If you are growing fennel for seeds, at the end of the first season, before frost, dig up the tap roots with about 3 inches of stem, and pack them for winter storage in moist sand in a place that is cool and humid. Don't overwater, but don't let them dry out. Return them to the garden in the spring, after danger of frost is past, planting them 24 inches apart. At the end of this second season, you can harvest seeds.

Maturation Time

• The leaves and tender shoots are ready to harvest about 2 months from the date seeds are sown. For harvesting larger bulbs, wait a bit longer.

Harvesting

• Seeds are ready for collecting toward the end of the second season, when they turn from green to tan.

Storing

• Dry the seeds on a screen or porous cloth in a shady, well-ventilated place.

Don't leave them exposed to air too long once they're dry—they tend to lose flavor. Put them in well-capped bottles.

Diseases and Pests

• Carrot rust flies.

Garden Tips

• Don't plant fennel among or close to other plants—they are said to dislike it intensely. Try planting it near a fence or beside some tall poles, to which the plants can be tied.

• Fennel, dried and pulverized, has flea-repellent properties.

Kitchen Tips

• Fresh fennel leaves make a very fine garnish for almost any meat, fish, or chicken dish.

• Used sparingly (because of its rather pronounced—but nice!—flavor), shredded fennel leaves are a tasty addition to a salad.

• Add fresh fennel to the water in which you poach or cook fish.

• The stalk and bulbous base of Florence fennel can be peeled, sliced, and cooked. Or slice it longitudinally, marinate with vinegar and pepper, and serve as a celerylike salad.

Field Pea

See *Bean*

Flea Beetles 🐞

Flea beetles include many species of small, oval beetles, most of which are specialized for certain plants. Very few garden plants are free from them. They get their name from their habit of jumping like fleas when disturbed. Flea beetles are ¹⁄₁₆ to ¼ inch long, shiny, and many colors—black, brown, bronze, metallic blue, or green. Some are striped.

They attack beans, beets, blueberries, broccoli, Brussels sprouts, cabbage, cauliflower, collards, corn, cucumbers, eggplants, garden cress, grapes, horseradish, kale, kohlrabi, melons, mustard, nasturtiums, peas, peppers, potatoes, radishes, rutabagas, spinach, strawberries, sweet potatoes, tomato seedlings, and turnips.

The adult beetles winter over in sheltered spots. In early spring they lay tiny white or orange, oval eggs at the bases of plants or in the top ¼ inch of soil. These hatch into larvae, which attack newly planted seeds. If the seeds have germinated, the larvae often injure the seedlings. The adults mainly chew tiny holes in the leaf surfaces of plants. Some flea beetles transmit bacterial wilt. Damage is greatest early in the season, when the plants are more vulnerable. A mature, healthy plant can generally withstand flea beetles' onslaughts.

Manifestation

• Seedlings whose roots and stems are attacked by flea beetle larvae grow more slowly or may even stop growing. Leaves attacked by adult beetles are peppered with tiny holes.

To Combat

• At the end of each season, remove weeds and garden debris, in which the beetles can overwinter.

• Planting seeds a little late in the season, after the larvae have hatched, may well save your plants.

• If you have stinging nettles growing in the vicinity of your garden, don't remove them—they are the hosts to many species of insects that feed on flea beetles and their larvae.

• Plants that deter flea beetles are clover, ragweed, and tobacco. Interplant these among your vegetables. Chopped clover, in particular, is very effective against the beetles when used as a mulch.

• Like many other garden pests, flea beetles are attracted to beer. Set out wide-mouthed jars containing a little beer, and when a large number of the beetles have entered, clap the covers on, shake the jars, strain out the beetles, and return the beer to the jars for further collection.

• Flea beetles don't like wet surfaces or high humidity. Mist or spray your plants often with plain water if you see flea beetles—this will temporarily interrupt their feeding.

• You can also make deterrent sprays against flea beetles: (1) Steep chopped clover leaves in water, as you would tea, then strain and use as a spray. You can also mix the clover and water in your blender, then strain and use. (2) Another effective blender mixture is made of garlic, hot peppers, onions, and water. Mix, strain, and spray.

• For severe infestations, dust with rotenone powder.

• Once the growing season is well advanced, flea beetles are usually not much of a menace.

Fruit Flies

Most fruit flies are orchard pests, but those of the genus *Drosophila*—the same ones that are a nuisance in the kitchen, where fruit or garbage is exposed—can also be a minor nuisance in the garden. The tiny flies, as well as their larvae or maggots, are drawn to the fruits of berry bushes and to any fruits that have been slightly damaged, particularly tomatoes. Fruit flies are generally not a problem if damaged fruits are removed from the garden. Predators of fruit flies and their maggots are birds and ladybugs.

You can make a fruit fly trap by putting bits of fruit in a jar, pressing a funnel into the opening, and standing the jar near the fruit under attack. When you see plenty of flies inside, pour in very hot water, then empty the jar and begin again. Empty the jar frequently, because fruit flies breed rapidly.

Fusarium Rot, Fusarium Wilt

Fusarium rot or fusarium wilt is a soil-borne fungal disease that, once present, can remain in the soil for years. It normally becomes active when the soil temperature is high—80° to 90°F. The fungi are also encouraged by a low potassium and high nitrogen soil content. The disease can attack beans, eggplants, onions, peas, shallots, squashes, tomatoes, and watermelons particularly, at any stage of development from seedlings on. Fruits, especially those lying on the ground, are especially vulnerable.

Manifestation

• Attacked seedlings turn yellow and die quickly. With more mature plants, the bottom leaves turn yellow and droop, while the stems begin to turn brown at the base. The whole plant may wilt and eventually die. Developing fruits show circular marks of rot, which can spread to the entire fruit.

To Combat

• If you're starting seedlings indoors, be sure to use sterile soil.

• Fusarium wilt can die out in the soil if you deny it host plants for a few years. If it has already struck, practice crop rotation, and don't sow any susceptible plants in the spot for at least 3 years.

• Slip a rock or a brick under each maturing fruit to raise it from the ground.

• Don't let tomato vines lie on the ground: Tie them to stakes, or use cages to keep the fruits from contact with the soil.

• Some varieties of garden vegetables, such as tomatoes, are wilt resistant—all those with the letter *F* after their names in seed catalogs or on seed envelopes.

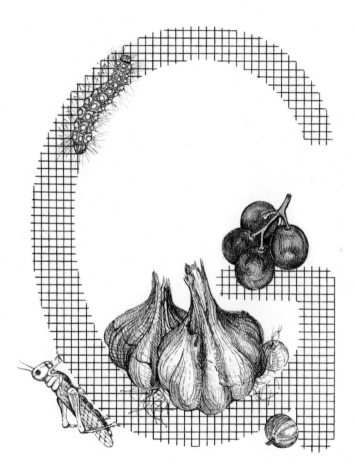

Garbanzo

See *Bean*

Garden Cress

Also called mustard cress, peppergrass, or upland cress, garden cress is an easily grown annual herb of the mustard family whose pungent sprouts can be eaten about 10 days after germination.

When to Plant
• Sow garden cress outdoors every 2 weeks from early spring until well into the fall. Indoors, it can be planted the year round.

Where to Plant
• Cress likes a very moist to wet soil (pH 6.0 to 7.5). Outdoors, it prefers some shade, but if planted in the sun it will grow well if the soil is never allowed to dry out.

How to Plant
• Indoors, because not all the seeds may germinate, sow them thickly in shallow containers of crumbly potting soil, pressing them down and watering well.
• Outdoors, scatter the seeds generously, then similarly scatter soil over them, not too deep. Sprinkle with water, and keep the ground moist.

Germination Time
• In bright light, in a temperature of around 70° F, the seeds will germinate in about 10 days.

Care During Growth
• Cress needs little care beyond seeing that the soil is kept moist throughout the growing season.

Maturation Time
• Cress is ready to use 10 days after germination, or 20 days after seeds are planted.

Harvesting
• Garden cress is best harvested after the first leaves appear, within 15 to

20 days afte. planting. Cut the seedlings at ground level, using a pair of small scissors.

• For more pungency and greater robustness, you can wait until the leaves are 3 to 5 inches long before picking. These are not as delicate, though, as younger leaves.

Diseases and Pests
• Clubroot, flea beetles, nematodes.

Kitchen Tips
• Garden cress added to salads gives them a wonderful tang.
• Crush some cress and mix with softened butter for one of the best herb butters there is. This makes a fine sandwich filling, too.
• You can grow garden cress on your kitchen windowsill.

. . .

Garlic

Garlic is a perennial herb grown under pretty much the same conditions as onions. Each head (bulb) should be separated into cloves and the cloves planted individually. You needn't buy these from a nursery—store-bought heads of garlic do very well in the garden. For planting, choose garlic cloves that are white and firm, showing no brown spots or other signs of rot.

Garlic cloves must have gone through a period of cold at some time before being planted. If you're in any doubt, keep them in the refrigerator a few weeks, then plant them. Generally, each clove of garlic planted in early spring will produce a bulb of garlic, containing many cloves, by the end of the summer. The bigger the cloves you plant, the larger the bulbs will be. Garlic can also be grown from seed. Fall plantings, where possible (see "When to Plant"), give earlier crops and extra-large heads the next season.

Elephant garlic is a giant form of garlic (some bulbs weighing as much as 1 pound) with a milder flavor than regular, or true, garlic. It is often eaten as is in salads. It is hardier than regular garlic, although, like true garlic, it requires a mulch in northern winters.

When to Plant
• In mild-winter areas, garlic seeds or cloves are usually planted in the late fall (October), while the soil is still workable. Northern gardeners will-

ing to gamble on fall plantings should mulch well, removing the mulch in early spring.
• In cold-winter areas (where the ground freezes hard), plant cloves

(also called sets) in the early spring, about the same time as lettuce, onions, and peas.

• Elephant garlic cloves planted in the late fall have a greater chance of surviving a cold winter than true garlic, but they should be covered with a deep mulch as soon as cold weather sets in; the mulch should be removed in the spring.

Where to Plant

• Plant garlic sets in loose, rich, loamy soil (pH 6 to 7) that is well drained, in full sun.

How to Plant

• Before planting, spade compost or dried or rotted manure well into the soil. Then separate the garlic bulbs into cloves, choosing large, well-formed ones. Plant each one, pointed end up, 2 inches deep, 5 inches apart (elephant garlic should be planted 8 inches apart), in rows 12 inches apart. Firm the surface lightly, and water if the ground is dry.

• If you are planting in the fall, mulch the garlic bed well.

Germination Time

• Garlic cloves sprout in 10 days to 2 weeks.

Care During Growth

• Like onions, garlic needs very little cultivation but requires moisture throughout its growing period. Never let the plants dry out completely.

• To get the biggest bulbs, break off any flower stalks that form.

• Stop watering when the stalks begin to droop and turn brown.

Maturation Time

• Garlic matures in about 120 days.

Harvesting

• Dig up garlic bulbs—don't pull them, use a garden fork—when the stalks get dry and yellow and begin to fall over (usually in late July or August). Do this on a sunny day. Leave the bulbs exposed to sun and air for a few hours, then rub off the dirt and let them finish curing for about a week in a well-ventilated place.

Storing

• Garlic can often be stored up to 1 year: Air-dry the bulbs in a shady place with good ventilation until the skins become papery—possibly up to 2 weeks. Then remove some but not all of the roots, leaving the stems on. Braid clusters of garlic bulbs together by their stems, and hang in a very cool, dry, shaded, airy location.

• Or store the bulbs loose, like onions, hanging them in mesh bags. Examine them from time to time, and remove any that are soft so they won't infect the rest.

Diseases and Pests

• Onion fly maggots.

Garden Tips

• Mature garlic bulbs left in the ground will usually reseed themselves year after year.

• Garlic planted in the fall and left over the winter produces more and better-quality garlic than spring plantings do.

• Garlic is often grown as an insecticidal companion crop: The cloves are planted in a ring around vegetables such as Brussels sprouts, cabbage, and cauliflower, to keep them free from aphids.

Kitchen Tips

• The yellow central strip of the garlic clove (lily) has the sharpest odor and taste. Halve the garlic clove, and you can remove the lily easily with the point of a knife.

• The quickest way to peel a garlic clove is to cut off each end, then cut the clove in half lengthwise. The skin will fall right off.

• Plant some garlic cloves in a pot on your kitchen windowsill. Snip off the green sprouts as you would chives. They'll continue to grow for months.

• If dry, garlic will keep in the refrigerator for weeks. Store it uncovered, possibly in a small open container on one of the door shelves.

• You can also store garlic for months in the refrigerator if you peel it, put it in a small jar, and cover it with salad oil. After the garlic is gone, use the oil for sautéing or in salad dressing.

• When you add garlic to flavor oil, vinegar, or salad dressing, impale each clove on a toothpick for easy removal.

• Pound garlic to a paste, and add to dishes calling for garlic flavor. No treatment releases the oils and flavors as well.

• Don't overcook garlic when heating it in butter or oil: If it browns, it—and the oil—will become bitter.

• Garlic is only "garlicky" when it's sautéed or used raw. You can boil lots of it in a soup or stock, and it becomes sweet and tender.

• Rub the inside of a cooking pan with half a clove of garlic if you want only the slightest hint of garlic in what you're cooking.

• Before you put salad in a serving bowl, squeeze the juice of a clove of garlic into the bowl—or put a clove through a garlic press—and rub the bowl thoroughly before adding the salad. The garlic will be transmitted gently to the greens without overpowering them.

• Don't bother to peel garlic for use in pickling brine. Just cut cloves in half lengthwise and drop them in.

• You can make your own garlic powder—it's much more flavorful than the kind you buy. Remove the skin, slice the cloves, and dry them thoroughly at room temperature. Then pulverize them in the blender, cover them, and pound with a hammer (or use a mortar and pestle). Bottle the powder.

Garlic Chives

See *Chives*

Globe Artichoke

See *Artichoke*

Gooseberry

Gooseberry bushes are very hardy. They are also attractive ornamental plants. They generally grow to 4 feet in height and about 4 feet in diameter. Although some varieties produce fruit the year they are planted, the bushes generally bear the year after being set out.

Because gooseberries, like currants, are host plants for a fungal disease that is fatal to white pine (five-needled pine) trees, they should never be planted within 1,000 feet of white pines. In some states growing gooseberries is prohibited in certain areas—consult the Cooperative Extension Service of the U.S. Department of Agriculture in your state before planting.

When to Plant
• Plant gooseberry canes in midfall or very early in the spring, as soon as the ground has thawed. Gooseberry plants that come in containers can go into the ground as late as early summer.

Where to Plant
• Although gooseberries do well in average soil, they do best where the soil is slightly acid (pH 5.5 to 6.5). They thrive in a moist but well-drained clay soil containing plenty of organic matter. They prefer partial shade.

How to Plant
• Plant the canes 5 feet apart all around, setting them 2 or 3 inches deeper than they were in the nursery. Cut off about half the tops as soon as the plants are set in the ground. Water well after planting.

Care During Growth
• Gooseberries tend to be shallow rooted. It's a good idea, for the first couple of years, to cultivate carefully now and then a few inches deep around the canes to encourage deeper root growth.
• Add well-rotted manure to the

gooseberry plot in either December or April of the first year after planting. From then on, little or no fertilizer will be needed, although you can add wood ashes occasionally. But always keep the plants mulched thickly with grass, hay, leaves, peat, sawdust, or straw.

• The fruit is borne on canes that are 2 and 3 years old. Keep removing the 3-year-old canes after they have fruited. This can be done in the winter or early spring. Also cut out canes that seem infested or sickly, and wherever there seems to be too much crowding. Remove any suckers growing outside the rows.

Maturation Time
• Gooseberry plants are mature 2 to 3 years after canes are planted.

Harvesting
• Gooseberries are light green at first, then turn pink to red when they're ripe. If you're going to use the berries for sauces or jam, pick them before they're completely ripe.
• The branches are extremely thorny—wear tough gloves on both hands. Hold the cane carefully with one hand, and remove the hanging berries with the other.

Diseases and Pests
• Most gooseberry diseases can be controlled by dusting or spraying with rotenone and by removing and burning any canes that look sickly. If mildew appears, this is probably the result of overcrowding and the consequent cutting out of sunlight and air: Thin some of the branches, including the tops.

Garden Tip
• If the bushes become very overcrowded, divide them, cutting down through the roots and either transplanting the divisions elsewhere or discarding them. This should be done in very early spring, while the plants are still dormant.

Kitchen Tips
• Pick gooseberries while they are still green, and simmer with a little sugar and water till soft, then puree. Use this in place of other berries or fruit in a trifle recipe. Or it makes a wonderful dessert when served with sweetened whipped cream.
• Substitute gooseberries for any berry or fruit in a pie.
• Gooseberries, traditionally used to make jams and jellies, make excellent conserve: Cook 1 quart of gooseberries with the chopped rind, juice, and pulp of an orange, simmering till nearly tender. Add 2 cups of sugar and ½ cup of any small or chopped fruit (dates or raisins, for instance), and simmer for another ½ hour. The result is great with meats or chicken, or served at breakfast.

Grape

Many grape varieties are very hardy in the North. Among these are Caco (red), Swenson Red, Concord (blue), and Niagara (white). As a rule, grape vines produce fruit the second or third year after planting. A mature vine can produce up to 20 pounds of grapes annually. Grapes must be trellised.

When to Plant
• Plant the vines in early to midspring.

Where to Plant
• Grapes mature faster when planted in a warm spot (along a fence or the side of a building), on a gentle slope, or where there is bottom heat such as is supplied by gravel. The soil should be coarse and deeply dug to provide excellent drainage, with a fair amount of—but not too much—organic matter (well-rotted manure or compost). Grapes prefer moderately acid soil (pH 5.00 to 5.75).

• Wherever you plant vines, arrange for future support as they grow—either a trellis composed of a series of posts with wires strung along the line of plants or an arbor (see "Care During Growth"). Grapevines must be exposed to plenty of air.

How to Plant
• Plant the vines in a straight line, in broad holes 8 inches deep and 6 to 8 feet apart. If you are planting more than one row of vines, the rows should be 9 feet apart. Place the roots in deep, and fill the holes with compost or rich soil. Firm the soil well, water thoroughly, and provide plenty of mulch.

• Cut back the tops of the plants to two or three strong buds.

Care During Growth
• Early in the spring, cultivate shallowly around the trunks of the vines. Continue doing so about once a month until the end of July. Throughout this period maintain a rich mulch, but don't fertilize further.

• The time to put up a trellis of some sort is usually the third year after vines have been planted. If you are using posts and wires, put the posts at the beginning and the end of the line of plants, and at intervals between these, usually three vines apart. Attach two lines of wire horizontally along the posts, the lower one 2½ feet above the ground, the upper one 3 feet above the lower.

• Train the vines to the wires by tying the main trunk (the most vigorous shoot) of each plant permanently to the wires and fastening the side canes sideways as they grow. These will be pruned in time and new canes tied likewise. Generally only four canes per plant are left each year to produce fruit.

• At the end of the winter, before spring growth starts, cut off all old canes that have already borne fruit. The object is to stimulate the growth of young canes and nurture these throughout the growing season.

• When you see grape clusters forming, thin them here and there—you'll get fewer but larger bunches of grapes.

• At the end of June, remove some excess foliage so that more of the plant's energies will go into the production of fruit.

Maturation Time

• Grapes are mature in middle to late summer and autumn. Concord (blue) grapes are ready to pick 150 to 160 days from the appearance of buds; other blue varieties (Beta, Van Buren, and Bufflo) ripen in 110 to 140 days.

Harvesting

• Don't let grapes get too ripe before you pick them—overripe grapes are very attractive to bees.

• Don't pull, twist, or tear bunches from the vines. Cut them off with clippers or sharp shears.

Diseases and Pests

• Bacterial diseases, bees, birds, downy mildew, flea beetles, grapeberry moths, Japanese beetles, leaf-hoppers, mealybugs, mummy berry, scale, thrips, whiteflies.

Garden Tips

• Grapes are very attractive to birds. You can often shield grapes by taking small, sturdy paper bags, cutting off two corners at the bottom of each (to allow for drainage and ventilation), and fastening a bag around each bunch of grapes. Use rubber bands, staples, string, tape, or whatever works best for you.

• It's also possible to cover grape bunches loosely with pieces of netting. Or cover the entire arbor with bird netting, weighing it down at the edges with stones and rocks.

• Don't fertilize too much—you'll get more foliage and late-maturing but fewer grapes.

• Where winters are severe, mulch heavily just before freezing weather is due. Pine needles are good for this, as are leaves, hay, and other organic mulches. The mulch should be at least 1 foot deep. Remove it in the early spring.

• It's a good idea to leave one or two suckers at the base of each grapevine to act as possible replacement for any trunks that are winterkilled.

• Many wild grape varieties are dioecious (each plant having either male or female flowers), but almost all cultivated grapes are monoecious (both sexes on one plant) and hence self-fertilizing. On rare occasions a grapevine may have flowers but no grapes: This is probably a male or a female plant.

• A warm summer will result in sweeter grapes; a cool season will give grapes on the sour side.

Kitchen Tip
• Grapes are delicious when served slightly frozen. Put a bunch of seedless grapes in the freezer for about 45 minutes, then serve.

Grape-Berry Moths 🦋

The grape-berry moth is a small, brown-and-gray moth that lays eggs on the stems and flowers of grapevines in late spring. The eggs hatch into ½-inch-long caterpillars that spin webs on young grape clusters, feeding on the new grapes inside. These larvae form cocoons on the grape leaves, pupate, and emerge as moths in late July. This second generation of moths lays eggs that hatch in August into larvae that attack ripening grapes. At the end of the season, the larvae fall to the ground and pupate in cocoons over the winter on fallen grape and other leaves, as well as garden refuse. They emerge as moths in the spring and begin the process all over again.

Manifestation
• Young, berry-sized grapes are webbed together, turn dark, and fall. More mature grapes shrivel after the caterpillars attack them and likewise fall to the ground.

To Combat
• In early spring, compact the soil around your grapevines and water thoroughly to seal the soil surface, thus covering cocoons before the moths have a chance to emerge.
• As the season progresses, clip off any webbed grape bunches you see, as well as any leaves bearing cocoons, and burn them or bury them deeply.

• At the end of the season, rake up and burn all fallen leaves around your vines, or leave them and bury them by cultivating deeply the next spring.
• Both rotenone and Bacillus thuringiensis (Bt) are effective against grape-berry moths if sprayed before the larvae have a chance to enter the grapes. Start as soon as you see blooms on your vines. Spray with rotenone every 7 days for 2 weeks, or with Bt every 3 days for 3 weeks. You may need to spray again later, when the second generation starts its cycle.

Grasshoppers 🦗

Sometimes also called locusts, grasshoppers can be extremely destructive during certain years. In a bad year very few plants escape their onslaught. Different species vary from 1 to 2½ inches in length; their colors range from black to dark gray, brown, or green. Many kinds of grasshoppers can fly long distances, and their specialized hind legs allow them to leap as far as 30 inches. All have specialized mouth parts for biting and chewing.

Grasshopper eggs winter over about an inch below the soil surface, in protective pods. The eggs hatch in early spring into young insects, called nymphs, which immediately start feeding on vegetation, molting several times until they reach the mature grasshopper stage. In the fall, the females lay eggs

Manifestation

• Normally, grasshoppers attack the leaves of plants, but no part of a plant is safe when the insects arrive in masses.

To Combat

• Entice grasshopper enemies to your garden:

Wasps, which are attracted to buckwheat, carrots, all varieties of daisies, dill, goldenrod, Jerusalem artichokes, parsley, and parsnips

Praying mantises (you can purchase their eggs from many plant nurseries)

Birds (especially Baltimore orioles and cuckoos)

• Jars one-fourth filled with a 9-to-1 solution of water and either molasses or corn syrup, placed here and there in the garden during grasshopper time, will often trap lots of insects.

• Plow the soil well under in the fall, deep enough to cover any grasshopper eggs so the young can't emerge in the spring.

• Rotenone, sprayed or dusted, is effective against grasshoppers.

Gray Mold

See *Botrytis blight*

Green Peach Aphids 🐞

These aphids, also known as spinach aphids, are about ½ inch long and pale yellow-green. Not only do they attack plants, but they can transmit mosaic virus to them. Green peach aphids feed on many vegetables, including beets, cabbage, celery, cucumbers, eggplants, lettuce, peppers, potatoes, spinach, and tomatoes, as well as ornamental plants and fruit trees. They lay their eggs in fruit trees, and, on hatching, winged forms develop that fly to adjacent gardens.

Manifestation
• Look for these aphids, which are larger than the general run of plant aphids, on young growth, both leaves and fruits. The leaves of attacked plants eventually wilt, and the plants as a whole remain stunted.

To Combat
• Interplant catnip, coriander, marigolds, onions, or tansy among your vegetables.
• The same measures for combating aphids in general (see *Aphids*) apply to green peach aphids.

Green Worms (larvae of white cabbage butterflies)

See *Cabbage worms*

Grubs (larvae of beetles)

See *Beetles*

Gypsy Moth Caterpillars 🐞

Gypsy moths lay oval-shaped masses of light brown eggs in the fall, which remain dormant over the winter, then hatch as small caterpillars in the spring. These attack the foliage of trees and smaller plants, and reach a length of 2 to 2½ inches. In July they pupate in cocoons, from which moths emerge in August. The moths live just long enough to lay more egg masses on the trunks and limbs of trees, on rocks, fences, and tractors and other vehicles, where the egg masses spend the winter and again give rise to caterpillars in the spring.

The dark, grayish, mottled, hairy caterpillars can often be seen suspended from trees by silken threads, waiting to be blown by the wind or carried by passing animals to other locations. They can do great damage to trees and have been known to attack the foliage of garden plants. They are especially fond of cranberries.

Manifestation

• Trees and plants lose their leaves to these voracious eaters. Plants often die. Trees usually survive these on-slaughts, although, if there is a succession of bad gypsy moth seasons, trees can die from excessive and constant defoliation.

To Combat

• Destroy the egg masses whenever you see them. Do the same with the hanging caterpillars.

• Remember not to destroy ground beetles, which are natural enemies of all caterpillars.

• Bacillus thuringiensis (Bt) is very effective against gypsy moth caterpillars. When you see any young larvae on your plants, spray weekly. This must be done up to June, before they begin to spin cocoons and pupate.

. . .

Hellebore Powder 🕷

Hellebore powder is an insecticidal powder made from the acrid, poisonous roots of a Northern Hemisphere flowering plant of the lily family, *Veratrum*. Although poisonous to insects, this powder when properly used is not dangerous to pets or humans.

Hornworms 🕷

Also called tomato hornworms or tomato worms, hornworms are the larvae of a large gray or brown moth with a line of orange spots on each side of its body. Female moths lay a series of separate pale green eggs on the undersides of leaves; these hatch into hornworms in about a week. The worms themselves, about 3 inches long at full size, are bright green with white diagonal stripes on each side of their bodies. Hornworms, difficult to see because their color is so much like the green of the vines or plants on which they feed, attack chiefly eggplants, peppers, potatoes, and tomatoes.

Manifestation
• Leaves shrivel and turn yellow. Stems shrink, turn brown, and die. The dark-colored droppings of the caterpillars can often be seen on the foliage, calling attention to the well-camouflaged worms themselves.

To Combat
• Handpick and destroy hornworms wherever you see them. Since they're difficult to spot among green foliage, look for their dark-colored droppings on and around leaves. Check for them in both spring and fall.
• But if you see small white clusters of what look like eggs on the back of any hornworm, don't destroy it—it is being parasitized by either braconid or trichogramma flies (sometimes called wasps), which lay their eggs in or on hornworms and other cater-

143

pillars. These white eggs will become larvae that not only destroy their host but go on to destroy other harmful garden caterpillars.

• Spray plants with cold water—this makes the hornworms thrash about so you can easily see them.

• Borage and marigolds are said to deter hornworms and can be used for companion planting.

• Some gardeners plant four-o'clocks in and around the beds of plants susceptible to hornworms—the flowers attract the hornworms, which are more easily seen on these plants than they are on many of the plants they traditionally attack.

• Bacillus thuringiensis (Bt) spray is also an effective hornworm control.

Horseradish

Horseradish is a vigorous, easy-to-grow, hardy perennial that is usually treated as an annual because if left in the ground the white, parsniplike, pungent roots multiply, becoming excessively tangled and hard to use. It's best to dig up and save some of the pencil-thin roots or make lengthwise root cuttings for planting the next spring (see "Storing").

When to Plant

• Plant small roots or cuttings early in the spring (new roots can take a light frost) for harvesting in the fall.

• Or plant roots in the fall, shortly before the soil freezes, then cover with about 5 inches of mulch. You will harvest larger roots the following fall.

Where to Plant

• Plant horseradish in the sun, in ordinary, loose garden soil (pH 6.5 to 7.5), provided it's not too sandy. Horseradish prefers a rich loam and plenty of moisture.

How to Plant

• Set the roots in the soil vertically, the narrow end down and the wider, top part 2 to 3 inches below the soil surface. Plant them 15 inches apart.

• If you are planting root cuttings, be sure a piece of the crown and a wedge-shaped slice of the main root are included in each cutting. A good length for these is 6 to 8 inches.

Care During Growth

• Horseradish needs little care.

• If you want very large roots, carefully uncover the top part of the plant when the leaves are about 1 foot long and remove all but a couple of the crown sprouts at the top of the root, then cover with soil once more. Don't disturb any other part of the plant.

Maturation Time
• Horseradish roots mature in 150 days.

Harvesting
• Horseradish roots produce most of their tangy taste and growth during September and October, so don't dig up the plant until late October or even November.
• After harvesting, save the thin roots—or longitudinal cuttings made from the large roots—for replanting.

Storing
• Horseradish roots lose their pungency in time, so don't plan on long-term storage; grate as soon as possible after picking
• If you are storing roots for planting the next spring, keep them quite cold—around 35° F—and in the dark.
• It's also possible to keep the roots in the garden and dig them up through the winter as needed: Cut the leaves back to the ground after the first frost and mulch at least 5 inches deep after the first frost.

Diseases and Pests
• Aphids, flea beetles.

Garden Tips
• Nasturtiums are often planted as a trap crop to lure aphids away from horseradish leaves.
• Colorado potato beetles are said to detest horseradish, so try planting horseradish among your potatoes.

Kitchen Tips
• Mix grated horseradish with finely minced, cooked, or pickled beets to make a delicious relish.
• If you make your own grated horseradish (mixed with white vinegar), store it in dark glass jars or in jars covered with anything impermeable to light. Horseradish tends to turn grayish when exposed to light.
• Grated fresh horseradish mixed with applesauce is a great accompaniment to beef and pork dishes as well as to cold leftover meats.
• A little grated fresh horseradish is wonderful for flavoring a fish sauce. Used sparingly, it can be added to salad dressing, too, especially for coleslaw or chef's salad.

. . .

Huckleberry

Huckleberry is grown exactly like blueberry. There are two chief cultivated forms:

a perennial bush (genus *Gaylussacia*), which yields clusters of fruit that resemble large blueberries but are darker and more tart. The fruit of some types is almost black. The perennial huckleberry, like the blueberry, is often grown as an ornamental evergreen—a bush can grow to a height of 3 feet in a single season.

an annual huckleberry (*Solanum nigrum*), also called the garden huckleberry, sunberry, or wonderberry, with black fruit that is slightly bitter when raw, but, when used in pie fillings or cooked in other ways, tastes very like blueberries. The leaves of this plant are poisonous, as is the unripe fruit in some wild forms.

For all further details on huckleberries, see *Blueberry*.

Hyssop

A very hardy, semievergreen, shrublike perennial in the mint family, hyssop has strong, sweet leaves that are used in soups and salads. Its dark green foliage also makes it attractive as a low hedge. It grows 18 to 24 inches in height, producing fragrant blossoms of blue, pink, or white from June through October. Hyssop self-sows freely.

When to Plant

• Hyssop seeds can be sown either in the spring (early May, generally) or in the late fall, when cold weather starts. The seeds will remain dormant through the winter and germinate the next spring.

• Hyssop plants are placed in the garden in early May.

Where to Plant

• Plant in sun or partial shade in any garden soil (pH 6 to 7), provided it is well drained.

How to Plant

• Press seeds ¼ inch into the soil fairly close together in a straight line if you are using the plants to form a hedge or garden border. Cover lightly with soil, and moisten well, using a fine spray.

• For faster growth, you can plant hyssop from nursery stock. Place the roots in the ground to the same depth as the plant grew in the nursery, and pack with soil.

Care During Growth

• When the seedlings are 2 inches high, thin them to stand about 1 foot apart.

• In the fall, when the plants have finished blossoming, cut the stems back to ground level. They'll become bushier the following year.

Harvesting

• Remove hyssop leaves for use in soups or salads (and the blossoms, as well, for potpourris) throughout the growing season. Cut the leaves and foliage from the top and sides, thus pruning and shaping the plants.

Garden Tips

• Hyssop blossoms are very attractive to bees and butterflies. If you need improved pollination in your garden, position hyssop plants with this goal in mind.

• Hyssop tends to become woody and less attractive after a few years. If you see this happening, dig up the plants, divide the roots, and replant. Or start with new plants or seeds.

• Plant hyssop among cabbages—it is said to protect against cabbageworms.

Kitchen Tips

• To make hyssop tea, pour boiling water over several green leaves in a teapot and let stand for a few minutes.

• Add a few longitudinally sliced hyssop leaves to a salad for a mintlike flavor.

• Use hyssop in soups and stews and in fruit compotes.

Inchworm

See *Cabbage loopers*

Indian Cress

See *Nasturtium*

Japanese Beetles

The beautiful, ½-inch-long Japanese beetle, a shiny, metallic green and bronze in color, damages many plants: asparagus, beans, berries, corn (injuring the silk), eggplants, grapes, and rhubarb, as well as fruit trees and many garden flowers, particularly roses. In addition, the grub of this beetle is a major pest of lawns, feeding on grass roots. Infestations maintain a certain intensity over a number of seasons and then for some reason diminish, only to increase again.

Manifestation
• Attacked leaves look skeletonized, often with nothing but their ribs remaining. The shoots of young vegetables are eaten away. The beetles are easily seen at work—they are active during the day, especially in hot, sunny weather.

To Combat
• Hand picking, if done daily, is always effective in keeping the beetles somewhat in check. Drop the beetles into a can of water mixed with kerosene or detergent or a can of ammonia or alcohol.

• Japanese beetle traps do a fine job

of destroying hundreds of the pests. The beetles are attracted to the yellow color and the odor of the bait. Some traps contain a natural sex attractant; some have floral scents. The beetles enter but cannot escape. The bags are disposable.

• Probably the best control to date is a powdered bacterial disease vehicle called milky spore disease. When applied to the soil where Japanese beetle larvae live, it destroys them. The spores are self-perpetuating and in 2 or 3 years can entirely dispose of the grubs in that location. You can purchase this control at garden supply stores.

• Many birds are great eaters of Japanese beetles and their grubs, brown thrashers, robins, and starlings, especially.

• Gardeners report that planting garlic around susceptible vegetables will deter the beetles. The same is true for planting rue around raspberries.

• Forsythia, honeysuckle, and privet repel Japanese beetles. Try laying branches of these around your garden. Or put any of these in a blender with water, strain, and spray the solution on susceptible plants.

• Okra is said to attract Japanese beetles, but the leaves are poisonous to them.

• Both rotenone and pyrethrum sprays are effective Japanese beetle controls.

Jerusalem Artichoke

Also called sunchoke, the Jerusalem artichoke is a hardy species of perennial sunflower whose crisp tubers are eaten as a vegetable, cooked or raw. Raw they have much the quality of water chestnuts. They are very easy to grow, are extremely productive, and will survive all but the coldest winters without mulching. A single plant whose tubers are left in the ground will continue to produce year after year and spread rapidly. The plant can grow to a height of 8 feet or more.

When to Plant

• Plant tubers or pieces of tubers early in the spring, after danger of heavy frost is past, up to the beginning of early summer, for harvesting in the fall. Or plant in the fall not long before the soil freezes, for a bigger harvest the following year.

Where to Plant

• Jerusalem artichokes like a sunny spot but will grow in almost any soil.

It doesn't hurt to rake in some well-rotted manure or compost first. The most important thing in choosing a site is to bear in mind that, left to their own devices, the tubers will spread like wildfire. Choose an area where they won't invade other garden beds.

How to Plant
• If the tubers you're going to plant are large, cut them into several pieces, each containing a small knob or "eye." Set each one 5 inches deep and 12 inches apart. If you are planting in rows, the rows should be 3 feet apart.

Care During Growth
• Jerusalem artichokes need little care. Cultivation isn't necessary.
• Once the plants reach a height of 1 foot, some gardeners mound dirt around the stems to help keep them upright.
• Once fall frosts hit, cut the tops back to soil level. If you plan to leave the tubers in the ground for digging over the winter, lay down a 10-inch layer of hay, salt-marsh hay, or straw to keep the soil soft.

Harvesting
• The time to dig up the tubers is in the late fall, when the first frost hits and the tops begin to blacken. This is about 100 days after planting.
• If you want to keep the tubers from spreading rampantly the next year, dig up the entire plants, then replant tubers in the spring.
• If you want to leave some in the garden for digging fresh throughout the winter, be sure to mulch (see "Care During Growth") so the soil won't freeze hard.

Storing
• For storing Jerusalem artichokes in the ground, see "Care During Growth." Be sure to set stakes as markers here and there so you'll know where to dig through the snow for the tubers.
• For above-the-ground storage, bury the tubers in moist sand, where they'll keep pretty well provided the temperature is close to freezing.

Kitchen Tips
• The tubers of this vegetable (it isn't really an artichoke, and it doesn't come from Jerusalem) are delicious, with a nutty flavor.
• For most uses it isn't really necessary to peel Jerusalem artichokes. Give them a good, hard rubbing under running water and then serve raw in salads or cook them. If you do want to peel them, either use a potato peeler or rub the skins off gently with a fine grater.
• The artichokes are easier to peel before they're cooked, but if you cook them first, peel them while they're hot; otherwise too much flesh comes off with the skin.

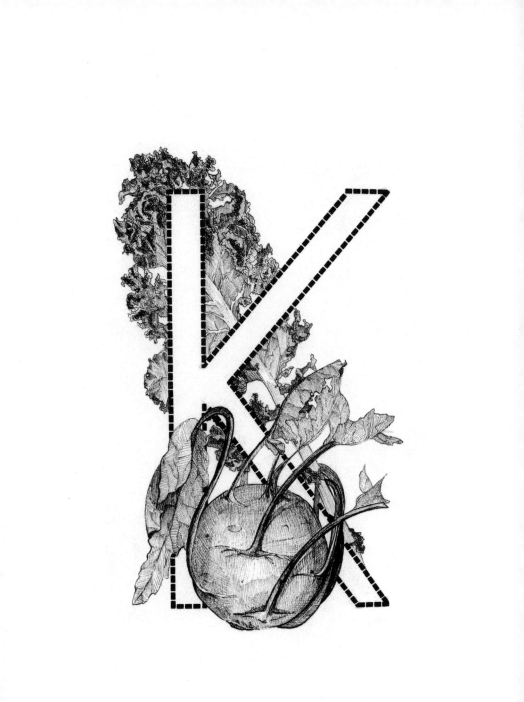

Kale

The most winter hardy of all the brassicas, kale can safely withstand severe frost. If left in the garden, it needs almost no protection over most winters. Although it grows well in the heat of summer, it prefers cool temperatures and improves in flavor as the days grow colder. It tastes best after a frost. Kale is particularly rich in calcium.

Chinese kale (gai lohn), also called Chinese broccoli, is likewise extremely hardy. Instead of the large leaves of most kales, it has small leaves and buds, reminiscent of broccoli. The growing conditions are the same for Chinese as for regular kale.

When to Plant
• You can plant and harvest kale throughout the growing season. Starting in the spring, sow seeds as early as the soil can be worked. For a fall and winter crop, sow seeds about 10 weeks before the first expected frost. It's also possible to sow in early autumn for a late fall and winter crop.

Where to Plant
• Kale will grow in most average garden soils, but it does best where the pH is 6 to 7 (slightly acid to neutral). It also benefits from plenty of nitrogen, afforded by compost, humus, or well-rotted manure.
• Kale will tolerate partial shade.

How to Plant
• If you are planting seeds, sow them ½ inch deep. Seeds or seedlings should be 12 inches apart, in rows 24 inches apart.

Germination Time
• Seeds germinate in 5 to 10 days at a soil temperature of 68° F or over.

Care During Growth
• Kale grows slowly at first. Be sure it gets plenty of moisture. When the plants are well up, thin them to 15 inches apart.
• If you sow seeds early in August for fall harvesting, be sure to keep the beds moist against the summer heat

until the seedlings are well established.
• Removing the side buds of Chinese kale will stimulate new shoots to branch out, as with broccoli.

Maturation Time
• Wait 55 to 70 days for complete maturity, although very young tender leaves can be harvested at any time.

Harvesting
• Although you can harvest kale whenever the leaves seem large enough for greens, those picked in hot weather tend to be leathery. Except for very young leaves, it's best to wait for cold weather before harvesting. A good frost will sweeten the kale overnight.
• Harvest the leaves rather than the entire plant unless the plant is small and tender. Because they are exposed to more sunlight, the outer leaves contain more vitamin C. Pick the young leaves at the top last to keep the plant producing.
• Plants can be left in the garden through the winter—you'll be able to harvest fresh leaves in early spring.
• When kale plants left in the garden develop seedstalks, harvest the leaf buds before they open—they taste very much like broccoli.
• Harvest Chinese kale as you would broccoli.

. . .

Storing
• Wash kale before storing, shake off all the moisture possible, then keep it close to 32°F. But don't let kale actually freeze while it's in storage.

Diseases and Pests
• Aphids, blackleg, cabbage loopers, cabbageworms, cutworms, flea beetles.

Garden Tips
• Kale can survive garden temperatures of 10° F if the fall cooling has been gradual.
• Don't plant kale in the same place 2 years in a row.
• If you must transplant kale for any reason, remove the lower leaves first. This way the root system will become established more easily.
• If you bring frozen kale into the house for eating, cook the leaves immediately, before they thaw.
• Good companion plantings for kale are said to be beets, celery, dill, lavender, mint, onions, potatoes, rosemary, sage, and thyme.
• Nasturtiums are often grown as a trap crop to keep aphids from attacking kale.
• Flea beetles are often deterred from kale if you interplant the kale closely with ragweed, tobacco, or tomatoes.

Kitchen Tips
• Cook kale just as you would spinach, but a few minutes longer.

• If you cut out the center ribs of young kale leaves, you can use the leaves, cut into strips, as salad greens. If you like your salad crunchy, cut the ribs in small pieces and include these as well.

• Add drained, finely chopped, cooked kale to sliced potatoes that have been sautéed with a little bacon, and cook the mixture until it becomes a little browned. Serve with grilled frankfurters.

Kohlrabi

A member of the cabbage family, also called stem cabbage, turnip cabbage, and turnip-rooted cabbage, kohlrabi is the fastest growing of the brassicas. Although it tolerates heat, it is a cool-weather crop. It can take light frosts—in fact, a few frosty nights in the fall make it sweeter. Kohlrabi is generally resistant to most diseases and pests.

When to Plant
• Although seeds may be started indoors about 5 weeks before setting into the garden, kohlrabi is such a fast grower that you may as well plant seeds directly in the garden.
• Plant as soon as the ground can be worked after the last frost. From then on you can plant seeds every 2 weeks until midsummer (the later plantings will give you a fall crop). Or make a second sowing at the beginning of midsummer.

Where to Plant
• Kohlrabi will grow in any ordinary, light, sandy soil if it is well drained and properly enriched. Three weeks before sowing seed, mix some rich compost or well-rotted manure into the bed. Kohlrabi prefers a cool location and a pH above 5.5. It

likes full sun but can tolerate partial shade.

How to Plant
• Plant 2 seeds together ½ inch deep, spacing them 8 inches apart, in rows 12 inches apart. Mist every morning until the seeds germinate.
• If you are planting transplants, space them 8 inches apart in rows 12 inches apart.

Germination Time
• Seeds germinate in 5 to 7 days.

Care During Growth
• When seedlings reach 2 inches in height, remove the weaker of the 2 at each planting site. (The thinnings may be transplanted elsewhere.)
• Kohlrabi requires a steady supply of water throughout its growing period.

• Don't cultivate—kohlrabi roots stay very close to the surface. Mulch instead, when the plants are about 6 inches tall. Use compost, grass clippings, shredded newspaper, or straw, and continue mulching up to the base of each bulb as it grows. This practice conserves moisture and holds down weeds.

• Keep the beds of midsummer sowings moist, especially during hot weather. Add more organic compost in early September.

Maturation Time

• Kohlrabi generally reaches maturity 45 to 60 days from the day of planting seed, depending on the variety.

Harvesting

• You can start harvesting kohlrabies when the round, swollen stems above the ground reach a diameter of 2 inches. They're at their best when they're this size.

• Use a sharp knife (a serrated one is easier) to cut the vegetable just below the bulb and above the root. Remove the leaves.

• The harvest period generally lasts a couple of weeks.

Storing

• For near-future use, store kohlrabies in a cool cellar or in your refrigerator. Otherwise, cut the bulbs into slices or large dices, blanch about 2 minutes in boiling water, drain, dry, wrap, and store in the freezer.

Diseases and Pests

• Diseases and pests are not usually a problem, but occasionally kohlrabi is attacked by aphids, blackleg, cabbage loopers, cabbage maggots, cabbageworms, cutworms, and flea beetles.

Garden Tips

• Take care never to let the soil dry out—aridity contributes to tough and bitter kohlrabi.

• Be sure to pick while the vegetables are smaller than a tennis ball, or they'll end up tough, stringy, or woody.

• Kohlrabi always has a new spurt of growth when cool weather comes at the end of summer. For this reason, make a late planting for harvesting in October or November.

• Good companion plantings for kohlrabi are said to be beets, celery, dill, lavender, mint, onions, potatoes, rosemary, sage, and thyme. (Aromatic plants—mint, onions, sage, and thyme, particularly—are thought to repel cabbageworms.)

• Nasturtiums are also recommended by many gardeners for planting as a trap crop to attract aphids away from kohlrabi.

Kitchen Tip

• Although most people cook kohlrabi, it makes an interesting salad ingredient. Peel fresh young kohlrabies with a potato peeler, and slice them thin. They are very crisp and tasty, either in a salad or marinated and served cold.

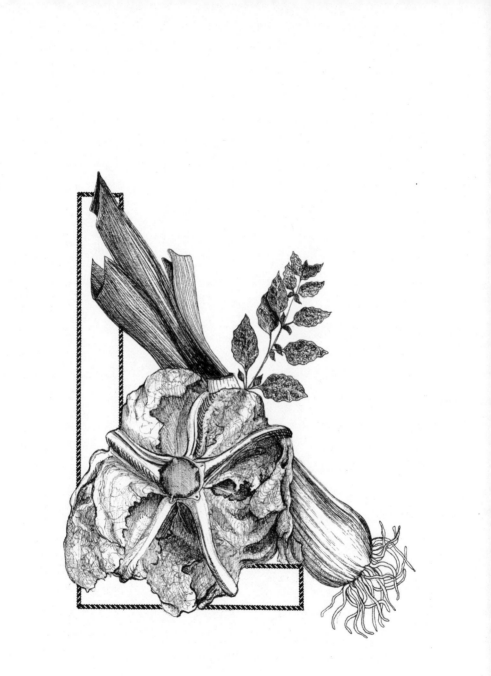

Lacewings

Also called lacewing flies, these insects are slender and beautiful, with gauzy, pale green wings and brilliant, red-gold eyes. Their flat, yellowish, hairy larvae with pincerlike jaws are called aphis lions, and they are treasured by gardeners because they eat aphids, mealybugs, and cottony-cushion scale insects. Lacewings are attracted to pollen- and nectar-producing plants. You can buy lacewing larvae from many nurseries.

Ladybugs

Ladybugs, also called ladybug beetles, are valuable predators of many destructive garden insects. They devour aphids in both larval and adult forms, fleas, fruit scales, leafhoppers, mealybugs, and thrips, as well as the eggs and larvae of other plant-destroying insects. Ladybugs are attracted to pollen- and nectar-producing plants. You can buy live ladybugs from many nurseries.

Lamb's-quarters

Also known as white goosefoot, pigweed, white chenopodium, and dirty dick, lamb's-quarters are the only plant in this book for which you cannot buy seeds. They are a weed growing in many gardens—but a deliciously edible weed. They're worth cultivating if you have them. When young, they make tasty, tender greens, served raw in salads or steamed like spinach. They're much richer in vitamins A and C than spinach.

Lamb's-quarters are extremely prolific. They appear early in the spring and last until frost. They can reach a height of 5 feet, and their appearance in any garden is usually a tribute to the gardener: They prefer rich soils. If you want to give them a chance in your garden, just don't let them grow too thick. Thin them out, and eat the thinnings.

Harvesting
• Pick when the plants are 4 to 8 inches high to use whole in salads or, instead of lettuce, in sandwiches. They're best when young.
• Or pick the tender, new leaves that grow at the tops of the plants. Single leaves may be picked at any time, even from mature plants, broken up, and added to soups.

Garden Tip
• Country people have prized lamb's-quarters for years, not only for their edibility but because they make good companion plantings for corn, eggplants, peppers, potatoes, pumpkins, and tomatoes. Apparently they contribute to the health of these vegetables—corn and peppers particularly.

Leaf Crops

See *Lettuce; Mustard greens; Spinach; Swiss chard*

Leaf Curl

Leaf curl is both a fungal disease, primarily of fruit trees, and a viral disease (see *Mosaic virus*) afflicting raspberry bushes. There is at present no cure for it—the emphasis must be on prevention.

Manifestation
• Leaves become puckered, thick, and dark, and the edges curl in and downward. Sometimes they fall prematurely. Fruits may fail to develop or, if they do develop, are cracked and misshapen.

To Combat
• Clear up garden debris, especially old leaves and dead branches from raspberry bushes, which may harbor the virus. Keep your bushes healthy and vigorous by giving them the water and nourishment they need.
• Be sure the plants you buy are disease-resistant and virus free.

• • •

Leafhoppers

There are many species of these wedge-shaped insects that hop or fly at the slightest movement. They suck sap from the leaves of an enormous variety of plants and may also carry viral diseases from plant to plant. Like aphids, leafhoppers excrete a sweet, sticky honeydew which attracts ants and bees, and on which a sooty mold often grows. Leafhoppers attack the leaves of beans, beets, celery, corn, cucumbers, eggplants, grapes, lettuce, melons, parsnips, peanuts, peppers, potatoes, pumpkins, raspberries, rhubarb, spinach, squashes, strawberries, and tomatoes. They are difficult to eradicate since they migrate south in the winter and return to the North in the spring.

Manifestation
• Leaves become stippled with pale dots, turn yellow, and fall off. Vines may be damaged and stems stunted.

To Combat
• Because leafhoppers migrate, spraying gives only temporary relief. However, pyrethrum spray kills them on contact.
• Sheets of shiny aluminum foil spread over the garden soil do much to inhibit leafhoppers from visiting plants in the area.
• Birds are great leafhopper eaters. Encourage them by erecting birdhouses and birdbaths nearby.

• Ladybugs also eat quantities of leafhoppers.
• The larvae of lacewing and syrphid flies (you can order their eggs from many garden supply houses) devour leafhoppers greedily.
• Wasps and yellow jackets kill leafhoppers.
• Plant some blackberry bushes within a few hundred feet of your grapevines. These bushes are often hosts in early spring to an insect whose eggs are parasitized by another insect, *Anagrus epos*, that later parasitizes the eggs of grape leafhoppers. They can often completely rid grapevines of leafhoppers.

Leaf Miners

Leaf miners are the larvae of many kinds of insect species, flies or moths. They spend their larval stage attacking the leaves of several kinds of plants, principally beans, beets, spinach, and Swiss chard. From late April on, small, white eggs, usually laid side by side or in small clusters, can be found on the undersides of leaves.

Manifestation
• Leaves become spotted, blotched, or curlicued with narrow white trails. Eventually leaves may drop off.

To Combat
• Keep the area around susceptible plants free from garden debris.
• Look for eggs on the undersides of leaves, and destroy them with cotton swabs dipped in alcohol.

• Remove and destroy any leaves that show leaf miner trails.
• If leaf miners are a major problem, make cheesecloth tents or cloches of fine screening over your vegetable beds.
• Spraying with a soapy water solution often controls leaf miners while plants are young and less able to resist major damage. Rinse with clear water 1 hour later.

Leaf Mustard

See *Mustard greens*

Leek

Leeks are a biennial, although they are generally cultivated for harvesting during and at the end of the first season. They go to seed in the second year of growth. There are several varieties (tall growing, early, and late), but they're all generally long-season vegetables, needing 120 to 150 days to reach full maturity (they can, however, be harvested at any time if size isn't important). Leeks are winter hardy, don't mind a light frost in the fall, and can withstand temperatures below 0° F if they're well mulched.

When to Plant
• If you want large leeks (bulb diameter 1½ inches or more), start seeds indoors toward the end of winter for transplanting to the garden in midspring.
• Plant seeds outdoors in early spring for early harvesting; or plant in midsummer (for hot-weather planting, see "Garden Tips") for late fall harvesting or winter mulching.

Where to Plant
• Leek seedlings don't like a lot of hot sun—try planting them where they're a little shaded in the morning. Or plant something like peas or other shading plants to the east of them.

Choose a different site for the leek bed every second year to protect young plants from onion fly maggots. Leeks like nitrogen—mix in plenty of humus or other organic matter before setting in seeds or transplants. They also like a cool, shaded soil that holds plenty of moisture—they need lots of water while they grow. They prefer a near-neutral soil (pH 6.5 to 7.0).

How to Plant

• Sow seeds ½ inch deep, 6 to 8 inches apart in rows 18 inches apart. Or set transplants 8 inches apart in rows 18 inches apart.

• Some gardeners dig trenches 6 inches deep, setting the transplants 6 to 8 inches apart and covering the roots with 1 inch or so of soil, gradually filling the trenches with more soil as the leeks grow upward. This blanches the lower parts of the leeks and also encourages them to grow taller.

Germination Time

• Seeds germinate in 10 to 20 days, depending on soil temperature.

Care During Growth

• Throughout their growth, remember to water liberally—leeks always need plenty of moisture.

• Once the plants are 4 inches high, start hilling up the earth around the stems and continue as long as you see growth in height. This stimulates them to grow taller and also blanches the stalks, giving them better flavor. To avoid getting grit into the stem, hill up only to where the leaves branch from the stem.

• Besides hilling, mulch the plants with leaves, grass clippings, and other organic matter to help conserve moisture and eliminate weeds. As in hilling, mulch up to but not beyond where the stem branches into leaves.

• A couple of times during growth, fertilize with dilute fish emulsion or manure tea.

Maturation Time

• You can get a fairly good-sized leek in 90 days, but you can pull leeks at any time during the growing season and treat them as you would scallions. If you're after 1-inch-minimum-diameter stems, count on at least 120 days from seed to harvest.

Harvesting

• Generally, the time to harvest mature leeks is when the stems (the part below where the leaves branch out) are 1 inch in diameter and 5 to 6 inches long.

• Or you can leave the leeks in the ground and help yourself to them at any time during the winter and very early the next spring. But you must mulch deeply (even 1 foot) when the weather gets very cold and before the ground freezes.

Storing

• Leeks will keep very well for several weeks in a cold place if they're wrapped loosely.

• For longer storage, remove them from the garden with their roots attached. Cut the leaves back, preserving a few inches of the green only, and stand the plants roots down in a box in a cool place. Pack them with sand, sawdust, garden soil, or vermiculite, and keep the packing medium moist (not wet). They'll keep for about 2 months.

• You can also store leeks by freezing them. Wash and slice them, and blanch for 1 minute in boiling water. Drain, let the pieces dry, then pop them into plastic bags. Don't let them thaw before you use them; they'll become mushy.

Diseases and Pests

• Onion fly maggots, thrips.

Garden Tips

• If you don't have much garden space, you can plant leeks very close together. They won't grow to a great size, but they'll still be tasty, and you'll have lots of them.

• Leeks germinate best in soil that isn't too warm—if you're planting in hot weather, start them indoors, where they're away from the hot sun, and, when you're ready to transplant

them to the garden, set them in deeply.

• When harvesting, don't pull up the roots: Cut the leek stems level with the ground and the leeks will grow new tops.

• Leeks bought at the market often have roots attached. If you leave ½ inch or so of the stem, you can plant these roots, burying them so that the tops are even with the ground. They'll start growing immediately.

• Leeks left in the ground over the winter can be eaten in the spring until they send up flower stalks. If you cut off the stalks when they start to grow, you can prolong the plants' edible life.

• Let a couple of plants go to seed. You can collect the seeds, refrigerate them, and plant them the next year.

• You can dig up leek plants after they've gone to seed: Look for bublets buried at the bases of the stems. These can be replanted at once, and you'll often get a winter crop the same year.

• Good companion plantings for leeks are said to be carrots, celery, and regular onions.

Kitchen Tips

• Wash leeks very carefully under cold running water to remove the dirt and sand lodged between their flat leaves. Trim and slice them lengthwise. If they're very thick, slice them lengthwise in quarters. Again hold them under cold running water.

• Tie leeks in bunches, and cook them in boiling water as you would asparagus, until they're just tender. Serve with a sauce.

• Substitute leeks for onions in soups and stews—they give incomparable flavor!

• A leek cooked and pureed with other vegetables for the base of a cream soup adds great, rich taste.

• Put a couple of white leek bulbs in a pot of moist dirt and keep this in your kitchen. They will sprout green shoots that you can cut and use just as you would chives or scallions.

Lemon Balm

Lemon balm is a hardy perennial of the mint family, sometimes also called bee balm or sweet balm, but not to be confused with *Monarda didyma*, the wild and garden bee balm, also a mint, which is grown for its bright flowers. Lemon balm has a lemonlike fragrance. Its bright green, slightly furry leaves and tender sprigs are used fresh in salads and fruit cups. They are also steeped for tea. They can be dried for similar use.

The plants grow in clumps from 2 to 3 feet high. Lemon balm self-sows plentifully.

When to Plant
• Plant lemon balm after the last sharp frost of early spring.

• Or start seeds indoors in very early spring, and transplant seedlings to the garden when they're about 3 inches tall.

Where to Plant
• Lemon balm will grow in a wide variety of soils (pH 6.0 to 6.5), as long as the location is damp but not waterlogged. It thrives in sun or partial shade.

How to Plant
• Set seedlings 18 inches apart to allow room for the leafy tops to spread.

• If you are sowing seeds directly in the garden, sprinkle them sparingly.

Germination Time
• Seeds germinate in 12 to 15 days.

Care During Growth
• When seedlings are 2 inches high, thin to 18 inches apart.

• Lemon balm needs almost no care

beyond seeing that the ground is kept moist. In the late fall, you can cut the frost-killed stems level with the ground, shred these over the bed, and cover with compost. This is all the fertilizing the plants need.

• After several seasons, if the plants are growing too thick, divide and separate the clumps early in the spring, setting the divisions 18 inches apart.

Harvesting

• You won't get full growth the first year, but you can harvest some leaves throughout the summer. You can also, several times during the first season, cut the plants down a few inches from the top for aromatic and tender stems and leaves. These prunings also encourage growth.

• The most fragrant oils are in the leaves shortly before flowering.

• If you're picking leaves for drying, choose late morning on a dry, sunny day.

Storing

• To dry leaves for storing, spread them while they're still fresh in a hot, dark, and airy room. When they're thoroughly dry, pack them in tightly closed containers.

Kitchen Tips

• The leaves of lemon balm, chopped or finely shredded, add a very nice lemon-minty flavor to cookies, custards, puddings, soups, and stews.

• Use the whole leaves arranged in any style as a garnish for chicken, fish, or vegetables.

• You can steep lemon balm leaves, alone or with leaves of other fresh garden herbs, in boiling water for a few minutes to make a refreshing herb tea.

• Use the leaves of lemon balm as a garnish for any iced drink.

• • •

Lemon Verbena

A vigorous-growing, tender woody perennial whose long, narrow, lemon-scented leaves are used in poultry stuffing, fish sauces, tea, and potpourris, lemon verbena can be grown from cuttings (which root easily) or, rarely, from seed. Where summers are long, the bushes may reach a height of 3 feet. You can plant lemon verbena in the garden for the summer season, but it must be moved indoors for the winter, since it is very frost sensitive. Being deciduous, it will lose its leaves in the fall, but they will eventually replace themselves.

When to Plant
• Take cuttings from an established bush in late summer and maintain them indoors over the winter. Plant seeds or set out transplants well after the last frost in spring.

Where to Plant
• Any good, moist garden soil (pH 6 to 7) will do. Lemon verbena likes shade.

How to Plant
• Plant seeds 5 inches apart in rows 2 feet apart.
• Set out plants 2 feet apart on all sides.

Care During Growth
• Lemon verbena is initially a slow grower, but it speeds up greatly as the season advances.
• If you've planted seeds, thin the seedlings, when they reach 4 inches in height, to 2 feet apart.
• At the end of summer, before cold weather starts, cut the plants back to 1 foot in height, dig them up, and pot them for indoor winter storage (see "Storing").

• In early February, remove potted plants from storage, place them where it's cool and light, and water as needed. Return them to the garden when all danger of frost is past. Trim off all weak shoots.

Harvesting
• Leaves are usually cut for drying. This can be done throughout the growing season, but the leaves are at their most aromatic in the late summer or early fall, just before the plants flower. Choose a sunny, dry day for harvesting.

Storing
• To store lemon verbena over the winter, place the potted plants in a cool, mildly dark place at temperatures from 55° to 65° F. Water slightly from time to time—just enough to keep the plants from drying out.
• To store leaves for tea and other uses, spread them to dry on a screen in a hot, shaded place with good air circulation. When they're dry, place them in jars or bottles. They'll remain flavorful for at least six months.

Lentil

See *Pea*

Lettuce

Lettuce is a hardy crop that loves cool, moist weather and thus does best in spring and fall. It can stand quite a bit of cold. Seeds germinate best at 65° to 70° F, although they will germinate in soil as cold as 40°. The plants generally prefer daytime temperatures of about 60° and nights as cool as 50°. Lettuce doesn't grow well in hot weather. Heat and dryness stimulate it to bolt to seed.

There are three main types of lettuce:

Head lettuce, also called crisp heading. The heads are firm and round, resembling cabbage. The best-known varieties are Great Lakes, Iceberg, and Mission. Head lettuce is the most difficult to grow because it demands cool summer nights. It also requires more room.

Leaf lettuce, also called loose-leaf and loose-head lettuce. The heads are less compact and the leaves less crisp than those of head lettuce. The chief varieties are Grand Rapids, Oakleaf, Ruby, Salad Bowl, Black-seeded Simpson, and Slobolt. There are also special types of leaf lettuce called butterhead—these are softer, more tender, with "buttery" leaves. Chief among these are Augusta, Bibb, Boston, Buttercrunch, and Tom Thumb (a miniature variety). The leaf lettuces stand heat fairly well and are slower to bolt.

Cos, or romaine, lettuce. Elongated, upright heads with looser leaves are slightly coarser than those of the other two types. Cos lettuce stands heat well, but the mature plants can't take extreme cold.

When to Plant

• Don't sow too many seeds at one time; divide them into at least 4 plantings, 2 weeks apart, to have a constant crop without too many maturing all at once.

• *Head lettuce:* Seeds can be planted indoors in a sunny window in very early spring and seedlings transplanted to the garden 5 to 6 weeks later. Or direct-seed as early as the ground can be worked, usually from midspring to early summer. A second outdoor sowing can be made in midsummer for fall harvesting if your summers aren't too hot.

• *Leaf lettuce:* Sow seeds outdoors in early spring, as soon as the soil is workable, and continue sowing every 7 days until early summer. For a fall crop, you can sow seeds from late summer to early autumn.

• *Cos:* Sow seeds outdoors from midspring to midsummer.

• *Note for all lettuces:* For midsummer plantings, it's sometimes advisable to start seeds indoors, where it is usually cooler. Transplant to the garden when the weather cools a bit. (Also, see "Garden Tips" on how to chill seeds for summer planting.)

Where to Plant
• All lettuces like loose, moist, well-drained soil with plenty of nitrogen. Soil in which legumes and clover have been grown is excellent for lettuce, as is the addition of fresh or aged manure, compost, and straw to the soil before planting. Although lettuce needs some sun, choose a shady part of your garden, where the plants will be shielded from the hot midday sun. (See "Garden Tips" for alternative spots for growing lettuce.) Lettuce grows well in soil with a pH of 6.5 to 7.5.

How to Plant
• Most lettuce seeds should be sown thinly, either in ¼-inch-deep furrows or broadcast. Cover the seeds only lightly—never more than ¼ inch—or not at all. They germinate best when they receive some light.
• Early every morning, mist the seeded area, and keep the ground lightly moist.
• If you are transplanting seedlings to the garden, plant them 9 inches apart for leaf lettuce and 15 inches apart for head lettuce. Bury the seedlings up to their seed leaves but no higher.

Germination Time
• Seeds germinate in 7 to 14 days.

Care During Growth
• Thin the seedlings when they're 3 inches high. Separate leaf lettuce plants by 9 inches and head lettuce by 15 inches.
• Lettuce plants shouldn't touch one another when they mature, but too much space between the plants may lead to drying out in hot weather.
• Lettuce needs a steady supply of water. If the weather is cool, you can allow the soil to dry slightly between waterings, but once hot weather arrives, always keep the soil lightly moist.
• Since lettuce likes cool soil, it's a good idea to mulch with grass clippings, hay, or straw as soon as the seedlings are well up.
• When hot weather arrives, you may need to shield your lettuce to prevent its bolting to seed. Use anything that will keep it in shadow during the hot part of the day. Try draping cheesecloth lightly over the plants. And make sure they get ample water.
• Lettuce planted for a fall crop will benefit from fertilizing with fish emulsion or manure tea in early September. Continue to keep the plants well watered.

Maturation Time

(Times are approximate, depending on variety, weather, and your taste.)
- *Head lettuce:* about 80 days.
- *Leaf lettuce:* about 43 days.
- *Butterhead lettuce:* about 65 days.
- *Cos:* about 65 days.

Harvesting

- You can often start picking leaf lettuce about a month after planting seed. Pick only the larger outside leaves, allowing the inner ones to continue to grow; in this way you can harvest throughout the growing season.
- If you do use the entire plant, don't pull out the whole thing—cut off the top portion, leaving a 2-inch stub. This method will encourage the growth of new leaves.
- The best time to pick lettuce is early in the morning, while there is still dew on the plants. That way there'll be less wilting.

Storing

- Lettuce keeps best in a cold place—at about 35°F.
- Avoid storing near apples, bananas, melons, or pears, whose gases can cause brown spots on lettuce.

Diseases and Pests

- Bacterial diseases, birds, Botrytis blight, cabbage loopers, cabbage-worms, corn earworms, cutworms, damping off, green peach aphids, leafhoppers, powdery mildew, slugs, thrips, tipburn, whiteflies.

Garden Tips

- It's a good idea to change the location of your lettuce bed every year.
- Lettuce seeds won't sprout when soil temperatures are in the 80s.
- Put your packet of lettuce seeds in the refrigerator for a week before planting outdoors in warm weather.
- Mix lettuce seeds with some fine soil to make distribution easier.
- Sow seeds of more than one variety of lettuce at one time—if the weather isn't friendly to one type, at least some other is likely to thrive.
- For summer planting, sow seeds late in the day on a cool day, moisten the soil well, and cover with a light grass-clipping mulch.
- If the sun is too hot for growing lettuce, cover each plant with a bottomless plastic milk jug during the hottest part of the day.
- Lettuce will bolt to seed if you have a succession of nights when the temperature stays above 70°F.
- You can tell when lettuce is about to bolt: The leaves become dull.
- Cool weather in the fall always gives a new spurt to lettuce growth.
- To save garden space, plant lettuce in the broccoli bed. By the time the lettuce has finished producing, the broccoli is thriving.

• A light frost will toughen lettuce leaves somewhat, but they'll still be crisp and nutritious.

• Try planting some lettuce seeds in the garden in very late fall (close to the first frost) for spring sprouting. It's a bit chancy, but you might end up with an extremely early spring crop.

• Plant lettuce in the tomato patch or among other tall-growing vegetables, like corn. These will shade the lettuce from the heat of the sun and give you a longer harvest season.

• Good companion plantings for lettuce are said to be carrots, cucumbers, onions, radishes, and strawberries.

Kitchen Tips

• Leaf lettuce has more of vitamins A and C than head lettuce.

• The best way to wash a head of lettuce is to fill a large bowl or pot with cold water and pump the head, stem side up, up and down in it. Use a couple of changes of water if necessary.

• Very crisp, shredded head lettuce or romaine can be substituted for shredded cabbage in coleslaw.

• Wash wilted lettuce in cold water, shake it fairly dry, cover, and refrigerate. In about 12 hours the lettuce will have freshened up surprisingly.

• The leaves of refrigerated lettuce will be less likely to "rust" if you wrap them in dry paper towels before refrigerating.

• Most lettuces make excellent hot greens, cooked as you would spinach. You have to flavor them a bit with celery salt, nutmeg, pepper, and perhaps some garlic, but they can make a fine dish. Also, try creaming lettuce, or stuffing lettuce leaves as you do cabbage.

• Don't throw away coarse outside lettuce leaves. Use them as greens in soups and stews.

• Some finely shredded lettuce is very good added to a vegetable soup shortly before you serve it.

Loganberry

See *Blackberry*

Lovage

Lovage is an aromatic, hardy perennial herb of the carrot family. Its flavor is similar to that of celery, though more potent. It matures into a sturdy plant that may grow as tall as 6 feet. Lovage stems and leaves are used fresh in summer drinks, soups, fish dishes, and salads, and the dried stalks and leaves in many cooked dishes.

When to Plant
• Seeds may be planted indoors in flats in late winter or very early spring, or 10 to 12 weeks before the last heavy frost. Transplant seedlings to the garden when they are 4 to 6 inches high, after danger of frost is past.
• Seeds can be sown directly in the garden from mid- to late spring, or in mid- to late autumn for early-spring sprouting.

Where to Plant
• Lovage does best in moderately moist, organically rich soil (pH 6.0 to 7.5). Plant it in full sun or light shade.

How to Plant
• Sow seeds ½ inch deep, 6 inches apart.
• Set plants or seedlings 12 inches apart.
• You can also divide already existing plants in the spring, after danger of frost has passed, cutting down through the roots and planting the divisions at the same depth as the original plant grew. Separate the transplants by 12 inches.

Germination Time
• Seeds germinate in 21 days.

Care During Growth
• If you have planted seeds, thin the seedlings to 12 inches apart when they are 5 inches tall.
• Once established, lovage needs very little care. It's a good idea to apply a straw mulch in the late fall to guard against winter injury.

Maturation Time
• After the first year, plants mature in 40 days.

Harvesting
• You can pick tender leaves and stems at any time during the growing season, to use fresh or to dry.

Storing
• Once the small stems and leaves have been dried, store them in jars. Dried lovage will retain its flavor for at least 6 months.

Kitchen Tips
• Lovage not only suggests the flavor of celery but also has a hint of anise. Its leaves and stalks can be used as you would celery.
• Add a few lovage leaves to soups during cooking.
• Lovage seeds give a very nice flavor to bread.

Mâche

See *Corn salad*

Marjoram

Although opinion differs as to whether marjoram and oregano are actually different kinds of marjoram, they both belong to the mint family and have similar cultures.

Probably because of the different varieties, pot marjoram—known also as oregano, common marjoram, wild marjoram, and wintersweet—has at least three botanical names: *Origanum vulgare*, *Origanum onites*, and *Origanum heracleoticum*, the last being the one whose highly aromatic leaves are most used in salads, soups, and tomato dishes.

Sweet marjoram has two botanical names: *Origanum majorana* and *Majorana hortensis*. Its delicate-flavored leaves are used in salad dressings and cooking.

Both marjorams are tender perennials that are usually treated as annuals in the North, growing to a height of about 1 foot.

When to Plant

• Plant seeds indoors in early spring and set the transplants in the garden about a month later.

• Or sow seeds indoors in midspring, when the danger of heavy frost is past.

Where to Plant

• Marjoram needs full sun and likes a rich, sandy, moist soil (pH 5.5 to 6.5).

How to Plant

• If you are planting seeds indoors or in a window box or cold frame, space the seeds 6 inches apart, covering them with ¼ inch of fine soil. Transplant to the garden when the seedlings are about 3 inches high. In the garden, space the seedlings 8 inches apart (12 inches apart for pot marjoram).

• Marjoram seeds are very small. If

181

you are planting them directly in the garden, mix them with a little sand or fine soil and broadcast them over the growing bed. Cover with a thin layer of fine soil. Later, thin the seedlings as previously described.

Germination Time
• Seeds germinate in 14 days.

Care During Growth
• Marjoram needs little care, beyond keeping the soil moderately moist.
• Toward the end of the season, when the plants begin to bloom, cut them back a few inches below the blossoms and you'll get further growth, extending the harvest time.

Maturation Time
• Marjoram plants are mature in 45 days.

Harvesting
• You can pick marjoram leaves all through the season for using fresh. If you want to dry them, wait until after the plants blossom, then cut the stems off above the second set of leaves.

Storing
• For drying and storing, cut the stems with their leaves and blossoms and spread them on a screen or stretched netting in a dry, warm place so they'll dry rapidly. Remove the leaves when they're thoroughly dry, and store in small jars.

Garden Tips
• Oregano is rather slow growing when planted from seed; if you want quicker development, you can divide existing plants by slicing through their roots and planting the root divisions.
• You'll get bushier plants if you prune the tops back about 6 weeks after seedlings appear, to about 1 inch above the growing center.
• Oregano leaves are very attractive to bees. Plant oregano in your garden if you need a bee lure to pollinate other plants.

Kitchen Tips
• The leaves of oregano are used in many dishes containing tomato, such as sauces for pasta and pizza (often in conjunction with basil). They are also a very tasty addition to all kinds of stews and many gravies.
• Sweet marjoram seems to go with everything—use the fresh leaves in salads and all sorts of vegetable dishes. Egg dishes, also, have an affinity for sweet marjoram's flavor.

Mealybugs

Mealybugs are soft, white, flat, cottony-looking insects that suck plant juices, setting up colonies on the axils of leaves and branching stems of plants. They can also be found on the undersides of leaves, on stems, and on the surfaces of fruits and vegetables. If the infestation is large, the plants are stunted and in some cases ruined.

Like aphids, mealybugs secrete a sticky honeydew that leads to the growth of a black, sooty fungus. Ants are also attracted to the honeydew and often carry the mealybugs from one plant to another. Mealybugs attack many garden plants, including beans, blueberries, grapes, peppers, pumpkins, raspberries, strawberries, sweet potatoes, and tomatoes.

Manifestation

• The sticky honeydew and sooty mold can be seen on leaves and branches. Also, the presence of many ants can be a sign of mealybugs. Leaves become stippled, yellowed, and wilted; branches die back; and fruits drop prematurely.

To Combat

• At the first sign of these insects, pick them off the plants with a cotton swab dipped in rubbing alcohol. Repeat as often as you see the bugs.

• Hose down infested plants, then spray them with a solution of 1 ounce of any kind of soap dissolved in 1 quart of water. Hose the plants again with clear water about 1 hour later. Repeat in a day or two if necessary— a few such treatments will generally clear the plants of mealybugs.

• Rotenone and pyrethrum sprays are also effective.

• Ladybugs, lacewing larvae, and parasitic wasps are great mealybug eaters. You can buy the eggs of all of these from many garden supply houses.

Measuring Worms

See *Cabbage loopers*

Melon

All melons are heat-loving plants. They need warm, sunny days and warm nights, generally require a long growing season, and cannot tolerate frost.

There are several short-term varieties of all types of melons, including muskmelons (often called cantaloupe) and watermelons, which until a few years ago could rarely be grown successfully in northern gardens. The fruits tend to be smaller in size and mature in 62 to 70 days after sprouting. To get a jump on the growing season, either start seeds indoors or buy seedlings.

Honeydews, muskmelons, and watermelons are now available in bush as well as the usual standard vining varieties. Bush types generally produce fewer fruits than vining ones and stop bearing somewhat earlier, but since they're more compact, you can plant more in less space so that the ultimate yield may not be much less. However, the harvest season is shorter for bush types: 7 to 10 days, generally. Vining varieties give fruit for 21 days or more.

When to Plant
• Sow seeds indoors about a month before the last expected frost.
• Plant seedlings outdoors after the soil has thoroughly warmed and there is absolutely no danger of frost. The nights should also be warm, with soil temperatures ideally from 70° to 80°F. A general rule of thumb is to plant melon seedlings outdoors when peonies bloom.

Where to Plant
• When planting seeds indoors, be sure they'll get plenty of sun, or set them under grow lights. Night temperatures should be well above 55°F.
• Melons need a large growing area and like full sun. It's best to choose a southern exposure, sloping if possible, or a spot near a fence or trellis against which the vines can be trained. The best soil is a rich, moist but well-drained, sandy loam that is slightly acid to neutral (pH 5.5 to 7.0).

Melons need lots of nitrogen, phosphorus, and magnesium in the soil. Dig well-rotted manure or compost well into the soil, spading 1 foot deep and breaking up any clods.

How to Plant
• *Indoors:* It's a good idea to presprout seeds. Make a double layer of paper toweling, and sprinkle it well with water. Spread the seeds over this, roll the towel up carefully, and slip it into a plastic bag. Keep it in a warm place, where the temperature will not go below 70° F. Examine the seeds every few days, planting any that germinate. Fill 3-inch peat pots with a mixture of equal parts peat moss and rotted compost, and plant 3 or 4 seeds to a pot. When the seedlings are 1 inch high, discard the weaker ones, leaving 2 per pot.
• Before transplanting to the garden, harden the seedlings off by setting them outdoors during the day for about a week.

• *Outdoors:* If you are planting seeds, plant in either hills or furrows.

Hills: Plant 6 to 8 seeds 2 inches apart, ½ inch deep in a ring about 2 inches in diameter. Rings should be 4 feet apart on all sides. Thin the plants to the 2 strongest when they are 2 inches high.

Furrows: Make long furrows or trenches ½ to 1 inch deep and 4 feet apart (for watermelons, 6 feet apart). Plant seeds 6 inches apart in a straight line. When the vines are about 1 foot long, thin them to the sturdiest plants 2 feet apart (watermelons, 3 feet apart).

• If you are planting seedlings or transplants, space them 2 feet apart (3 feet apart for watermelons) in rows 4 feet apart (6 feet apart for watermelons).

• Try not to disturb the roots when transplanting, and water thoroughly afterward.

Germination Time

• Melon seeds germinate best at 70° to 75°F and will sprout in 5 to 10 days.

Care During Growth

• When you see seedlings, break the crust gently around the plants every couple of days to help them emerge. Remove weeds by cultivating gently, because most melons have shallow root systems.

• If necessary, protect the plants against cool nights with hot caps, cloches, inverted cans, plastic containers, or other coverings. Remove these during the day when the sun is warm.

• A mulch is particularly important for melons: It concentrates and holds heat in the soil, controls weeds, conserves moisture, and hastens fruit maturity. Use gravel, hay, or black plastic, placing it about the time the first fruit sets. If you are using plastic, hold it down around the plants with stones.

• Moisture and warmth are very important. Give the plants plenty of water right up to the time the fruits start ripening.

• For watermelons, pinch out all but 3 fruits to each vine. They'll be bigger and more flavorful, and will ripen sooner.

• If you're growing vining melons on the ground, keep them from direct contact with the soil. Place them on a bed of straw or on upturned flowerpots, coffee cans, berry baskets, or other containers. Better yet, train the vines to a fence or trellis (this saves a great deal of garden space), using twist ties. The melons should also be supported and tied to the trellis by slings or hammocks of mesh bags, netting, or nylon stockings—loose enough to allow the fruit to grow.

• About the third week of August, pinch off the tips of the vines so that the plants' energies will go into the developing fruit. Also, prune off the small, unripe fruits—the melons remaining will grow larger and ripen sooner.

Maturation Time

• Depending on variety, muskmelons take 60 to 120 days to mature; honeydew, 85 to 100 days; watermelons, 65 to 88 days—all from the date of transplant.

Harvesting

• For best flavor, always leave melons to ripen on the vine. If for some reason you must pick them before they're fully ripe, keep them out of direct sunlight to ripen, as you would tomatoes. (But picked early, their flavor will never match that of vine-ripened melons. This is particularly true of honeydews—any that are hard, green, and smooth will never ripen properly. And unripe muskmelons will never get very sweet.)

• As muskmelons ripen, their green rind turns to yellow-green and eventually grayish, the netting becomes more pronounced and coarse looking, and they develop a full, fruity aroma. A muskmelon is fully ripe when the scar at the stem end is sunk a bit and a crack appears completely around the base of the stem. There should also be a slight softness at the blossom end. The stem should slip

easily from the vine with a very slight twist or pull.

• The harvest period for muskmelons usually lasts 3 to 4 weeks.

• A honeydew is ready for picking when the outer skin has become cream colored and feels like soft, smooth leather. The blossom end should give a little when pressed.

• When you are harvesting honeydews, leave 1 inch of stem on the melons to keep them from rotting if they have to stand a little before being used.

• A ripe casaba melon is yellow (not greenish), and the blossom end should be a little soft when pressed.

• A watermelon is ripe when the covering turns from a bright to a dull green, the portion touching the soil turns from greenish white to cream color, and the tendrils nearest the fruit begin to blacken and shrivel. The fruit will make a dull, hollow sound when thumped. If you're unsure, you can cut a small, deep, wedge-shaped plug to examine and taste. If the melon is still unripe, replace the plug—chances are the fruit will continue to ripen normally.

• The harvest period for watermelons is about 2 weeks.

Storing

• Store ripe melons at around 50° F, unripe ones at 65° or 70°. No melon will last long in storage. Watermelons will keep for 2 to 3 weeks. Muskmelons and honeydews can be pared, diced, or cut into small balls and frozen.

Diseases and Pests

• Bacterial diseases, blossom-end rot, cucumber beetles, damping off, field mice, flea beetles, fusarium wilt, leafhoppers, mites, powdery mildew, squash bugs, thrips, vine borers, whiteflies.

Garden Tips

• Before you plant and after you harvest, fertilize the melon plot heavily with compost and rotted manure.

• To keep the soil warm and help melon plants thrive, excavate the plot about 1 foot deep before planting, and spread a 9-inch layer of fresh manure throughout. Cover with composted soil, then plant. The seeds will germinate faster, and the plants will flourish.

• Since melon plants love nitrogen, it's a good idea to grow them where you grew peas and beans before. These enrich the soil with nitrogen.

• Irregular pollination produces sparse and small fruit. If your growing season is short, hand pollination of melon blossoms is recommended. Snip off a male flower, remove its petals, and place it on the female blossom so that the pollen falls on the female flower's stigma. (Female flowers have a small bulb at the base.) Pollinate no more than six flowers on the same vine at the same time, and remove further flowers as they develop.

• Don't water too much after the fruits begin to ripen, or the plants will be stimulated to produce more vine growth.

• If your melons are attacked by animals, cover them with webbed plastic milk crates. Air, light, and rain can still enter, but animals will be kept at bay. Weigh down the crates if necessary.

• Melons placed on 2-pound coffee cans will also be safe from small animals, such as field mice. And the cans collect and retain heat, hastening ripening.

• Ample watering is important while melons are developing, but moderate dryness during final ripening promotes sweetness in the fruit.

• No melon will ripen further once it's been refrigerated.

• Removing the female flowers that develop during the first 2 weeks of blossom production will give a yield that may mature a bit later, but the melons will be larger and more numerous.

• Pinch out any blossoms that develop within 50 days of the first expected frost.

• Melons flourish in the corn patch.

Kitchen Tips

• Melons taste best when they're *thoroughly* chilled. Since it takes a long

time for cold to penetrate to the center, put a melon in the refrigerator at least 2 days before you serve it.
• Once a melon is cut, it absorbs odors from other foods easily. Wrap or cover it tightly before storing in the refrigerator.
• An ice-cream scoop is great for removing the seeds neatly and cleanly from the cut halves of melons.

• Want to eat a slice of watermelon without washing your face? Make cuts 1 inch or so apart down the slice through the meat as far as the white part of the rind. Spread the ends of the slice apart, and each "finger" of the melon will stand up for easy eating.

. . .

Mexican Bean Beetles

These beetles are often mistaken for ladybugs; both are a shiny, brownish red with black spots. Ladybugs, however, have a varying number of dots, whereas Mexican bean beetles always have sixteen. They are also a little larger than ladybugs, about ¼ inch long.

Mexican bean beetles lay yellow-orange egg masses on the undersides of leaves. The eggs hatch into oval-shaped, yellow larvae covered with black-tipped spines. The larvae feed on the undersides of the leaves for several weeks before pupating and giving rise to mature beetles. Both larvae and adult beetles chew holes in the foliage of beans: chiefly cowpeas, limas, snap beans, and soybeans. (Many bean plants seem to survive bean beetle onslaughts without difficulty.) Adult beetles overwinter in piles of bean leaves and stems.

Manifestation
• The beetles' chewing gives leaves a lacelike appearance. An unusually severe infestation can transform a plant into nothing more than a skeleton.

To Combat
• Mexican bean beetles are more likely to attack pole beans than bush beans.
• Pick off and destroy adult beetles wherever you see them. Look under the leaves (you can use a hand mirror for this) for egg clusters. Wipe these off with alcohol-soaked cotton swabs.
• A parasitic, nonstinging wasp called the Pediobius wasp is very effective at keeping Mexican bean beetles in check. You can purchase the wasp eggs from some nurseries. These wasps are also attracted to gardens where the following plants are grown: buckwheat, carrots, all varieties of daisies, dill, goldenrod, Je-

rusalem artichokes, parsley, and parsnips.
• Stinging nettle plants are hosts to many species of insects that prey on bean beetles.
• Interplant beans with rows of potatoes or rosemary: These are said to repel bean beetles.
• Make a soap-and-water solution (1 ounce of soap dissolved in 1 quart of water), and spray your bean plants from the sides and from below, wetting the leaves well, once a week.
• Both pyrethrum and rotenone sprays are effective against bean beetles.
• At the end of the season, remove and destroy all bean vines. You can compost them.

Mice

See *Rodents*

Mildew

Powdery mildew and downy mildew are fungal diseases that drain nutrients from plants. Downy mildew attacks grapes and lima beans chiefly; different strains of powdery mildew attack beans, celery, cucumbers, eggplants, gourds, lettuce, melons, peas, pumpkins, squashes, and strawberries, as well as many ornamental plants. Both types of mildew flourish in cool weather, especially when nights are damp and days are cool, and in shaded, crowded gardens that have poor air circulation. The spores, carried by the wind or by anything that touches the diseased plants, can infect other plants.

Manifestation

• Downy mildew produces whitish, cottony masses of fungus on the undersides of grape leaves, as well as on the new shoots and fruit. The grapes become hard and shrivel. The leaves may show pale blotches. When lima bean plants are infected, a whitish down grows on the pods, eventually enclosing them so that they turn dark and curl.

• Powdery mildew appears at first as round, pale spots on the undersides of leaves. The leaves may darken, turn reddish, and curl. The spots gradually enlarge, become powdery, and produce white, weblike strands that cover the leaves entirely. Plants often become stunted.

• • •

To Combat
- Choose disease-resistant varieties of susceptible plants.
- Don't crowd plants.
- Try not to wet the foliage when watering plants. Or water early enough in the day for the moisture on the leaves to evaporate before nightfall.
- If the infected plants are annuals, pull them up or bag and burn them. In the case of grapevines, cut out infected parts where possible, and dispose of them in the same way.

- Don't plant lima beans in the same spot 2 years running.
- Mix ¼ ounce baking soda with 1 gallon of water, and spray the solution on vulnerable plants once a week. This very much inhibits the development of mildew.
- Since mildew spores can overwinter in diseased pods or old stems and leaves, remove these from the garden. Burn them if possible.

. . .

Milky Spore Disease 🐞

Also known as milky disease, this is a natural control of many beetle larvae (grubs), especially the lawn-damaging grubs of the Japanese beetle. It is applied to lawns in powder form at 4-foot intervals, whereupon the disease spores infect and kill the grubs before they do much damage and before they emerge as full-blown beetles. The spore dust requires only one application, since the spores perpetuate themselves, returning to the soil when the grubs die and remaining ready to infect any others in the vicinity for season after season. When no beetles are present, the spores go dormant, but they become effective again if more grubs appear.

It may take as long as 3 years for milky spore to wipe out a grub infestation entirely, but from then on you need do nothing more about the problem. Milky spore disease is said to be harmless to plants, humans, and other animals, but read the directions on the package carefully.

Mint

Mint is a very rapid-growing, perennial herb of many species and varieties, the chief ones being peppermint (*Mentha piperita*) and spearmint (*M. spicata*). Except for catnip, most mints don't breed true from seed, so it's safer to start with plants. Thereafter, they self-propagate from surface or underground runners, and you can supply a whole neighborhood with transplants if need be. Mints are very hardy and can grow up to 3 feet tall. Their leaves, fresh or dried, are used in candies, jellies, potpourris, salads, sauces, and teas.

When to Plant

• Set out mint plants early in the spring, as soon as the ground can be worked.

Where to Plant

• Mint will grow in almost any moist, well-drained soil, but it does best in a deep, rich, slightly acid soil (pH 5.5 to 6.5) that's moist without being soggy. It can take full sun but prefers partial shade. Since mint spreads rapidly, choose a location for it not too close to your other plants.

How to Plant

• Mint plants can be set in rows or beds—it hardly matters, since they multiply rapidly from runners. Firm the soil around the roots, and water well immediately after planting.

Care During Growth

• Mint grows easily, with no care, and spreads rapidly. To keep it from escaping to the rest of your garden, sink boards or metal garden edging about 10 inches into the ground around the mint bed.

Harvesting

• Fresh leaves and tender stems may be cut throughout the growing season and used fresh or dried. For drying, pick the leaves and flowering tops just before mint begins to blossom—this is when they're at their most aromatic. The best time to pick for drying is late in the morning on a dry, sunny day.

Storing

• To dry for storing, cut the upper parts of the plants, tie them in small bundles, and hang them in a hot, shady spot until they're dry and brittle. Or remove the leaves and flower tops from the plants and spread them on a screen to dry in the shade.
• Store the dried leaves, small stems, and flower tops in tightly closed containers, away from light.

Diseases and Pests

• Fungus, rust (sometimes called mint rust).

Garden Tips

• If your mint plants are too thick or if you wish to divide some plants, dig up a plant and tear it apart gently, taking some of the root and some of the leafy stem attached to it. Transplant as desired.
• Good companion plantings with mint are said to be Brussels sprouts,

cabbage, cauliflower, kale, kohlrabi, tomatoes, and turnips.

• Mint plants are believed to deter cabbage moths.

• Mint leaves liquefied in the blender with four times their volume of water will make a spray that is effective against aphids. A second treatment may be necessary to finish the pests off.

Kitchen Tips

• Fresh mint leaves are great breath sweeteners. Chew a few.

• Sprinkle coarsely chopped, fresh mint leaves over cooked vegetables such as carrots, peas, and potatoes just before serving. Do the same with broiled fish and seafood.

• It goes without saying that mint leaves and roast lamb go together. But also sprinkle fresh-chopped leaves over lamb chops after you've broiled them.

• Sprigs of leaves, both peppermint and spearmint, are the very nicest garnish for almost any dish.

Mites

Plant mites, also called red mites, red spider mites, and spider mites, are of many kinds, but all of them are exceedingly tiny spiders. Most are reddish, although there are also green ones and yellow ones. They have soft bodies and piercing mouths for sucking up plant juices. Mites don't like humidity or moist soil and are primarily a problem when the weather is hot and dry. They attack most plants and lay spherical eggs, pale yellow to pale red, on the undersides of leaves.

Manifestation

• The presence of mites is often first revealed by the tiny fine webs they spin under leaves. You can see the mites themselves if you use a magnifying glass. Leaves become dull, turn gray, then yellow or brown, and drop off.

To Combat

• Frequent misting of plant foliage discourages mites.

• If you see mites, try a strong spraying with the garden hose. This usually dislodges them.

• A soap-and-water spray is effective against bad infestations—1 ounce of soap dissolved in 1 quart of water—followed in 1 hour by a plain water spray. Since this treatment kills only adult mites, repeat it periodically to get all the mites as they emerge from their eggs.

• Lacewings, ladybugs, and praying mantises are great mite eaters.

• Both pyrethrum and rotenone sprays are effective against mites.

Moles

Don't be too quick to get rid of moles if you know you have them. They do a great deal of good in the garden: They destroy vast amounts of cutworms, and they eat white grubs and other harmful garden pests. It's true that moles' mounds and ridges can make a lawn look unsightly, and although it's unlikely that they eat bulbs, their tunneling might somewhat disturb the roots of flowers and vegetables. Still, unless you know they're injuring your garden, think twice about removing them.

To Combat

• Cats catch moles.

• Young moles can often be drowned in their tunnels in the spring if you flood the mole runs with water.

• If you suspect that certain plants are under attack, plant garlic cloves around them. Moles are said to dislike garlic.

• Trapping is probably the best method to get rid of moles.

Mosaic Virus

Various forms of this virus are known as bean mosaic virus, cucumber mosaic virus, and tobacco mosaic virus (TMV). Clover and other leguminous weeds are its wild host plants, and the virus is transmitted by aphids, which move from these to garden plants. They also transmit the virus from infected to healthy plants. The chief garden plants attacked are beans, cucumbers, eggplants, peppers, potatoes, pumpkins, raspberries, summer squashes, tobacco, and tomatoes, as well as some garden flowers.

Manifestation

• Leaves become pale or patterned with mottled areas of dark and light green, misshapen or curled, and often die from the base upward. Plants are stunted, and any fruits they produce are small. The plants usually die.

To Combat

• There is no cure for mosaic virus—emphasis must be on prevention.

• Practice crop rotation wherever possible.
• When buying plants, be sure they are virus free.
• See *Aphids* for control of these pests, since they remain the prime carriers of mosaic virus.
• Milk is said to inhibit the progress of this virus—some gardeners report success from dipping their tomato seedlings in milk before transplanting them to the garden.
• If you have handled tobacco in any form (the virus can even be present in cigarettes), wash your hands before handling garden plants.

• Destroy the following weed hosts of the virus: ground-cherry, horse nettle, jimsonweed, and nightshade. And keep your susceptible plants away from clover.
• Always destroy diseased plants— burn them or bag them. Composting won't kill the virus.
• Don't leave any wilted vines in the garden at the end of the season— they may carry viral material over the winter.
• Lacewings and ladybugs, great aphid eaters, should be encouraged in your garden. They are attracted to pollen- and nectar-producing plants.

Moths

See *Borers; Cabbage loopers; Cabbageworms; Corn borers; Corn earworms; Cutworms; Grape-berry moths; Gypsy moth caterpillars; Hornworms; Leaf miners*

Mulch

A mulch spread over the garden bed and around plants inhibits weed growth and helps conserve moisture in the soil, saving lots of watering during dry spells. In addition, some mulches keep the soil cool, others warm it up, and some help enrich the soil. Mulches are divided into three types: organic, synthetic, and mineral.

Organic Mulches
• Any of the following are excellent organic mulches: brown paper, chopped corncobs or ground-up cornstalks, compost, dry grass clippings (from unsprayed lawns), evergreen clippings, fir bark, green manure crops, hay (especially from

animal bedding), newspapers (black and white only) either shredded or covered with grass clippings, nutshells, peat moss (humus), pine needles, rotted sawdust, salt-marsh hay, seashells, seaweed, shredded leaves, straw, strawy manure, well-rotted manure.

• Most organic mulches shouldn't be applied until the soil is thoroughly warmed and the plants well established.

• Organic mulches enrich the soil and tend to keep the ground cool, which is very desirable for cool-weather plants and those that don't like too much heat.

• Leaves make an excellent mulch, but they must be chopped or shredded, otherwise they tend to mat down and keep air out of the soil. (Oak leaves, however, do not mat down.)

• You can shred leaves by running your lawn mower over them.

• Don't mulch with wet grass clippings—they tend to generate too much heat and can kill tender plants. Spread lightly to avoid their matting down and becoming slimy.

• Before using sawdust as a mulch, compost it or allow it to rot.

• Newspapers make a good mulch. Wait until plants are up, then spread layers of paper around them, holding the sheets down with stones. Cover with grass clippings throughout the summer, and in the fall plow what remains of this double mulch into the soil. But don't use newspaper with colored inks—they may contain harmful chemicals, such as lead.

Synthetic Mulches

• Synthetic mulches consist of black plastic (black polyethylene sheeting), clear plastic, aluminized plastic film, and aluminum foil.

• Black plastic and the aluminum mulches, since they are opaque, keep weeds from sprouting.

• Both black plastic and clear plastic mulches attract and hold heat, keeping the soil warm during cool nights, although clear plastic warms the soil more. Clear plastic, however, won't keep weeds from sprouting.

• Aluminized film tends to keep the soil on the cool side.

• Plastic and aluminum mulches should be laid down in sheets over the garden bed before planting, with holes made for the seeds or seedlings and slits here and there to allow rain and air to reach the soil.

• You can use household aluminum foil as a mulch: Spread it with the shiny side up, and make holes through which you plant seeds or seedlings. Hold the sheets down with stones.

Mineral Mulches

• A good mineral mulch is gravel, which soaks up heat during the day and releases it gradually during the night—excellent for heat-loving plants.

• Coarse sand can be used as a mulch, especially on dense, clayey soils.

For a mulch for acid-loving plants, use any of the following: hay, hops, leached seaweed, leaf mold, peat moss, pine needles, shredded or rotted oak leaves, well-rotted sawdust, wood chips, or woodland soil.

Bag your dry leaves in the autumn and store them over the winter. By spring they'll be just right for a mulch.

At the end of the season, work your mulch into the soil—it will enrich the soil and improve its texture.

A 6-inch winter mulch is a good idea for all bulbs and perennials; it helps to retain moisture and prevents heaving from winter thaws. Use any lightweight mulch, such as peat moss, pine needles, or shredded leaves.

Mulches used for winter protection shouldn't be applied until the top few inches of soil are frozen hard.

Snow makes a fine winter mulch. You can spread other mulches over the snow.

A good winter mulch for non-acid-loving plants is any of the following: ground-up cornstalks, salt-marsh hay, or straw. You needn't remove these in the spring; dig them into the soil.

Mummy Berry

Mummy berry is a blight of blueberries and grapes, caused by a fungus that attacks plants when the blossoms begin developing. When the fruits start to mature, they shrivel and become hard ("mummies"). The spores of the fungus winter over in the mummified berries on the ground.

Manifestation

• Berries or grapes rot, turn brown or gray, shrivel, dry up, and fall to the ground.

To Combat

• You can rid an area of mummy berry fungus by removal of any "mummies" you see on plants and by conscientious sweeping up and removal of any on the ground at the end of the season. These can be deeply buried or composted.

• A 3-inch mulch of well-rotted manure and compost around plants will keep any spores in the soil from being blown elsewhere. The buried spores will disintegrate over the winter. Early in the spring, rake up and discard this mulch.

Mung Bean

See *Bean*

Muskmelon

See *Melon*

Mustard Cress

See *Garden cress*

Mustard Greens

Also known as leaf mustard and grown for their leaves, like spinach, mustard greens are very nutritious. They are frost hardy and can be grown for both an early spring and a fall crop. It's advisable to till the ground about 1 foot deep very early in the spring to help the soil warm up before sowing seeds.

When to Plant
• It is said that mustard greens should be planted when the leaves on oak trees are the size of a mouse's ears. In other words, sow in early spring, as soon as the soil is workable, about 4 weeks before the last expected frost. Plantings can be made at 10-day intervals until a month before warm weather arrives. For a fall crop, start planting again 8 weeks before the first expected frost. Mustard seeds germinate when the soil temperature reaches 45°F.

Where to Plant
• Mustard greens aren't fussy about soil (pH 6.0 to 7.5), but put them in a cool spot where they can get partial shade.

How to Plant
• Plant seeds ¼ inch deep and 2 inches apart, in rows 12 inches apart.

When seedlings appear, thin them so the plants stand 5 inches apart.

• You can also scatter the seeds sparingly in your chosen plot, covering them with a ¼-inch-thick layer of soil.

• It's a good idea to mist the newly planted mustard garden every morning, especially in hot weather, to aid in germination.

Germination Time

• Seeds germinate in just a few days.

Care During Growth

• Thin seedlings to approximately 5 inches apart on all sides (the thinnings are very good in salad).

• Mustard greens need no care at all once the plants are well established. Until then, keeping the beds moist is all that's necessary.

Maturation Time

• Greens are ready to harvest anywhere from 35 to 50 days after the seeds have been planted. A variety called mustard spinach matures in 28 days.

Harvesting

• You can harvest leaves or entire plants any time they look right to you:

4-inch-long leaves are fine for salads. For cooking, you might want them to grow slightly longer.

• If you have enough plants, harvest a few of the leaves from several plants instead of pulling entire plants. This way they'll continue to produce more leaves.

Diseases and Pests

• Aphids, blackleg, clubroot, cutworms, flea beetles, nematodes.

Garden Tips

• Mustard green seeds will germinate faster if you presoak them overnight before planting.

• Plant nasturtiums among mustard greens: They'll act as a trap crop, luring aphids away from the mustard plants.

Kitchen Tips

• Cook mustard greens as you would spinach (they have much more zip). Sometimes it's necessary to add a little water.

• Cooked and pureed, mustard greens are delicious with a little lemon juice and grated onion.

Nasturtium

Nasturtiums, also known as Indian cress, are semihardy, annual herbs with edible leaves, flowers, and seeds. Their flavor is sharp and cresslike, a tangy addition to salads and soups. The common nasturtium can grow as tall as 16 inches if unsupported, or can climb a trellis to as high as 8 feet. There are also dwarf varieties. Nasturtiums are easily grown, and in full sun will bloom continuously all summer and into the fall. Because these plants are very attractive to aphids, many gardeners plant them among their cole crops to act as a trap plant.

When to Plant
• Sow seeds outdoors from early spring, after danger of frost is past and the ground is warm, until early summer.

Where to Plant
• Nasturtiums grow best in alkaline soil (pH 7.0 to 7.5). If you are growing them for blossoms, the soil should be on the dry side: sandy or even gravelly, and not too rich. If you are growing them principally for leaves (for salads, soups, and so on), the soil can be more fertile, producing vigorous foliage but fewer flowers.

• Grown in full sun, nasturtium plants will produce more blossoms. Increasing the amount of shade produces larger leaves and fewer flowers.

How to Plant
• Sow seeds ½ inch deep, covering them firmly—nasturtium seeds need darkness to germinate. Plant 3 inches apart on all sides.

Germination Time
• Germination may take as long as 2 weeks, depending on soil and weather conditions.

Care During Growth
• When seedlings are 2 inches tall, thin them so they are 8 inches apart on all sides.

• The first blossoms will appear in 4 to 6 weeks. Keeping the flowers, especially the dead blossoms, picked will prolong the blooming season.

• Don't fertilize unless you want more

leaves than blossoms, and don't over-water.

Maturation Time
• Flowers appear 4 to 6 weeks after seeds have been sown.

Harvesting
• You can pick the leaves and flowers throughout the growing season, for use in salads and cooking, and in every way you might use watercress. The flower buds can also be picked and used as you would use capers: in salads, in pickling, for garnishes, and so on.
• The plants will continue to grow until the first fall frost.

Diseases and Pests
• Aphids, cabbage loopers, cabbage-worms, flea beetles.

Garden Tips
• Nasturtium seeds will sprout faster if you soak them for 48 hours before planting.
• Seeds should always be sown directly in the garden—nasturtiums don't transplant well.

• Pinching the plant tips will induce bushiness.
• Long-vining varieties of nasturtium planted beneath fruit trees can be trained to climb into the branches to help combat woody aphids.
• Nasturtiums planted among many garden vegetables—especially members of the cucumber family—will attract aphids and other plant pests and lessen the attacks on vegetables.
• Good companion plantings for nasturtiums are cabbage, cucumbers, radishes, and tomatoes.
• If winters aren't too severe, flowers left to go to seed may self-propagate the following year.

Kitchen Tips
• Don't forget—you can eat the flowers as well as the spicy leaves of nasturtiums in salads. The flowers also make a pretty garnish for many dishes.
• Nasturtium butter is delicious: Mince the flowers fine, and blend into softened butter. Use alone or with other ingredients in sandwiches or as a canapé spread.

Neck Rot

See *Botrytis blight*

Nematodes 🐛

There are hundreds of varieties of these microscopic parasitic, wormlike organisms, some specific to certain plants; hence they are known by many names: eelworms, meadow nematodes, potato root nematodes, root-knot nematodes, rootworms, roundworms, and many others. They are abundant in most garden soils and have different effects on different plants, although most of them attack the roots and underground portions of plants.

Although some nematodes are beneficial in gardens, most are not. They tend to increase in the soil, particularly where susceptible plants are grown season after season in the same garden bed. Plants particularly vulnerable to nematode infestation are all crucifers, cucumbers, okra, potatoes, snap beans, sweet potatoes, and tomatoes, as well as many ornamental plants.

Too small to be seen with the naked eye, nematodes live in moist soil, where they puncture stems and roots, sucking out juices and often leaving wounds through which harmful bacteria and fungi can enter. Despite all this, if the soil is rich and the plants initially healthy, most will survive nematode onslaughts.

Manifestation

• By the time nematode-disease symptoms become apparent, the infestation is fairly far along: Plants show a decline in vigor, they become deformed and stunted, and the foliage yellows and turns to bronze. You may see small or large swellings (galls) near the bases of plants, and, if you pull up an infected plant, you'll note galls in the roots and see that the root system has become shallow and sparse.

• To determine if nematodes are destroying any of your plants, dig up a suspected one, keeping the roots intact, and include some of the soil around it. Moisten it, wrap it in plastic, and mail it to your nearest agricultural experiment station.

To Combat

• Destroy all plants that you know to be infected, including end-of-season plant residue in the garden bed. Bag and dispose of them (don't bury or compost them).

• Practice crop rotation—try never to plant the same crop in the same bed sooner than every 3 years.

• Sowing plants that are immune to nematodes can in a few years wipe them out in a particular garden bed. Try sweet corn.

• Or plant rye—nematodes can't reproduce in the roots of rye plants, and they'll eventually die out. Also, fungi that kill some kinds of nematodes thrive in the vicinity of rye plants. If you till the rye under at the end of the season, chemical compounds are formed that are toxic to nematodes.

• Or keep the portion of your garden that has shown infestation free from all plant growth for 1 or 2 years.

• African marigolds (*Tagetes erecta*) have been reported to inhibit greatly the growth of nematodes. Plant some of these early, before your regular crop, then plow them under. You can do this every year to keep nematodes in check.

• Various solutions, poured into the soil around plants, will discourage nematodes: for example, fish emulsion solution and liquid seaweed (1 tablespoon seaweed fertilizer mixed with 2 gallons of water).

• In general, soils rich in organic matter are less likely to encourage nematode infestation. Nematode predators thrive in compost.

• Some seed packets announce that plants grown from their seeds are resistant to nematodes. Look for the capital letter *N* next to the name of the seeds.

. . .

New Zealand Spinach

This isn't a true spinach, although its fleshy, brittle, green leaves somewhat resemble those of common spinach. New Zealand spinach is prepared the same way as common spinach and is similar in taste. It differs from common spinach in being a strong, heat-resistant plant that produces throughout the summer. Yet it is also very hardy. The plants are large and sprawling, sometimes growing to a height of 2 feet.

Although New Zealand spinach is a warm-weather plant, its seeds (which take a long time to germinate) sprout best in cool soil.

When to Plant
• For a spring crop, sow seeds after danger of frost is past. Although the plants will produce all summer, you can get a fall crop of new and tender shoots (the best part of the plant) by making more plantings from midsummer to early fall.

Where to Plant
• New Zealand spinach will grow in average garden soil (pH 6 to 7), even

if it's somewhat on the dry side. It likes full sun to partial shade.

How to Plant
• To help break down the seeds' hard coat, soak them in warm water overnight before planting, or even for an hour in a solution of water and soap (not detergent).
• Plant the seeds ½ inch deep, 12 inches apart, in rows 2 feet apart (these sprawly plants take up a lot of room).

Germination Time
• Seeds rarely germinate before 14 days, but they can take a month!

Care During Growth
• New Zealand spinach needs no special care during growth.

Maturation Time
• New Zealand spinach can be harvested from 40 days after planting up to 70 days.

Harvesting
• The 3 or 4 inches at the ends of young stem tips, and the tender leaves, are best for eating. The plants will continue to produce new shoots throughout the season.

Diseases and Pests
• New Zealand spinach is resistant to most diseases and pests.

Garden Tips
• The hard casings of New Zealand spinach seeds can be broken, to speed germination, by lightly rubbing one side of each seed with a small file or sandpaper. Follow this treatment by a few hours of soaking in warm water, then plant.
• The plants will often reseed themselves from one year to the next if you cover them just before winter with a good mulch. Remove this in the early spring.

· · ·

Nubbins

See *Sterile-plant virus*

Okra

Okra is related to hibiscus and rose of Sharon, which its beautiful, cream-colored flowers resemble. Individual okra flowers last less than a day, but if you grow many plants in the bed, okra can be cultivated for its flowers alone. Okra is a tender, frost-sensitive plant, easy to grow in hot sun practically anywhere, but it won't grow where summers are very cool. The pods are used in soups, stews, and as a cooked vegetable. They not only add flavor but serve as a thickening agent. The seed pods are often dried and used in dried bouquets.

The plants start bearing when they are about 1 foot tall and continue until the first fall frost. Flowers appear about 50 days after germination. The plants can grow from 5 to 6 feet high, dwarf varieties from 2 to 3 feet.

When to Plant
• Wait to plant seeds until the soil and the nights are warm, and the average daily temperature is above 60°F. To be safe, especially in cool or northern sections, sow seeds outdoors over a 2-week period beginning in early summer. For a head start, plant seeds indoors in midspring and set out transplants in early summer.

Where to Plant
• Okra likes a rich, well-drained soil (pH 6.0 to 6.5) in a sunny location.

How to Plant
• Okra seeds are very hard shelled. Soak them overnight before planting.

See "Garden Tips" for several alternative ways of treating the seeds before sowing.
• Plant the seeds 1 inch deep, in groups of 2 seeds 1 inch apart, each group 15 inches apart. Plant in rows 15 inches apart. With dwarf varieties, each group of 2 seeds can be 12 inches apart, and the rows 12 inches apart. Cover with a thin layer of compost, and water thoroughly.

Germination Time
• Okra seeds germinate at about 70°F in 8 to 12 days.

. . .

Care During Growth

• If the weather is dry, water the bed daily. When seedlings appear, remove the weaker in each group of two.

• Don't let the bed get too dry. It's a good idea to lay down some mulch (grass clippings, leaves, and so on) after the plants are a few inches high to help conserve moisture and lessen the need to keep hosing the bed. Okra likes moisture!

Maturation Time

• Okra pods are ready to pick 50 to 70 days from the planting of seed.

Harvesting

• Pick the pods when they're young, up to 2½ inches long, before seeds develop. Longer pods become woody and are practically inedible. The pods should snap off easily. Keep picking every 2 or 3 days for a continuous harvest.

Diseases and Pests

• Okra is relatively disease and pest free. Wormwood tea (see *Repellents* for how to make) sprinkled on the plants when necessary will repel most insects.

Garden Tips

• The following successful methods of softening the hard seed coats of okra for quicker germination are reported by gardeners:

Pour boiling water over the seeds, and let stand overnight. Plant them the next morning.

Place the seeds in the freezer overnight, soak them the next morning in hot water for 1 hour, then plant.

Let the seeds stand in water for 24 hours before planting.

Place the seeds between 2 pieces of sandpaper and rub lightly to abrade the outer coverings, then plant.

Make a slight cut in each seed coat with a sharp knife before planting.

Soak the seeds at room temperature overnight in buttermilk. Then plant.

• If you pick okra pods when they're dry, the tiny spines on the plants will be less likely to sting.

• Okra leaves are said to be poisonous to Japanese beetles. If the beetles are a problem in your garden, plant okra here and there among affected plants.

• Bees are highly attracted to okra flowers. If you want more bees in your garden for pollination, plant okra as a lure.

Kitchen Tips

• One cup or more of sliced okra cooked with the vegetables in a soup or stew will give a tasty thickener. Vary the amount of okra to taste.

• You can pickle whole, fresh okra pods just as you do small cucumbers.

Onion

Onions are a hardy, cool-weather crop that do best in the spring and fall. They can be planted as seeds, sets (bulbs), or already-sprouted plants. They're generally divided into large bulb onions (Bermuda, Spanish, red Italian, and so on) and scallions, also known as spring onions, green onions, and white bunching onions. Scallions have small bulbs, often in clusters, and are grown mainly for their green stems.

Onion seeds cost less than sets or plants but are much more trouble to grow. Most home gardeners plant sets. It's possible to grow your own sets from seed—usually for next year's onions—but if seeds are planted indoors, early, and the summer days are long, the seedlings set in the garden can produce fairly large onions the same season.

Choose varieties known as long-day onions. The size of harvested bulbs is largely determined by the length of the summer days—the longer the days, the larger the bulb size. Cool weather and even moisture are necessary for good onion development.

When buying sets, look for small ones—generally ½ to ¾ inch in diameter. Too-large bulbs will bolt and go to seed rapidly. Keep sets cool and dry until you plant them. The refrigerator is a fine storage place for them.

When to Plant

• Sow seeds in flats indoors in late winter, or 8 to 10 weeks before the last expected heavy frost. Transplant to the garden as soon as the soil can be worked in early spring. The earlier you get the plants in the garden, the larger the onions will be.

• The time to sow onion seeds in the garden is said to be when the leaves of oak trees are the size of a mouse's ears. Actually, the best time is in early spring, when the soil is workable but still cool; this will give you fair-sized onions by summer's end. You can plant seeds as late as midspring for harvesting onions at the end of the season. Seeds planted in early midsummer will give you scallionlike greens throughout and at the end of the season, or onion sets for next spring's plantings.

• To get the biggest onions, plant sets or seedlings as early in the season as you can, preferably 4 to 6 weeks before the last expected frost. The leaves develop best in the cool weather of early spring, whereas the bulbs develop best in the heat of the summer.

Where to Plant
• Onions need full sun, although scallions will grow well in partial shade. They do well in soil that is very slightly acid to very slightly alkaline (pH 6.0 to 7.5). The soil should be loose, cool, moist but well drained, and moderately rich in organic material—humus, compost, or slightly rotted manure.

How to Plant
• If you are planting seeds indoors, fill flats with soil mixed with sphagnum moss, and sow the seeds thinly, about ¼ inch apart, thinning to 2 inches apart when the seedlings emerge. Keep the flats either in a sunny window or 6 inches below grow lights that are on at least 12 hours a day. When the stems are about ¼ inch in diameter, transplant the seedlings to the garden, 3 inches apart. Thin them later to 5 inches apart, using the thinnings for scallions and allowing the others to grow into large onions.
• Outdoors, before planting seeds, sets, or seedlings, till the ground well 6 to 8 inches deep, then smooth over.

• If you are planting seeds outdoors for sets or scallions, scatter them moderately thickly throughout the bed (you can mix the seeds with sand to make dispersal easier), and cover with ¼ inch of fine soil. Thin later to 2 inches apart on all sides. If you are planting seeds for mature onions, either strew the seeds thinly in rows 18 inches apart or scatter them over the bed, in both cases covering with ¼ inch of fine soil and thinning the seedlings later to 5 inches apart.
• If you are planting sets or seedlings outdoors, space them 4 inches apart in rows or furrows 12 inches apart. Place the sets or sprouted onions at a depth that allows the necks or "topknots" of the onions to protrude just above the soil level. Too-deep planting may cause the bulbs to rot. Firm the soil well around each bulb, and give the onion bed a thorough sprinkling.

Germination Time
• Onion seeds germinate in 10 to 14 days at about 50°F.

Care During Growth
• To form good-sized bulbs, onions need consistent moisture, so don't let the bed dry out. It's wise to mulch with grass clippings to help conserve soil moisture and combat weeds, which can often take over an onion bed.

• Add well-rotted manure or rich compost in early summer and again in midsummer.

• In midsummer, pull some soil away from each onion bulb so that roughly half the bulb is exposed to sun and air—you'll get larger bulbs this way.

• If you're growing onions for storage, go easy on watering after midsummer.

• You'll get larger bulbs by promptly cutting out any seedstalks that develop (usually toward late summer).

Maturation Time

• Planted from seed, mature onions will be ready to harvest in 120 to 150 days, scallions in 60 to 80 days, sets in about 110 days.

• Onions grown from sets or seedlings will mature in approximately 65 to 90 days, depending on variety and size.

Harvesting

• Scallions can be pulled any time they seem tall enough for use, usually when the leaves are 10 to 12 inches high. If you leave them in the ground longer, the bulbs will become larger.

• Sets grown from seed should be dug up when the bulbs are about marble size (¾ inch or so in diameter)—they'll shrink a little during storage. Dig them carefully, from below, in order not to damage them. Shake the soil from them, and cut off the leaves, preserving 1 inch or so of neck. Spread the bulbs in the sun for a couple of days, then in a dry, shaded place for 3 to 4 weeks, or until the coverings are dry and papery.

• Mature onions are ready for harvesting when their green tops wither and fall over, in mid- to late summer or early fall. The maturation of any laggards can be hastened by bending over the tops yourself and holding them down with a small stone or two. Dig the onions up carefully to avoid bruises or cuts, and lay them out in a single layer to dry in well-ventilated partial shade for a few days, or until the leaves become papery.

• Onions should be harvested before the first frost.

Storing

• Store onion sets in flat layers or very loosely where there is cool ventilation. Sets can also be spread in the vegetable tray of your refrigerator if they're kept dry (don't store with potatoes or other vegetables that will release moisture, or the sets will rot).

• After mature onions have dried, select sound, unbruised ones and gently rub off the stringy roots. You can braid the tops if you want to hang the onions in bunches, or cut the tops 1 inch above the bulbs and store the onions loosely in mesh bags or slatted containers. If stored where it's dry and quite cool (from 40° to 50°F is ideal), onions should keep well through the winter.

Diseases and Pests
• Bacterial diseases, damping off, fusarium rot, neck rot (see *Botrytis blight*), onion fly maggots, thrips.

Garden Tips
• Onion fly maggots stay within a confined area, so if you have trouble with them, move your onion patch every year.
• Japanese bunching onions seem to be resistant to onion fly maggots.
• To speed germination of onion seeds, dampen a double paper towel well, scatter the seeds evenly over the surface, roll it up, and place it in a plastic bag. Keep the bag where it's warm, around 70°F, and check daily to see when the seed coats begin to split. Plant at once.
• Onion seedlings are more sensitive to cold than sets. But once sets have produced leaves in the garden, they can take light frost. However, prolonged exposure to freezing will promote bolting to seed. So will alternating cold and warm periods, drought, or insect stress.
• Don't be alarmed if your onions seem to push up out of the soil as they grow. Only the roots on the undersides of the bulbs need to be below soil level.
• Alternating wet and dry periods

during early bulb formation can produce split or double bulbs. These don't store well, so use them first, or chop and freeze them.
• Generally, cool growing conditions produce sweeter onions. But a too-cold growing season inhibits good bulb formation.
• If onion sets are planted properly, with the necks above the soil line, the necks will dry faster after harvesting and will be less likely to rot during storage.
• Try planting onion seeds late in the fall, just before hard frost. They may sprout the next spring to give you extra-early onions. If your winters are severe, mulch well.
• Onions with thick necks don't store well, probably because the necks don't completely dry out before storing.
• Check on your stored onions now and then over the winter. Remove at once any that show signs of spoilage. You can probably use these in the kitchen.
• Good companion plantings for onions (which act as a slug repellent) are said to be beets, broccoli, Brussels sprouts, cabbage, camomile, carrots, cauliflower, kale, kohlrabi, leeks, lettuce, parsnips, peppers, strawberries, summer savory, tomatoes, and turnips.
• But don't plant onions with asparagus, beans, or peas.

Kitchen Tips

• Onions that show a bit of green spear should be used at once; otherwise they'll spoil.

• If you have an onion that's begun to sprout, put it in a pot with a drainage hole, fill the pot with soil (the onion should be only half covered), water it well, and set the pot in the light. If you keep the surface moderately moist, the onion will grow lots of green sprouts. Snip them as you would chives or scallions—the sprouts will continue to grow for weeks.

• If you slice or chop an onion when it's cold, you'll weep less. So keep 1 or 2 onions in the refrigerator, replacing them as you use them. Refrigerated onions keep very well if they're open to air and protected from dampness.

• An onion is easily peeled if the outside is thoroughly wet.

• To peel lots of onions, cover them with very hot water for a few minutes.

• If you need only part of an onion, don't peel it before cutting. The unused portion keeps better in the refrigerator if the skin is still on.

• An onion won't slip when you're slicing it if you cut it in half from top to bottom, then slice it, cut side down.

• You can squeeze half an onion to get onion juice: Leave the skin on and treat it as you would half an orange.

• To get a small amount of onion juice from a cut onion, sprinkle a little salt on the cut surface and scrape with a knife or spoon.

• To tame a strong onion, cut it into rings and soak in cool water for 1 hour. Really virulent ones should be covered with boiling water for 1 minute, then drained and soaked in ice water.

• Chopped onion frozen in a plastic bag will keep for months. Cook without defrosting. (This is a good thing to do with half a leftover onion.)

• To cook whole onions, cut crosses in the root ends and they won't be as likely to break or burst.

• If onions to be served boiled are very strong, cover them first with boiling water, boil 2 minutes, and drain. Cover them again with fresh water and finish cooking. They'll be sweet and pleasant.

• For stuffing, boiled onions will firm up if you drop them gently into ice water as soon as they're cooked.

• Put sliced onions in a low oven, and heat until golden brown and absolutely dry. Bottle, refrigerate, and use them in sauces, soups, and stews.

• Most dishes calling for onions—especially stews and casseroles—are immensely improved if you sauté the onions lightly first in oil, butter, or other fat.

• For a really out-of-the-ordinary dish, add a little honey to the butter in which you sauté onions. Be sure the mixture sizzles before adding the onions.

• Here's a shortcut for making French-fried onion rings: Dry the rings well on paper towels, then dip in prepared pancake batter and fry quickly in hot fat.

• For a low-calorie sauce or base for salad dressing, boil onions in a little water until they are very soft, drain well, and puree. Flavor as you like. This is a splendid thick base you can do a dozen things with.

Onion Fly Maggots

The brown, hairy onion fly, resembling the housefly, appears in late spring and lays its eggs at the bases of the leaves of young chives, garlic, leeks, onion, or shallot seedlings, or in the soil around them. The eggs hatch into yellow larvae or onion maggots, which burrow down and begin chewing the bulbs and roots of the plants. The maggots develop into flies, which mate, lay eggs, and produce maggots again. There are two or three generations of onion fly maggots in a season. Those resulting from the last hatching remain in the bulbs or the soil over the winter, developing into flies in the spring. Onion fly maggots do greatest damage to seedlings. Later attacks can affect bulbs in storage.

Manifestation

• Leaves become limp and yellow. Bulbs show tunneling and rot. Bulbs in storage may also show rot.

To Combat

• When you purchase onion sets, see that they are firm and have no signs of injury. Be sure the same is true of garlic and shallot cloves.

• Move your onion bed every year.

• If onion fly maggots are a major problem, cover your garden plot with fine cheesecloth or netting after you've planted the bulbs in the spring.

• Don't leave garden refuse about at season's end. Be particularly careful to remove any rejected garlic, onion, or shallot bulbs. Doing so will deprive the maggots of places to winter over.

Onion Thrips

See *Thrips*

Oregano

See *Marjoram*

Oriental Garlic

See *Chives*

Oyster Plant

See *Salsify*

Parsley

Parsley is a member of the carrot family whose leaves are used in salads, soups, stews, and garnishes. It is a biennial, producing seeds the second season, but is generally sown for first-season use. Because it is quite hardy and can generally withstand northern winters, you can harvest its leaves for two seasons. Parsley often reseeds itself. Eight to twelve plants are usually all a family needs.

The most common forms of parsley are the curled varieties, about 8 inches high, which are the hardiest; and Italian parsley, which is taller (12 inches), flatter leaved, more flavorful, often preferred by cooks. There is also Hamburg parsley, called turnip-rooted or root parsley as well; it is grown mainly for its roots—which taste like a combination of parsnip and celery—although the leaves are edible.

When to Plant

• If you want seedlings to go into the garden early and become well established before hot weather, sow seeds indoors in very early spring.

• Sow seeds outdoors as soon as the soil is workable. Parsley seeds will germinate at 50°F. Seeds planted in early spring will give you a summer crop. For a fall and winter harvest, sow seeds outdoors in the last week of August.

• Set out seedlings 4 to 6 weeks before the last expected frost in your area.

Where to Plant

• Parsley will grow in any average garden soil, from slightly acid to slightly alkaline (pH 6.5 to 7.5). It can take light sun but does well in partial shade. Avoid very hot, sunny areas.

How to Plant

• Soak seeds in warm water for a full day before planting. Drain and press them between paper towels to keep them from sticking together. Germination can also be hastened if you soak the seeds overnight, then drain and put them in the freezer for 3 days.

• If you are planting indoors, sow the seeds in flats, ¼ inch deep, and always keep the soil moist.

• If you are sowing directly in the garden, plant seeds in a straight line, ¼ inch deep, about 15 seeds to the foot. Rows should be about 1 foot apart. If you haven't presoaked the seeds, you can often hasten germination by dousing the seedbed daily with lukewarm water.

• Plant seedlings outdoors 6 inches apart, in rows 12 inches apart.

Germination Time

• Since not all seeds germinate at the same time, the appearance of seedlings will be spotty. Seeds germinate indoors in 10 to 14 days, outdoors in as much as 21 days.

Care During Growth

• Thin the seedlings to 6 inches apart when they're 2 inches high. After their appearance, keep the area moist and free from weeds. Little other care is needed.

Maturation Time

• Parsley is ready to pick about 70 days from the planting of seed.

Harvesting

• Pick parsley greens as soon as they're tall enough for use, throughout the season. Clip the stems at their bases, leaving the roots to produce more greens. You can often harvest parsley well into the winter, even under snow, if the plants are mulched in the fall.

• *Hamburg parsley:* Cut and use a few sprigs from each of the plants, leaving the roots to continue growing. The delicious roots can then be harvested late in the fall. But dig them up before the plants flower; otherwise the roots will be tough.

Storing

• You can keep parsley in near-fresh condition if you wash it, shake well, and put in a tightly closed glass jar in the refrigerator.

• Or rinse, shake dry, then wrap and freeze parsley sprigs. Use them straight from the freezer in cooked dishes.

• You can also dry the leaves and bottle them—the flavor isn't as good as when the parsley is fresh, but it's fine as long as the color remains a bright green.

Diseases and Pests

• Cabbage loopers, carrot rust flies.

Garden Tips

• If indoor seedlings become leggy, either they're not getting enough direct light or they're too hot.

• You can plant parsley in your garden from the roots that are sometimes on bunches you buy at the market.

• If the temperature cools gradually in your area in the fall, parsley plants can survive down to even 10°F! And if you mulch well, they'll often come through the winter and sprout again in the spring.

• Plant parsley seeds late in the fall, just before hard frost. They may sprout the next spring to give you extra-early parsley. If your winters are severe, mulch well after planting.

• Good companion plantings for parsley are said to be asparagus and tomatoes.

Kitchen Tips

• Parsley butter, if made from freshly cut leaves, is delicious. Cut the leaves very fine, and mix with softened butter for a great sandwich filling alone or in combination with other fillings.

• A fast way to mince parsley very fine is to cut the leaves from the stems, force the leaves into a tight ball, and, holding the ball firmly with one hand, slice down through it with a sharp knife, working from the outside inward and making the slices very close together.

• Use a full-leaved sprig of parsley for brushing or sprinkling flavored oil or melted butter on fish or vegetables.

• Pot up some parsley plants from your garden in mid-September for growing indoors on a sunny windowsill over the winter.

Parsnip

Parsnips are biennial, very hardy root vegetables that, although they flower and produce seed in the second spring of growth, are generally grown for their roots, which are harvested in the fall of the first season, or through the winter and into the early spring of the second season. Parsnip roots get sweeter the longer they stay in the ground: Not only can they stand freezing, but they need at least one sharp frost for their starches to change into sugar. They can become almost as sweet as sweet potatoes. Parsnip roots can grow to 10 inches or more in length.

When to Plant

• You can plant parsnip seeds outdoors as soon as the soil can be tilled. There's no great hurry, though—since the best time to dig parsnips is in the late fall or during the winter, you're not looking for an early harvest. A good rule of thumb is to plant seeds about the time daffodils bloom, or, even better, up to early summer.

Where to Plant

• Parsnips like a deep, fine, loamy, well-drained soil with plenty of potassium and phosphorus and a pH level as close to neutral (7.0) as possible. The deeper and finer the soil, the more encouragement the roots will have to grow long and full. Parsnips do well in semishade.

How to Plant
• Sow seeds ¼ inch deep, approximately 1 inch apart, in rows 18 inches apart. Moisten the soil after planting, and keep it moist until seedlings appear.

Germination Time
• Parsnip seeds take 2 to 3 weeks to germinate.

Care During Growth
• Parsnip seedlings resemble those of celery. When they're 3 inches tall, thin them, leaving the strongest ones, to 6 inches apart.
• Keep the soil cultivated, and water weekly (unless it rains) to keep the roots from becoming tough. Parsnips grow slowly.

Maturation Time
• Parsnips are generally ready for harvesting about 100 days after the planting of seed, but it's best to wait until there have been a few good cold nights or, even better, until after the first hard frost.

Harvesting
• Dig parsnips in late fall or, if you mulch where winters are very cold,

throughout the winter and into early spring. If you're digging them for storing aboveground, be careful not to cut into them or bruise them: Only sound parsnips keep well. And dig them, don't pull them, or the roots may break.
• If you leave parsnips to winter in the ground, you must dig them out in spring as soon as the ground thaws; otherwise, once the tops start to grow, the roots become bitter.

Storing
• One of the best places to store parsnips through the winter is right in the garden. Cut the foliage to the ground, then cover (where winters are very cold) with about a 10-inch mulch of hay or leaves. You can dig beneath the mulch all winter long to harvest them.
• For aboveground storage: Cut off the green tips to about 1 inch above the roots, brush off the dirt, and bury the roots in barrels or boxes of sand, sawdust, or leaves in a dark, humid place where the temperature is between 32° and 40°F. Dryness will cause parsnips to shrivel.
• You can also store parsnips in the refrigerator.

Diseases and Pests
• Bacterial diseases, black spot, carrot rust flies, leafhoppers.

• • •

Garden Tips

• Parsnip seeds more than 1 year old aren't very viable.

• Don't plant parsnips in recently manured ground.

• Other mulches you can use for overwintering parsnips in the ground are shredded cornstalks, wood shavings, and oat straw.

• The sweetest parsnips are those that are dug up in the spring, as soon as the ground thaws.

• Mark the rows with stakes of some kind so you'll know where under the mulch and snow to dig your parsnips during the winter.

• Rotate your parsnip bed every 2 years to combat soil-borne diseases, such as black spot.

Kitchen Tip

• Don't think the use of parsnips need be confined to soups and stews. They're a fine vegetable in their own right—treat them as you do carrots, except that they require a shorter cooking time.

Pea

Peas are a hardy crop that thrives during cool weather; they can even withstand frosts and, though fairly drought tolerant, generally don't do well during warm weather. Like other legumes, they're soil builders, adding nitrogen to the ground in which they grow. Almost all pea plants develop tendrils, which aid them to climb strings, trellises, and other supports. But there are dwarf bush types that need only a little climbing.

For a long harvest, either make succession plantings so your peas don't mature all at once (this is possible where summers are cool) or, better, plant early, midseason, and late varieties at the same time. These mature at different intervals throughout the summer. Late varieties cope better with end-of-summer heat than other types of peas.

Peas are usually classified in two types: standard peas, the kind you shell for the mature peas inside; and snow peas, also known as Chinese peas, with subvarieties called sugar peas, sugar snaps, or snap peas. You can eat the entire pods of snow peas, with the small immature peas inside. They can be eaten raw, in salads, or cooked as you would green beans. The pod walls of snap peas, although edible, are thicker and fleshier than those of other snow peas. These peas can be eaten whole or shelled.

Most snow peas and their varieties, although the pods can be eaten early, can—if left to mature on the vine—be cooked just as you would string beans.

And if left still longer on the vine, they can be shelled at the end of the season and treated like standard peas. The vines of sugar snaps are twice as productive as those of standard peas, provided you pick the peas regularly.

Lentils, although not actually peas, are in the same family and have exactly the same culture.

When to Plant

• If you need to harvest peas extra early, you may want to start seeds indoors, in early spring. The plants can then be set out from late spring to early summer. But peas don't transplant well—it's recommended that you sow seeds directly in the garden.

• Because peas grow best during cool weather and seeds will germinate in soil as cool as 40°F, get your seeds in as soon as the ground thaws and the soil can be worked in the spring. Sow again 2 or 3 times at 10-day intervals. If you're planting early, midsummer, and late varieties at the same time, they can all go in in early spring.

• For a fall harvest of standard peas, sow seeds again in midsummer (see "How to Plant").

Where to Plant

• Peas grow well in average soil as long as it's well drained and has plenty of potassium (potash). The soil should be slightly acid to neutral (pH 6 to 7). Lentils can stand a little more alkalinity in the soil—pH up to 8. They all like sun.

How to Plant

• To speed germination, soak the seeds in water overnight before sowing.

• You can save a great deal of garden space by planting peas along a wire fence or trellis. Pea vines trained upward also get more sun and are easier to harvest. Plant the seeds in a line ½ inch deep and 2 inches apart, firming the ground well after planting.

• Otherwise, plant peas ½ inch deep and 2 inches apart in double rows, 3 inches apart, each set of double rows 24 inches apart. If you're planting in midsummer for a fall harvest, the sets of double rows should be only 12 inches apart, so the plants will shield one another during the hot weather.

Germination Time

• Seeds germinate in 7 to 14 days.

Care During Growth

• Mist the newly sown pea patch daily, especially in hot weather, to speed germination. This is best done in early morning.

• Provide strong support for tall-growing, vigorous vines, particularly sugar snaps. Very few need help attaching themselves to supports.

• There's no need for much extra watering until the plants start to flower. In fact, you'll encourage a deeper root system—peas tend to have shallow roots—if you hold back on watering in the beginning. The time to see that the plants have plenty of water is from the appearance of first bloom until harvest. But don't overdo it—peas don't like to be waterlogged.

• Mulch with grass clippings or other light mulch when the plants are 6 inches high. This is especially important during the hot, dry days of summer.

• A side dressing of liquid manure and wood ashes is a good idea as soon as you see flowers forming.

Maturation Time

• Most standard varieties develop mature pods in about 65 days. Early-season peas are often ready in 60 days, midseason varieties in 75 days, and late varieties in 90 days.

• Snow peas are often ready in 50 days.

Harvesting

• Snow pea varieties should all be picked when the pods are very young and tender—2 to 2½ inches long. If left on the vine longer, they can usually be picked, shelled, and eaten as standard peas (but the vines will bear fewer pods).

• Pick pods daily once they mature or reach the stage of development you like: This will keep the vines producing. Be sure they get water during the picking season.

• Peas planted in late summer will give a smaller yield than a spring harvest.

• Peas can stand a light frost. Don't be afraid to allow pods of standard peas to mature fully in the fall. Pick your last crop before an anticipated heavy frost.

Storing

• Wash snow peas, snap peas, and other edible-podded peas, tumble-dry in a dishtowel, then pack in plastic bags and freeze. They freeze very well.

• Dried peas and lentils stored in a dry, cool place will stay in excellent condition for many months. If thoroughly dried, they can be kept in plastic bags.

• Regular shelled garden peas can go straight from the pods into plastic bags in the freezer.

Diseases and Pests

• Birds, cabbage loopers, corn earworms, cucumber beetles, damping off, flea beetles, fusarium rot, powdery mildew, root rot, thrips, whiteflies.

Garden Tips

• Don't plant peas in recently manured ground.

• Wrinkled seeds often produce plants with the sweetest peas.

• Although tall-growing pea vines need trellising the most, even dwarf bush types do better with something to attach to. You can use string or yarn, netting, chicken wire, or collections of branches.

• All vegetables, except the onion family and potatoes, are good companion plantings with peas.

Kitchen Tips

• After picking, don't shell peas until you're ready to cook them.

• Just as in corn, the sugar in peas begins to turn to starch as soon as they're picked.

Peanut

Peanuts are an excellent source of protein. Most peanuts require fairly hot summers and four months of frost-free growing season. Spanish peanuts are the best for growing in the Northeast—they're highly productive and mature more quickly.

When to Plant

• The ground must be warm before peanuts are planted. In cooler areas, seeds can be started indoors in early to midspring and set in the garden in late spring if the weather is warm. The earlier the better so they can have the long growing season they need—but not if there's a chance of frost.

• Put transplants in the ground in late spring or early summer.

Where to Plant

• Sow peanuts in ordinary, light, well-drained soil (pH 5 to 6) where they'll get plenty of sun. Avoid nitrogenous fertilizers.

How to Plant

• It's not necessary to remove peanuts from their shells before planting, but if you want to plant single seeds, crack the shells with care so as not to break the thin skin surrounding the seeds.

• If you are planting indoors, sow 2 to 3 seeds per pot, 1½ inches deep. Thin to the strongest single plant before transplanting to the garden, 12 inches apart in rows 3 feet apart.

• Plant seeds outdoors 1½ inches deep, 4 to 6 inches apart, in rows 3 feet apart.

Germination Time

• Peanut seeds germinate in 18 days.

Care During Growth

• When plants are 6 inches high, thin them to 12 inches apart. When they are 12 inches high, hill the soil up around each one, as with potatoes. This way the plants will form peanuts earlier.

Maturation Time

• Depending on the variety, peanuts are generally ready to harvest in 110 to 120 days. Some varieties of Spanish peanuts mature in 100 days.

Harvesting

• Peanuts are ready to harvest when the pods are hard and dry and the nuts inside fill the shells well. The papery skin around each separate nut is brown.

• You can wait until the first frost before harvesting if you wish. Dig up the entire plant, and allow it to air-dry thoroughly before removing the pods.

Diseases and Pests

• Leafhoppers.

Kitchen Tip

• To roast peanuts, put them in a 350° oven for about 20 minutes.

Pepper

Peppers are very tender perennials, grown in the North as annuals. They require a long growing season and, though sensitive to cold, don't like excessive heat. The common sweet bell pepper prefers a medium range of temperature—70° to 80°F during the day, 60° to 70°F at night. It will not grow at temperatures below 55°F or above 85°F.

It's hardly advisable to sow pepper seeds directly in the garden, since they need a guaranteed growing season of at least 110 days. It's better to buy seedlings at planting time, or grow your own indoors.

A green pepper is a yellow, orange, or red pepper that hasn't fully ripened. The most common sweet pepper varieties are bell peppers, long Italian and "banana" peppers, and cherry peppers. All of these go through a green stage, some maturing through yellow to orange and most, eventually, to red. There are also "hot" peppers or chili peppers, green maturing to orange or red. Most hot peppers grown in the North, or where the climate is cool, seldom become very pungent.

When to Plant

• Start seeds indoors in very early spring, or about 7 weeks before the last average frost date.

• Or plant seedlings outdoors when the nights have become definitely warm, usually in early summer. If in doubt, wait.

Where to Plant

• Peppers like a deep, rich, moist, sandy loam that is well drained. They like phosphorus and plenty of humus in the soil, and do best in slightly acid soil (pH 5.50 to 6.75) and partial shade.

How to Plant

• *Indoors:* For fast germination, soak seeds overnight in warm water, then roll them up in a damp paper towel tucked into a plastic bag and keep in a warm place until they sprout. Then plant immediately: In flats, sow seeds ½ inch deep and 3 inches apart; in peat pots, sow 2 seeds to the pot, covering them with ½ inch of soil. Pinch off the weaker of the two seedlings when they are 3 inches tall. Use rich potting soil mixed with sand and keep in a mildly warm place (about 75°F), such as a sunny windowsill.

• *Outdoors:* Peppers don't take easily to transplanting, but there are ways to minimize transplant shock. Twenty-four hours before placing them in the garden, give them a good watering with diluted fish emulsion. If the seedlings are in flats, cut the flats into cubes with a seedling in the center of each cube. Try not to disturb the roots when you transplant. Each seedling should be set lower in the ground than it was in the flat. If the seedlings are in peat pots, bury each entire pot deeply enough that its edges are completely below the soil surface. If there are any blossoms on the plants at transplanting time, pinch them off.

• Peppers seem to grow better and produce more fruit when they're rather tightly spaced. This arrangement helps maintain moisture levels, prevents sunscald on the fruit, and makes the plants grow taller. So space seedlings 12 inches apart in rows 15 inches apart.

Germination Time

• Pepper seeds germinate in 14 to 21 days, although presoaked seeds will sprout in 6 or 7 days if the temperature is 68°F or higher. But sprouting is uneven at any time.

Care During Growth

• If the weather turns cool after you've transplanted peppers to the garden, cover the plants with plastic gallon jugs that have had their bottoms removed. Leave the tops open or remove the jugs during the day to allow adequate ventilation.

• Peppers that don't get enough moisture will be bitter. Water well daily during hot, dry periods to increase sweetness and yields. Never let the plants dry out.

• A mulch of black plastic or gravel attracts heat, controls weeds, and helps maintain moisture levels during the early part of the growing season. But don't use other types of mulch too early—they tend to keep the ground cool; wait until you see the first peppers. At this time, when the weather becomes hot, you can use aluminized plastic film, white plastic, grass clippings, shredded leaves, or hay around the plants— these definitely increase yields.

• After you see the first fruits, feed the plants liquid manure or a fish emulsion solution. And keep them watered.

• When cold fall weather first appears, you can keep pepper plants producing if you cover them at night with plastic, newspapers, or anything handy to shield them from the cold. Remove this protection during the warmer parts of the day.

Maturation Time
• Peppers can be picked 62 to 80 days from the date of transplanting, depending on variety and degree of ripeness desired.

Harvesting
• Most peppers, if left on the plants, will turn red (yellow, orange, or brown in some varieties) when they're mature. Peppers picked green have an unripe taste, but if you want to use green peppers, wait until the skin is shiny and waxy looking, or until you see the first signs of orange in the coat. Most bell-type peppers shouldn't be picked until they are 2 or 3 inches in diameter. Peppers picked when underripe are quick to shrivel.

• When picking, don't pull or twist the pepper. Use a knife or pair of sharp scissors to cut it free, leaving a piece of stem attached. This way it will stay fresh longer.

• Pepper plants continue producing as long as you pick the fruits, weather permitting. But try to get the last ones off the plants before the first frost hits. Any peppers picked after frost don't keep well.

Storing
• Peppers will keep for as long as 3 months in a cool place (45° to 55°F) that has high humidity. Pack them carefully to allow good ventilation.

Diseases and Pests
• Aphids, blossom drop, blossom-end rot, Colorado potato beetles, corn borers, corn earworms, cutworms, damping off, flea beetles, green peach aphids, hornworm, leafhoppers, mealybugs, sunscald, tobacco mosaic virus, verticillium wilt, whiteflies.

Garden Tips

• Unless your soil is organically rich, prepare the pepper bed before transplanting—mix in some leaf mold or well-rotted sawdust.

• If the seedlings you're growing indoors look weak or leggy, either the temperature is too high or they're not getting enough light.

• If the soil and night temperatures are below 60°F for more than a day or so when you set out peppers, they'll drop their blossoms—a major setback!

• Pepper blossoms can also drop before forming fruit if the plants haven't been getting enough water or if night and day temperature remains above 80°F for several days running.

• To encourage bushy growth of pepper plants (the leaves shield the fruit from sunscald), pinch off the tops when you set out seedlings.

• When using plastic mulch, place stones to hold it down around the plant stems.

• Tie pepper plants to stakes when they get tall to keep them from falling over.

• Banana peels provide phosphorus and potash for pepper plants. Bury bits of snipped-up peel around the plants—about 2 peels per plant.

• It's possible to spread tobacco mosaic virus to pepper plants if you've touched cigars, cigarettes, or any form of tobacco before handling the plants. Wash your hands first.

• Pepper plants are perennials—at the end of the season you can dig them up, put them in pails or large coffee cans with drainage holes punched in the bottoms, and set them in a very sunny window. They'll continue to produce blossoms and peppers all winter. Pollinate the blossoms with a cottom swab, going from flower to flower, two days in a row. Set the plants out again in the spring, when the weather has become warm.

Kitchen Tips

• Green or sweet red or yellow peppers don't keep well under normal kitchen conditions, so don't pick them too far ahead of time.

• If you're going to stuff peppers, cut them in half crosswise instead of lengthwise; then you can place the halves upright in cupcake tins before you fill and bake them. They're easier to handle and hold their shape better when cooked.

• To peel green peppers (for antipasto or marinated peppers, for instance), wash and dry firm fruits and broil them on a rack about 5 inches from the heat for about 10 minutes, or until the skins begin to wrinkle and brown. Turn them now and then. Let them cool, then hold them under cold water. The skins will peel off easily.

• • •

Pepper Grass

See *Garden cress*

Peppermint

See *Mint*

Plant Lice

See *Aphids*

Potato

Potato plants aren't vigorously hardy. They're usually grown from cut sections of mature potatoes, each section (called a seed tuber, or seed potato) containing one or two eyes (buds). The sections are planted separately, each giving rise to a new potato plant. Each section should be roughly the size of a golf ball.

Potatoes you intend to cut up into sections should already show sprouting at the eyes. In fact, longer sprouts—even several inches long—produce higher-yielding plants. Sections cut from older potatoes also produce better plants. After cutting a potato into sections, let the pieces dry at room temperature for 1 to 3 days before planting—this way they'll be less likely to rot in the ground.

You can also use small, full-formed seed potatoes, about the size of large marbles. You can grow these yourself or buy them. As with cut potato sections, they should be presprouted before planting. (Expose them to temperatures around 45°F for about 2 weeks.)

Potatoes can also be grown from seed, started indoors and later transplanted to the garden as you would treat tomatoes, but the potatoes produced by this method are smaller—at best, 2 to 3 inches long.

Each potato plant, properly hilled (see "Care During Growth"), should produce 2 to 3 pounds of potatoes.

When to Plant

• Plant seed potatoes when the soil has begun to warm and the danger of a hard frost is over. Potatoes start out best in slightly warm soil, and you'll get a better yield if you plant on the late rather than the early side.

Where to Plant

• Potatoes do well in most garden soils but do best in a light, loamy, sandy soil that's moist without being waterlogged. It's a good idea to mix in some compost or aged manure before planting. Potatoes tolerate soil that's moderately acid straight up through moderately alkaline (pH spread from 5.5 to 7.5). They should have full sun.

How to Plant

• Dig trenches or furrows 6 inches deep and 30 inches apart, and place the seed potatoes inside, 12 inches apart. Cover with soil or a mixture of soil and straw.

• Or dig a line of holes 12 inches apart and 6 inches deep, plant the potatoes, and likewise cover with soil or a soil-straw mixture. In either of these methods, be sure there is room for the elongated sprouts to lie flat. Each node on the long sprouts will become a feeder root and help the plant produce more.

• Some gardeners place potato sections on top of the soil, covering them with a rich mulch. This method can work, but plants may need more frequent attention to prevent drying out.

• If you have grown potato seedlings from seeds, transplant them to the garden in groups of 3 close together, the groups 12 inches apart, in rows 30 inches apart. When the seedlings are 4 or 5 inches high, cut off the two weaker in each group at soil level.

Germination Time

• Potato seeds germinate in 10 to 21 days.

Care During Growth

• Shoots from planted seed potatoes will appear above the soil in about 3 weeks. As soon as the sprouts emerge, start hilling them up with soil or a leaf-and-hay mulch or compost, so that only about 6 inches of the green tops remain visible. Continue this for several weeks, until the hills around the plants are about 1 foot high. You must keep the light from reaching the developing potatoes or portions of their skins will turn green, making the potatoes bitter and inedible. This mulch also helps retain moisture. A plastic mulch is likewise useful for moisture retention and keeping down weeds.

• Potatoes thrive on potash—mix into the mulch, from time to time, fish emulsion, dried fish scraps, liquid or well-rotted manure, seaweed, or wood ashes. Add a little bonemeal occasionally.

• Continue watering, especially during August, for large tuber development. Once the plants begin to blossom, you can cut back somewhat on watering.

Maturation Time
• Potatoes grown from seeds will mature 100 to 120 days after the seedlings have been set out. (They will be small.) You can harvest "new" potatoes (potatoes that have not yet matured into large ones) about 90 days after seed potatoes have been planted. You can dig large ones—often up to 6 inches long—in about 120 days.

Harvesting
• "New" potatoes may be dug in the summer shortly after you see the plants begin to blossom. It's usual to use a garden fork to pull up potatoes, but often you can just pull the whole vines. Or you can reach in and under the vines to pull out the largest potatoes only, leaving the others to mature further. Fully mature potatoes are ready to be dug after the tops of the plants have begun to brown and die down. You can also leave them in the ground until the possibility of a freeze looms—but get them out before the freeze.
• If you're digging for potatoes you intend to store, be careful not to bruise or cut into them.

• Discard any potatoes that show green skin.

Storing
• For the most successful storing, wipe off excess dirt and let potatoes dry for about 1 week at 60° to 70°F where it is dark and there is plenty of ventilation. Then store in uncovered cartons in a very cool (temperature around 40°F), dark place with high humidity (80 to 90 percent).
• Examine potatoes occasionally, and discard any that seem soft or shriveled or have green patches (a sign of exposure to light). Should any sprouts develop during storage, rub them off.

Diseases and Pests
• Aphids, bacterial diseases, blister beetles, cabbage loopers, Colorado potato beetles, corn borers, corn earworms, cucumber beetles, flea beetles, green peach aphids, hornworms, leafhoppers, leaf curl, nematodes, potato scab, slugs, tarnished plant bugs, thrips, verticillium wilt, whiteflies.

Garden Tips
• What is true for most vegetables is particularly so for potatoes: Change the location of your potato bed each year.
• Some growers believe an alkaline soil, as well as a soil that's too dry, promotes potato scab.

• The longer the shoots on seed potatoes before planting, the bigger the harvest.

• If any potatoes have started to sprout, you can often eat the potatoes and still plant the sprouts. Cut the peel slightly thick in the area of the sprout, and plant this section, cut side down, about 3 inches deep in rich soil or compost. Keep slightly moist. The soil must be well warmed for these to "take."

• Never use fresh manure in your potato bed.

• Most early varieties of potato don't store well.

• Horseradish and beans are said to deter potato beetles. Try planting these here and there in your potato bed.

• Other good companion plantings with potatoes are said to be Brussels sprouts, cabbage, corn, eggplants, kale, kohlrabi, lamb's-quarters, marigolds, and radishes.

Kitchen Tips

• Keeping potatoes in the refrigerator inhibits the growth of eyes. But they must be kept dry.

• Potatoes with a good starch content (mealy ones) are best for baking. These usually have tough skins, such as Idaho and russet. To test whether your potatoes are mealy, cut one in half crosswise and rub the two halves against each other briskly. A potato with plenty of starch will produce a frothy juice as you rub it.

• Long and slow baking will give a drier, mealier potato, regardless of the kind.

• Two ways to shorten the baking time of a potato: After scrubbing, remove a slice from each end and oil the cut ends slightly, then bake. Or run a long steel nail lengthwise through each potato and leave it in during baking.

• You can freeze raw, unpeeled potatoes for later boiling and mashing: Wrap them individually, airtight. When you need them, let them defrost at room temperature, then peel. (They peel easily.)

• Peeling cold cooked potatoes is easier if you wet them first.

• The best mashed potatoes in the world are made from *baked* potatoes. Bake as usual, scoop out the interior, and add some hot milk or cream and maybe a little butter as you beat. (Eat the delicious crispy skins as you work.)

• Potatoes baked in aluminum foil are really steamed, not baked.

• Grate raw potatoes into soup and simmer for a few minutes if you need a thickener.

• Save the water in which you've cooked potatoes and use it in yeast dough for wonderful bread and rolls.

. . .

Potato Beetles

See *Colorado potato beetles*

Potato Scab

See *Scab*

Powdery Mildew

See *Mildew*

Praying Mantises

These upright, tall, green insects are very valuable in gardens. They eat aphids, beetles, caterpillars, flies, grasshoppers, and many other injurious pests. In the fall, the females produce pale brown egg cases about 1 inch wide and attach them to the twigs of low-growing shrubs. Praying mantis egg cases can be ordered from nurseries.

Pumpkin

Pumpkins are really a species of winter squash. Pumpkins are heat-loving plants and, although they can stand cool nights, are extremely frost sensitive.

The standard vining varieties need a large growing area (unless you trellis them), but there are bush and semibush cultivars that can be grown in small gardens. Bush pumpkin plants produce fewer fruits than vining ones, but, because you can plant them closer together, they'll give a respectable total yield.

Each pumpkin plant bears both male and female flowers. The female ones have a small bulge at the base. The first few blossoms to appear are generally male.

When to Plant

• Although you can plant pumpkin seeds indoors in early spring for transplanting to the garden 6 weeks or so later, the seedlings don't take easily to transplanting; their roots are very fragile.

• It's better to plant seeds outdoors. Do this when iris is in bloom—late spring or early summer. Earlier planting, when the ground is on the cold side, may cause the seeds to rot.

Where to Plant

• Pumpkins like a fertile, moist soil that's moderately acid (pH 5.0 to 6.5). They prefer full sun—they need at least 6 hours of direct sunlight a day—but can take a little shade during a small part of the day.

How to Plant

• If your soil isn't rich, dig in some compost, aged manure, or both, before planting.

• For vining types, form 6-inch-high mounds of soil 5 feet apart on all sides. Insert 3 seeds, or seedlings, equidistant from one another in each mound, 1 inch deep.

• For bush or semibush types, plant seeds, in mounds 2½ feet apart.

Germination Time

• Pumpkin seeds germinate in 7 to 10 days.

Care During Growth

• When seedlings are 2 inches high, thin to the strongest plant in each hill.

• Pumpkin seedlings are very tender—protect them from hot sun, winds, and cold nights with a light cover of grass clippings or straw.

• Pour water—very important throughout the growing period—around the base of each vine during dry periods. Use tepid water if possible. Avoid watering from above, which encourages mildew and other leaf diseases.

• Black plastic mulch or gravel attracts heat and increases fruit size. If you are using plastic, set stones around the base of each plant to hold it down.

• When you see the first fruits, pour 1 cup of compost tea or liquid manure at the base of each plant at 2-week intervals until September.

• After 3 or 4 fruits have set, remove all other blooms and pinch out the growing tip at the end of each vine. This increases fruit size and makes fruits ripen sooner. Continue removing blooms as they appear unless you don't want large fruit. For small fruit you can continue to let blooms develop until mid-August. Pinch off any later ones; they won't have time to ripen.

• Place a board or mat of some sort under each pumpkin to hold it off the ground as it develops.

Maturation Time

• Pumpkins mature in 90 to 120 days, depending on variety.

Harvesting

• Pumpkins are ready to harvest when they're completely orange. The harvest period generally lasts about 1 month, but for best taste leave them on the vine as long as possible—up to the first light frost, in fact. But don't leave them longer—a heavy frost will ruin the crop.

• Use a sharp knife to cut a pumpkin from the vine, leaving about 4 inches of stem attached. Pick up a pumpkin from underneath—never by its stem. If the stem snaps off, the pumpkin won't store well and should be used as soon as possible.

Storing

• Cure pumpkins for 10 to 14 days before storing. You can do this outdoors (called field curing), covered, if the temperature falls to 40°F or thereabouts, or indoors, at 75° to 80°F. Outdoors curing is safe if you have a warm spell after harvesting, but beware of a freeze.

• After curing, which hardens the outer surface, store pumpkins where it's dry, moderately cool (50° to 60°F if possible), and dark. Arrange them on a shelf or other surface where they won't touch one another.

• Only pumpkins with hard rinds and no bruises or scratches will store well.

• You can also refrigerate pumpkins for short-term storage (1 or 2 weeks).

Diseases and Pests

• Bacterial diseases, cucumber beetles, damping off, leafhoppers, mealybugs, mosaic virus, powdery mildew, squash bugs, thrips, vine borers, whiteflies.

Garden Tips

• Any time you see the leaves of pumpkin vines wilting before 11:00 A.M., they're telling you they need water. (A little afternoon wilt in hot weather is normal.)

• You can trellis pumpkin vines. The foliage will be less prone to mildew, there'll be less insect infestation, and you won't have to worry about rotting. Tie the vines to the trellis where necessary as they grow, and make strong slings and hammocks to hold the developing fruit.

• The yield of a pumpkin vine will be increased if you remove all the female flowers for the first 3 weeks. Pumpkins will mature a little later, but the sturdier plant will produce more of them.

• If you're after a single, extra-large pumpkin, remove all fruits and blossoms from the vine after the first fruit has set.

• Clear the pumpkin patch of all vines at the end of the season and burn them—they may harbor many pests.
• Good companion plants for pumpkins are corn and lamb's-quarters.

Kitchen Tips
• Don't throw away the seeds you've scooped out of a pumpkin. They're very good to eat if you dry them in a low oven, then salt and continue toasting till they're light and tan colored.
• To remove strings from cooked, mashed pumpkin, beat with an electric mixer—the strings will adhere to the beaters.
• Pumpkin blossoms make delicious eating. Wash, drain well, dip in batter, and fry in deep fat. Use as an unusual meat garnish or with butter, syrup, or honey as a breakfast dish.

• Winter squash (Hubbard, acorn, or butternut) can be used in place of pumpkin in any recipe.
• Peel and seed a pumpkin, cut it into chunks, then slice it thin and dry the slices in a very low oven. When dried, the slices can be ground into flour in the blender. This is marvelous to use as part of the white or whole wheat flour in muffins, bread, or other baked items.
• You can make pumpkin soup the same way you make potato soup. It cooks even more quickly. (Add a little milk at the end, but don't boil the soup.)
• Why not cook and serve pumpkin as a vegetable? It's as good as squash and can be served in all the same ways.

Pyrethrum

This organic insecticide is made from the pulverized dried flowers of several species of chrysanthemum, including *Chrysanthemum cinerariaefolium* and *Chrysanthemum coccineum*, also known as pyrethrum, painted daisy, or painted lady. Like rotenone, it is both a stomach and a contact poison to insects, especially effective against soft-bodied ones. It also has the advantage of leaving little residue on food crops. It is not harmful to humans or other mammals.

Pyrethrum is acutely toxic to fish, however, in the event you have a fish pool in your garden. It is also mildly toxic to honeybees, but if sprayed in the early evening, when bees are least active, it is fairly safe, since it breaks down in about 6 hours. For this reason, frequent spraying may be necessary. Avoid purchasing compounds with the word *pyrethroid* in them: These are synthetic versions of the natural chemicals in pyrethrum, and many are highly toxic to bees.

Quassia 🪲

Quassia is a very bitter plant extract of the roots and bark of the tropical tree *Quassia amara*. Mixed with water, it makes an effective spray against aphids and other insect pests.

Rabbits 🪲

It appears that rabbits will eat almost anything that grows in a garden. Even one or two of them can cause great damage.

Manifestation
• Seedlings and new growth at the tops of plants are the first things to be attacked. As the season advances, rabbits go after soft stems, roots, and fruits.

To Combat
• A rabbit-proof fence is probably the surest way to thwart the critters.
• Cats hunt down and catch young rabbits, thus keeping down the rabbit population. Rabbits will also think twice about coming into a cat-protected garden.
• A sprinkling of ground black or red pepper over and around plants will often keep rabbits away from them.

The pepper won't harm the plants or the soil. You'll need to sprinkle after each rain.
• Dried blood meal sprinkled on the soil around plants (but not on the plants themselves) is said to deter rabbits. In any event, the soil will benefit from this substance.
• Rabbits are said to love soybeans. If you have no other way of combating the animals, try a planting of soybeans to keep the rabbits away from your other plants.
• Bait box traps with carrots and catch the rabbits.

. . .

Raccoons 🦝

Raccoons, although they're carnivorous mammals, love corn. If you have raccoons in your vicinity, your corn is endangered.

To Combat
• Even fences won't keep raccoons out of your corn patch. They climb them. But you can run a strand of electrified wire about 1 inch above the fence top—this is very effective.
• Dust your corn silks periodically with ground hot red pepper.
• Run your hands daily over the ears of corn from the time they near ripening until you harvest them—raccoons are put off by human scent.

• Some gardeners maintain that growing squashes around the corn patch keeps raccoons out—the animals appear to dislike walking through the vines.
• Try planting more corn than you'll need for yourself: The raccoons may be satisfied with only part of your crop.
• Try setting traps. But be warned that most raccoons are too smart to fall for them.

Radicchio

See *Endive*

Radish

Radishes are easy to grow: They are quick to sprout and quick to ripen. They are hardy, prefer cool weather, and can withstand light frosts. They don't grow well during hot periods.

There are early, summer, and winter varieties of radishes. Most come in shades of red, although there are white varieties and black ones. Early radishes are fast maturing; summer ones grow more slowly but can withstand heat more easily; winter radishes, which are larger and generally sharper in taste, need a longer growing time, maturing just before frost.

When to Plant

• Sow the seeds of early radishes as soon as the ground can be worked in spring. Since they're at their best for only a few days, make successive plantings at 10-day intervals until midspring.

• Plant summer, or midseason, varieties from late spring to midsummer.

• The seeds of winter radishes should be planted in late midsummer. They do their best growing in the cool weather of fall.

• Try planting some early radish seeds about a month before the first expected frost.

Where to Plant

• Radishes will grow in almost any soil, but they prefer a loose, not-too-coarse, sandy loam that is acid to neutral (pH 5 to 7). The long, white radish (icicle type) needs a more deeply spaded bed. Radishes do well in partial shade.

How to Plant

• Plant radish seeds ½ inch deep in shorter rows than you'd plant most vegetables, since it's advisable to stagger plantings. Plant 8 to 10 seeds per foot, evenly spaced, in rows 10 inches apart.

Germination Time

• Seeds germinate in 3 to 7 days, at temperatures as low as 65°F.

Care During Growth

• If you have planted more thickly than recommended, thin seedlings to 1 inch apart when the first leaves have formed.

• Radishes need a steady supply of water to remain crisp.

• Seeds sown in late summer for fall or early-winter harvesting need moisture to germinate. Continue watering as long as the summer heat lasts.

Maturation Time

• Depending on variety, radishes mature 20 to 35 days from the day seeds are planted. Fall-winter radishes generally take longer to ripen.

Harvesting

• The harvest period for any batch of radishes is usually 1 week.

• Pick radishes as soon as the roots have swelled to the size you like—usually when they're ½ to 1 inch in diameter. Cut the leaves off close to the radish as soon as it's been picked—they draw moisture from the root.

Storing

• With the exception of fall-winter radishes, most varieties don't store well for long periods. You can keep them in the refrigerator for 2 to 4 weeks, but they gradually lose flavor.

• Late-season radishes can be stored in a cold place (close to 32°F) in containers of peat moss, moist sand, or moist sawdust. They'll last fairly well for a couple of months.

Diseases and Pests

• Radishes don't usually have problems with pests and diseases, although the following have been known to attack them: aphids, blackleg, cabbage loopers, cabbage maggots, cabbageworms, clubroot, cutworms, damping off, flea beetles, nematodes, scab.

Garden Tips

• Don't use fresh manure in the radish garden—it promotes top growth at the expense of the roots.
• The faster radishes grow, the better their quality.
• You're not likely to harvest good radishes during very hot weather.
• Radishes given too little water, or left in the ground too long, become woody and unpleasantly sharp.
• If radishes crack, it's probably because of alternating wet and dry periods.
• Try planting radish seeds in the late fall, just before frost, for early-spring sprouting. It's chancy, but this method sometimes works.
• Because radishes seem to repel most pests, try interplanting them with beans, cabbage, cucumbers, lettuce, nasturtiums, peas, potatoes, squashes, and tomatoes.
• If you haven't been able to get your radishes out of the ground before they begin to flower, leave them for their ornamental value: They have beautiful, dainty flowers in pink, white, and pale blue.

Kitchen Tips

• To make a radish rose, cut the peel down from the top in thin, narrow strips, almost but not quite to the bottom. Then put the radish in water and it'll open.
• Stuffed radishes make a very attractive and tasty hors d'oeuvre: Make radish roses, and, when they've opened, use a sharp, pointed knife to remove the white inner part, which can be set aside for other uses. Drop the roses in ice water while preparing your stuffing. This can be made of any kind of cheese (Roquefort is nice) mixed with a little wine and thoroughly mashed. Press the mixture into the cavities of the well-drained and dried roses, and sprinkle with a little paprika.

Raised Beds 〈🖌

Raised bed gardening is very successful in most northern areas. Raised beds are quick to warm up in the spring, allowing for earlier planting. They also allow room for more and deeper root growth and better drainage.

To form a raised bed, make elongated mounds of soil about 1 foot high (they can be higher if you wish) and 1½ feet wide at the base. Level off the top for planting. You can have several mounds, each the length of your garden bed, with walking room between them.

Raised beds usually have less problems with slugs. But if you live in a dry area, raised beds may not be for you: Because of their excellent drainage, they dry out more quickly than the rest of the garden.

Raspberry

Raspberry bushes are hardy, grow and multiply vigorously, and generally need little care. The roots are perennial, but the fruit-bearing canes are biennial. With the exception of everbearing reds, berries develop on canes that grew the year before, whereupon those canes die. The roots have already produced new canes for berry production the next year. The bushes generally reach 4 to 5 feet in height. Raspberries are self-pollinating.

For most home use, 10 to 15 plants are enough to start with. Although some everbearing varieties may produce a small crop the first year of planting, raspberries won't come into full production until the third year. Be sure you buy virus-free stock.

Garden raspberries fall into two classes: the reds (which include yellow) and the blacks, also called black caps (which include purple—a hybrid cross of red and black). Red raspberries are the easiest to grow and are somewhat more cold resistant than blacks. Red raspberries increase by suckers from their roots; blacks increase by tip rooting (see *Propagating* under "Care During Growth").

Some red raspberries, called everbearing, produce two crops a season, one in midsummer and one in late fall. Various raspberry cultivars mature at different times through the season—by planting different varieties with an eye to maturity dates, you can have raspberries from spring until frost.

When to Plant
• Where winters aren't severe, dormant raspberry bushes can be planted either in early spring or in midfall. Black raspberries are better planted in early spring. In the North, all raspberries should be planted in early spring, after the last frost.

Where to Plant
• Raspberries do well in almost any moist, well-drained garden soil, but

they do best in a deep, loose, organically rich soil. Moisture is essential; so is good drainage. An elevated spot, if you have it, decreases the likelihood of spring frost injury. Raspberries like moderately acid to neutral soil (pH 5.5 to 7.0) and need at least half a day of full sun, although they can tolerate partial shade.

• Virus-free raspberries should be planted as far away as possible from already-established raspberry bushes.

How to Plant

• Remove all grass and weeds from the soil, and work well into it compost, dried manure, humus, or lawn clippings.

• If plants are bare rooted, soak them in water for about 4 hours before planting. They should go directly from the water to the planting hole.

• For each plant, dig a hole wide enough to allow you to spread out the roots, and fill it with water. Set in the plant, spreading the roots well, so that it stands 1 inch deeper than it did in the nursery. Cover with soil, packing it down tightly, and water once more. If the soil level goes down after watering, add more soil. Then cut the plant back to about 6 inches in height.

• Plants should stand 3 feet apart, and, if you are planting in rows, the rows should be 6 feet apart.

• Finally, mulch well with several inches of organic matter (see *Mulching* under "Care During Growth").

• Black and red raspberry plants should be separated from each other by at least 50 feet.

Care During Growth

• At the first sign of new growth, apply compost or aged manure. Remove weeds whenever you see them, but don't cultivate too deeply—raspberry plants have shallow roots.

• Start watering daily at the first signs of new growth, and continue watering through dry periods. This is most important from May until harvest if you want plump berries.

• You can increase the growth rate of raspberry bushes by feeding them fish emulsion solution or manure tea every 2 weeks.

• When new shoots are about 1 foot long, you may want to remove some of them to give more strength to those remaining.

• Many gardeners don't allow fruit to set the first year but remove all flower clusters so the plants' energies go into building strong roots.

• Cut or pull off any red raspberry suckers that come up between the rows unless you want to use them for propagation.

• You'll get more fruit if you keep black raspberry plants low growing. Prune about 3 inches off the tips of canes when the plants are about 2 feet high.

• Dried manure should be applied early every spring.

• *Mulching:* An 8-inch-deep mulch, especially important when warm weather arrives, should be begun when the plants are about 1 foot high. Start after a good rain, using composted or shredded leaves, hay, wood chips, straw, well-rotted barnyard manure, seaweed, or wood ashes. Mulching conserves soil moisture. In the fall, for winter protection, increase the mulch to at least 1 foot by adding leaves. These need never be removed, for they enrich the soil.

• *Trellising:* If you have a great deal of room, you can let the canes sprawl. But trellising is a great space saver, and most tall-growing raspberry varieties benefit from being staked in some way, gaining increased air circulation and exposure to sunlight and being less susceptible to fruit diseases. Trellising can begin at the end of the first summer, when the canes are tall enough to be tied or trained to a fence or wire supports.

• *Pruning:* Early in the fall, cut off at ground level all the canes that have borne fruit during the season (except those of red or yellow raspberry bushes, which shouldn't be pruned the first year). This annual pruning will leave the new canes that developed during the current season to bear berries the next year. Also, prune out any canes that look diseased or insect infested. All prunings should be burned. Cut back the new, healthy canes to about 2½ feet, either just before winter or early the next spring to encourage side growth and hence more berries. Early spring is also a good time to prune out winterkilled canes or any that look spindly or unvigorous.

• *Propagating:* Red or yellow raspberries produce shoots, or sucker plants, from their roots. To increase your plantings, leave a few of the suckers that seem the sturdiest. If you want to move these, cut them in early spring and root them as you would a houseplant cutting; then replant elsewhere. Give the transplants plenty of water and a little fish emulsion solution from time to time until they're well established. Black or purple raspberries increase by tip rooting: The canes naturally arch over until they touch the ground, whereupon they root and new plants develop. You can increase your number of blackberry bushes in much the same way you do the reds: Leave the new rootings to develop where they are. If you want to move them, cut the new plants in the spring, leaving two or three buds above the roots, carefully remove them with their roots, and transplant.

Maturation Time

• Most raspberry bushes are midseason developers, bearing berries from late early summer to early midsummer. So-called everbearing varieties (reds only) have a second crop in early fall.

Harvesting

• Raspberries on all bushes ripen at different times over about a 2-week period. They should be deeply colored, according to their variety, and ripe enough to slip easily off their cores with a gentle pull (they leave their cores behind). Any that don't pull off easily should be left to ripen further.

• Once berries start ripening, they should be picked daily. They don't last. Don't pick them unless they're dry—also, they crush easily, so don't pile them too high.

• Mature raspberry bushes should render about 1 quart of berries per plant during the season.

Storing

• Keep bruised or crushed berries separate from those in good condition.

• Raspberries are extremely fragile and have a shelf life of about 2 days. If you can't use them the same day they're picked, keep them in a cool place.

• Wash only before using.

Diseases and Pests

• In spite of the following list of enemies, raspberries don't generally have a great deal of trouble with insects and diseases: anthracnose, aphids, bacterial diseases, birds, borers, Botrytis blight, cane blight, Japanese beetles, leaf curl, leafhoppers, mealybugs, mosaic virus, scale, viral diseases, whiteflies, wilt.

Garden Tips

• Raspberry bushes that come bare rooted are extremely perishable. Don't let the roots dry out before you plant them.

• Eggplants, peppers, potatoes, tobacco, and tomatoes may carry fungal diseases that can infect raspberry bushes. For this reason, don't plant the bushes where any of these have grown within the previous 3 years.

• Never leave dead canes around raspberry bushes. Cut them out and remove them. If you see disease symptoms in live canes, cut them out and burn them too.

• The chief cause of moldy berries is prolonged humid weather. Too much shade, as well as prolonged humidity and overcrowding, can promote viral diseases.

• Everbearing red raspberry bushes can be made to produce a single but large and early fall crop if you prune all canes to 2 or 3 inches above the ground either after the fall harvest of the year before or before growth starts the next spring.

• Never use insecticidal sprays on raspberry bushes once the fruit has begun to form.

• Where winters are very cold, mulch raspberry canes after the ground freezes. Pushing snow up around them in midwinter also protects them against cold.

• Some gardeners report that planting garlic thickly around raspberry canes deters Japanese beetles. So does a planting of rue.

• Raspberry bushes tend to lose their vigor in time. For this reason it's recommended that you renew the plants by allowing suckers to root (for red raspberries) or encouraging tip rooting (for blacks) every 3 or 4 years, then remove the parent bushes.

Kitchen Tips

• Raspberries are among the most delicate of berries—handle them gently, and don't pile them on one another.

• For an unusual dessert, freeze washed and drained raspberries in a flat serving dish; then, at serving time, remove from the freezer and pour cream over them. The cream will freeze slightly to the berries. Try pouring wine over raspberries instead of cream.

. . .

Rats

See *Rodents*

Red Mites, Red Spider Mites

See *Mites*

Repellents ⟋⟍

Pest Deterrents You Can Make Yourself

To make a "tea" that repels most insects and doesn't harm plants, put about 1 cup, or 8 ounces, of well-chopped wormwood in a pail and pour enough boiling water over it just to cover. Leave it until it starts to ferment, stirring now and then. Sprinkle this solution on your affected plants—it's sticky, so it will adhere to the leaves and stems.

Make a soap-and-water solution (about 3 tablespoons of Ivory liquid or similar liquid soap to 1 gallon of water), and spray this on your plants to kill many insects. Some plants may not take kindly to this treatment; they will need a clear water rinse ½ to 1 hour later. Test first on a single leaf to be safe.

If you have a bad infestation on fruit-bearing plants (but not those with edible foliage), mix up this organic spray in your blender: 3 large onions, chopped; 1 garlic clove; 2 tablespoons hot red pepper; 1 tablespoon liquid soap; 1 quart water. Strain and spray. Because any mixture containing soap or detergent may irritate plants, either spray afterward with clear water or, better still, test on a leaf or two first.

Many seedlings can be protected against insect infestation if you add 1 teaspoon garlic powder to 1 gallon of water. Moisten the soil with this solution when transplanting young seedlings. You can also use this as a spray.

Save your used tea leaves, and scatter them around the bases of plants—they are often an effective insecticide.

Boil rosemary leaves in water, cool and strain, and use this as a spray—it's very good against many garden pests.

Sprinkle freshly ground pepper on the ground near your plants—it will keep off many harmful crawling insects.

Garlic and hot pepper, mixed in a blender with water, then strained and used as a spray, are often effective against most insects, but only for a day or two. Try repeated sprayings if you have a bad infestation.

Rhubarb

Rhubarb is an extremely winter-hardy perennial that needs cool weather for the stalks to mature and cold winter frosts to induce the dormancy period necessary to produce tender stalks in the spring. It can be grown from roots or seeds, although growing from seed will postpone the first harvest for an extra year. Rhubarb plants grown from roots (also called crowns or corms) will allow a moderate cutting 1 year after planting. But the plants won't come into full production until the third spring after planting. Rhubarb plants will yield harvests for 10 years or more.

The leaves of rhubarb contain large amounts of oxalic acid and are poisonous.

When to Plant

• Seeds or crowns go into the ground as early in the spring as the soil is workable. Crowns can also be planted in late fall, close to the time the soil freezes.

Where to Plant

• Choose a site where your rhubarb can remain undisturbed for years— once established, it doesn't take well to transplanting. A very heavy feeder, rhubarb needs well-drained, extremely fertile soil (work in plenty of decomposed manure or rich compost) that is spaded at least 1 foot deep. It prefers a near-neutral soil (pH 6.5 to 7.0) and needs full sun.

How to Plant

• If you are starting rhubarb from seed, sow seeds ½ inch deep, 4 inches apart, in rows 12 inches apart.
• If you are planting crowns, take care that they don't dry out before planting. Set them in the ground with the buds facing up, in holes 1 inch below the surrounding soil surface, covering them with loose mulch. They should be planted 3 feet apart in rows 3 feet apart. Firm the soil surface around them well, top-dress the whole area with well-rotted manure or compost, and water liberally.

Care During Growth

• If you're growing rhubarb from seed, water the seedlings well, con-tinually. Thin out the roots or transplant them to their permanent location the following spring.
• When you are transplanting, follow the procedure for planting crowns in "How to Plant." The transplants should also be kept well watered continually until they get established. Mulch with old hay, shredded leaves, or other organic matter to hold the moisture in.
• Encourage early spring growth by spreading compost or rotted manure or any high-nitrogen fertilizer around the roots in March and watering it in well. Follow this procedure throughout the growing season.
• Later in the season, remove all flower stalks as they form so the plants' energies will go into the roots for sturdy growth the next year.
• It's wise to divide rhubarb plants every 5 years, or when the stalks they produce remain small and tough instead of becoming large and juicy. Lift the crowns gently out of the ground very early in the spring, while the plants are still dormant, and divide them into pieces, each containing at least two "eyes" or buds, and with as much root attached as you can manage. Plant these as recommended under "How to Plant."
• Rhubarb plants usually go dormant in late summer or early fall. At this time you can cut the clumps to 1 to 2 inches above the ground.

Harvesting

• Don't harvest rhubarb the same year you've planted it. Even the second year, harvest lightly—take no more than a couple of stalks from each plant. By the third year the plants will be in full production.

• To keep production up year after year, never take more than half the stalks from any plant during a season.

• Harvest when the stalks are 1 to 1½ feet long. The best ones for all uses are the red ones.

• Remove each stalk by grasping it near the base and pulling gently sidewise and with a slight twist. Try not to injure the bud, which will later produce several stalks. The harvest period ends when emerging stalks stay small. From then on, throughout the summer, keep the plants well watered—they're storing up nutrients for next year's crop.

Storing

• Rhubarb will keep fairly well in a cool, humid place, such as a refrigerator, for about 1 week, although it loses its crispness. It freezes very well.

Diseases and Pests

• Japanese beetles, leafhoppers.

Garden Tip

• Do you want fresh rhubarb during the winter? Dig up some clumps after a good frost but before the ground freezes too hard for digging. Plant them shallowly in containers, in soil mixed with a little sand, and leave them outside until the soil freezes hard. Then bring the containers into a cool cellar, or wherever the temperature can be kept between 50° and 60°F, and keep them moderately moist. Water frequently, but don't let the soil get soggy. In about 1 month you'll have very tender rhubarb stalks, which, removed judiciously, will give you fresh rhubarb all winter. Set the plants back in the garden in the spring—they'll reach full production again in 2 years.

Kitchen Tips

• To make a 9-inch pie, you will need 6 cups of diced rhubarb.

• Young, early-season rhubarb is the best for pies. The more mature stalks are inclined to be tough and stringy in a pie. Use them for stewing.

Rocket

Also known as arugula, roquette, rucola, and rugula, this is a fairly hardy, annual, cool-weather herb of the mustard family, much prized for salads. It doesn't like summer heat, but the tender greens grow well and quickly in spring and fall.

When to Plant

• Start as early in the spring as the soil can be worked, and plant seeds every 3 weeks except in midsummer. Start again in early fall, and plant weekly until the end of the month.

Where to Plant

• Plant in soil (pH 6 to 7) that has been enriched with compost, aged manure, and wood ashes. Rocket needs sun but will take a little shade.

How to Plant

• Rocket thrives when it grows thickly. You can sow the seeds liberally in 6-inch-wide bands 1 foot apart. Or strew them thickly over the bed, thinning where necessary later. Cover the seeds very lightly with fine soil, and water with a fine spray.

Germination Time

• Seeds germinate in about 10 days.

Care During Growth

• Rocket needs practically no care, except to see that it is watered during dry periods.

Maturation Time

• Thirty days after planting seed, you can pick a few leaves or thin out some of the plants for use. Rocket reaches full size in about 65 days.

Harvesting

• Don't wait for hot weather before harvesting, or the leaves will turn bitter. Pull out the entire plant and cut off the roots.

Garden Tips

• Fall plants covered with cloches of some sort often live through the winter and start growing again early in the spring.

• If plants are left in the ground to bolt to seed (in summer), they'll usually self-sow for a late-fall or early-next-season crop.

Rodents (Mice and Rats)

The chief damage mice and rats do to gardens is gnawing and eating bulbs and succulent roots. Such destruction is fairly rare, but when it occurs your best control is a cat. You can, of course, always set traps.

You can protect bulbs by planting them in individual wire-mesh baskets, available from plant supply houses. Be sure to pack the soil well in and around them You can also cover bare bulbs with about 2 inches of soil and then place a large square of ½-inch-mesh hardware cloth over each bulb, turning it down around the edges and again packing the soil well in and around the bulb.

Root Maggots

See *Cabbage maggots*

Root Rot 🐛

Root rot is largely caused by fungi that, when introduced to a particular location, continue to exist in the soil and proliferate when conditions are right for them. The spores abound in compacted, wet soil and will enter any nearby roots. Beans, celery, and peas are particularly vulnerable to root rot.

Manifestation

• Plants are dwarfed, a greenish decay appears at their bases, and the foliage turns yellow. Later the leaves wilt and drop off.

To Combat

• Good drainage is particularly important—if the soil in your seedbed is too dense, cultivate it well, mixing in some shredded straw or vermiculite to encourage aeration.

• With crop rotation, you can starve out the fungi in a few years by not planting vulnerable vegetables where the fungi are. Root rot of peas, for instance, is caused by a fungus specialized for that plant only, so don't plant peas in the same spot for at least 3 years.

• Anything that wounds a root may make it vulnerable to root rot. Be careful in handling seedlings, and don't cultivate around them too harshly.

• Look for varieties of vegetables that are resistant to root rot.

Rootworms

See *Nematodes*

Roquette

See *Rocket*

Rosemary

Rosemary is a tender, perennial herb of the mint family whose slender, aromatic leaves are used, fresh or dried, in cooking and dried in potpourris. It is usually grown as an annual in the North, but it can be transferred to pots and brought indoors over the winter, going back to the garden each spring. Where winters aren't excessively cold, if grown in a sheltered place and well mulched, rosemary can survive outdoors for many years.

Although rosemary can be started from seed, it takes at least 3 years to grow into a usable plant. It's best to buy plants or root cuttings from already established ones (see "Garden Tips").

Rosemary, which looks like a small pine tree, rarely flowers before the second or third year. It has pink blooms. In the North it grows to about 1½ feet tall; in warmer areas it can reach as high as 4 feet.

When to Plant
• Place plants or rooted cuttings in the garden when the soil is warm, in May.

Where to Plant
• Rosemary will grow in any garden soil, even a poor one, that is relatively dry and not too highly acid (pH 5.5 to 6.5). A sheltered spot is preferable if you're going to mulch it and leave it over the winter. Plant rosemary in full sun.

How to Plant
• Set plants or rooted cuttings deep enough in the soil to cover the roots thoroughly, up to perhaps ½ inch of stem. Set the plants 1½ feet apart. Water once, immediately after planting.

Care During Growth
• Rosemary needs little care, beyond mulching with shredded leaves or other organic matter in the fall, to protect it against winter injury.
• Don't water too often, only when the ground seems excessively dry.
• Pinching out the tops will stimulate lateral branching.
• Where winters are quite cold, it's wise to pot the plants in the fall and bring them indoors for winter protection. Treat them like houseplants.

Harvesting
• You can pick off leaves from time to time for cooking use.

Storing
• To dry rosemary, cut off stems with their leaves from the top or sides and spread in a warm, dark place until the

leaves are thoroughly dried. Strip the leaves from the stems.

• Place the dried leaves in closed containers to use in soups, stews, gravies, and so on. They'll stay flavorful for 1 year.

Garden Tips

• Rosemary plants can be easily started from cuttings at any time of the year, although September is generally best. Cut off about 4 inches of young, green stems, with their leaves, from an established plant; stand them in a pot of moist sand or vermiculite; and keep them where there is light but not direct sun. See that the potting medium is always moist. Roots should develop in about 6 weeks. Place each rooted cutting in a pot of rich soil that has been mixed with a little sand, and keep indoors over the winter, transplanting to the garden in May.

• You can also form new plants outdoors by weighting down to the ground, with a stone, the lower branches of an established plant. Cover the point of contact with a little soil and keep moist. Roots will form and make new plants, which you can transplant elsewhere by severing the new plants from the mother plant.

• Rosemary, planted with beans, cabbage, and carrots, is said to repel bean beetles, cabbageworms, and carrot rust flies. Other good companion plants are cauliflower, kale, kohlrabi, sage, and turnips.

Kitchen Tips

• The fresh little needles (leaves) of the rosemary plant can make a salad dressing unusually delicious. Cut them into fine bits, add to the dressing, and shake well.

• Rosemary, once dried, tends to become splintery. Put it in a pepper grinder, and grind it over the dish you're adding it to. It's much easier on the tongue this way and much more pungent.

Rotenone

Rotenone is a natural toxin extracted from the roots of tropical plants such as *Lonchocarpus*, *Derris*, and others. Like pyrethrum, it is both a stomach and a contact poison to many insects. It is also poisonous to fish and other cold-blooded organisms, but it appears not to affect mammals, including humans (except as, possibly, a throat irritant). Rotenone is even less toxic to bees than pyrethrum and has the advantage of leaving no poisonous residue on plants. Unfortunately, though, it also kills beneficial insects, such as chalcid wasps and ladybug larvae, both of which are important insect predators in a garden.

Rucola, Rugula

See *Rocket*

Rust

This disease is caused by a parasitic fungus of which there are many, many kinds. Some form of rust can attack practically every kind of plant. Many rusts are specific for certain plants: There are references to blackberry rust, mint rust, sunflower rust, and so on. Some species of this fungus pass through a stage of their life on one host, then complete their life cycle by transferring to another host. Rain and wind can carry the spores from plant to plant. Spores may also be carried on seeds.

Manifestation

• Although the spots and discolorations caused by these fungi are usually rust colored, the colors can vary, according to the organism and the plant attacked, from yellow to orange, red, rust, brown, and black, as well as combinations of all these. They appear as powdery speckles or pustules (blisters), often with jellylike protuberances, on leaves, stems, buds, and fruit. The plants are often stunted.

• If you spot any signs of rust early in the spring, remove the infected plants at once to keep rain or wind from spreading spores.
• If an entire bed seems stricken, remove all the plants and dispose of them, leave the bed bare, and start a new bed of plants somewhere else.
• Try to buy rust-resistant seeds and plants.
• Rake up and burn all plant debris at the end of the season.

To Combat

• There's no known cure for rust at this time.

. . .

Rutabaga

Also called Canadian turnips, Macombers, Russian turnips, Swedes or Swedish turnips, winter turnips, and yellow turnips, rutabagas are easy to grow. Because they prefer cool weather, rutabagas are best treated as a fall crop. They can take light frosts.

When to Plant

• Sow seeds outdoors about 100 days before the first expected frost. Sowing earlier isn't advisable, since the root in its later development doesn't do well in summer heat.

Where to Plant

• Rutabagas grow well in ordinary, even rather infertile, garden soil, although they probably appreciate a fine loam. They prefer slightly acid to neutral soil (pH 5.75 to 7.0) and can take partial shade.

How to Plant

• Spade the bed about 1 foot deep, then plant seeds ½ inch deep, 8 inches apart, in rows 12 inches apart.

Germination Time

• Seeds germinate in 6 to 7 days.

Care During Growth

• Rutabagas need very little care. If the weather is hot and dry, just see that they are watered.

Maturation Time

• Rutabagas mature in about 90 days.

Harvesting

• The harvest period for rutabagas lasts about 2 weeks. The best time to dig them is after one or two light frosts (not heavy ones—if they freeze they won't store well). Their weight at harvest should be about 1 to 1½ pounds.

Storing

• Store rutabagas in containers of moist peat moss, sand, or sawdust in a cold, moist cellar, as close to 32°F as possible, but don't let them freeze. Humidity is necessary to prevent wrinkling of skins.

• Or, after harvesting, dip the rutabagas in melted paraffin, let them dry, and store in a cool place. This treatment will keep them fresh and usable for months.

Diseases and Pests

• Rutabagas are resistant to most enemies, but occasionally there may be infestations of aphids, blackleg, cabbage loopers, cabbageworms, cutworms, flea beetles, scab, and various fungi.

Garden Tips

• If you must transplant rutabagas for any reason, remove the lower leaves first. This lessens the drain on the root systems' energies while the plants are adapting to their new location.

• It's a good idea to rotate crop sites each year so that soil infestations will be less likely to continue to affect the crop. Also, keep rutabagas away from where other brassicas are growing or have recently grown.

• Look for cabbageworms or cabbage loopers in June; pick and destroy them. A good control for these is Bacillus thuringiensis (Bt).

• Plant nasturtiums here and there throughout the rutabaga patch—they can act as a trap crop, luring aphids away from the vegetable.

Kitchen Tips

• Prepare rutabagas in most of the ways you would white turnips except that rutabagas require slightly longer cooking.

• A little sherry added to mashed rutabaga just before serving gives the dish a fine touch.

• Rutabagas are great sautéed with a little onion.

Ryania

An insecticide available in both powder and liquid spray form, derived from the roots and bark of a tropical shrub, *Ryania speciosa*, ryania is especially effective against cabbage loopers, Japanese beetles, and squash bugs.

Sabadilla

A botanical insecticide, sabadilla is a powder made from the seeds of a South American lily. It is a very effective control for blister beetles, squash bugs, and tarnished plant bugs, among others.

Sage

A perennial herb of the mint family, the species of sage with lavender-blue flowers, often called garden sage, is the one used for culinary purposes. It is a very hardy, low-growing shrub, usually 18 to 20 inches high, whose leaves are used either fresh or dried. There is also a more compact dwarf form with smaller leaves, growing to about 12 inches in height. Sage plants, which can be harvested whenever the leaves seem the right size for use, usually bloom the second season. They often seed themselves. Propagation is from seeds, crown divisions, or stem cuttings, although seeding is the more usual.

When to Plant
• Plant seeds outdoors in early to midspring.

Where to Plant
• Sage likes an ordinary garden soil (pH 6.0 to 6.5), not too damp, in sun or partial shade.

How to Plant
• Mix a packet of seeds with a pound or so of garden soil and strew evenly over the bed. Cover lightly with more soil, and give the plot one good watering.

Germination Time
• Seeds germinate in 12 days.

Care During Growth
• When the seedlings are 2 inches high, thin out the plants to stand about 6 inches apart (sage does well when slightly crowded). You can use the thinnings in salads and sauces or dry them (see "Storing").

265

• Sage needs little care. Water only when there is a run of dry weather.
• It's a good idea, in June, to cut the plants back halfway, to keep them more compact.

Harvesting

• You can pick separate leaves, for using fresh, throughout the growing season. Or cut as much as 6 inches of the top growth from each plant a couple of times during the season. The plants will continue growing.
• Once sage blooms, the leaves are no longer as delicate or fragrant.

Storing

• Sage should be washed before the leaves are removed from the stems. Use cool water, and shake dry. Then strip the leaves, and spread them loosely on screens in a shaded, well-ventilated place. Stir them daily to hasten drying. When they are thoroughly dry, pack them in airtight bottles or other containers.

Diseases and Pests

• Sage is practically problem free.

Garden Tips

• Sage, with its gray-green foliage, will form an attractive, low, compact hedge if planted close together (about 4 inches apart) and kept clipped. It makes a nice garden border.
• Sage is said to deter many insects, such as cabbageworms and carrot rust flies, so use it as a companion plant for beans, Brussels sprouts, cabbage, carrots, cauliflower, kale, kohlrabi, rosemary, and turnips.
• Although classified as perennials, sage plants usually die down in four or five years, so replanting is necessary. In any case, they tend to become woody after the third year.

Kitchen Tips

• Fresh sage has a nice pungency that deserves more use in the kitchen. Try using it in fish and chicken sauces. Cut the leaves into fine strips. You can even add a few fresh leaves, cut very fine, to a bowl of salad greens.
• You can make sage tea by pouring boiling water over fresh or dried sage leaves and letting it steep until the flavor pleases you. Add a little lemon or lime juice.

Salsify

Also known as oyster plant, vegetable oyster, or common salsify, this hardy root vegetable is generally classified as a fall crop because it needs a long growing season. The tapering root, creamy white inside, is 8 inches or more long and resembles parsnip. It has a flavor similar to oysters. Salsify is very easy to grow. There is also a closely related plant known as black salsify, or scorzonera, whose root is covered with a black skin. It is grown like common salsify.

When to Plant
• Plant seeds early in the spring, as soon as the ground can be worked.

Where to Plant
• Salsify grows best in a deeply prepared, loamy soil (pH 6.5 to 7.5) containing plenty of phosphorus and potash. It will grow in both sun and partial shade.

How to Plant
• Loosen the soil well to a depth of about 1 foot, and sow the seeds ¼ inch deep, 4 inches apart, in rows 12 inches apart.

Germination Time
• Seeds germinate in 14 to 21 days.

Care During Growth
• Remove weeds by hand pulling or cultivate gently, taking care not to injure the roots.
• Very little other care is needed except watering during dry periods.

Maturation Time
• Salsify matures in 110 to 120 days.

Harvesting
• Salsify can be harvested in the fall, preferably after one or two light frosts. As with parsnips, frost improves the flavor. If you cover the roots with a 10-inch mulch of leaves or straw, you can harvest salsify through the winter and into the next spring. If you're digging them for storage, be careful to avoid bruising or cutting the roots. Leave on only about 1 inch of the green tops.

Storing
• For storing by overwintering in the ground, see "Harvesting."
• If you're planning on storage elsewhere, dig the roots in the fall before a heavy frost, choosing only sound ones, and let them dry. Arrange them in a bin in a cool cellar (32° to 40°F) where it's dark and the humidity is high. Too dry an atmosphere will cause the skins to shrivel.

Kitchen Tips
• In the spring, when the salsify first starts to grow, you can pick off some of the young leaves—these are delicious in salads.
• Salsify darkens quickly when you peel it. Immediately after peeling, drop it into water containing a little lemon juice or vinegar (2 tablespoons to 1 quart of water).

• Salsify takes a long time to cook to tenderness—1 hour or more. Most recipes assume you've already boiled it to tenderness.

Savory

Winter savory (*Satureia montana*) and summer savory (*Satureia hortensis*) are hardy members of the mint family and similar in fragrance and flavor, although winter savory is more pungent. Both are grown for culinary use, as well as for their flowers in garden borders or rock gardens.

Winter savory, probably the more decorative of the two, is a woody, perennial, evergreen shrub that grows to 12 to 15 inches in height and has white or purplish flowers. Summer savory is an annual with pink, lavender, or white flowers. It can grow to a height of 18 inches. Both are easily grown from seed. Winter savory can also be propagated from cuttings or root divisions.

When to Plant

• Sow seeds of both types of savory early in the spring, as soon as danger of frost is past.

• Winter savory rootstocks can be divided early in the spring, as soon as the ground can be worked, as well as in early fall. You can also make cuttings of young shoots in the spring, as soon as they look long and robust enough to be handled easily.

Where to Plant

• Savory will grow in any ordinary garden soil that is slightly alkaline (pH 7.5 to 8.0), although it does best if a little compost is mixed in. It should have full sun.

How to Plant

• Place cuttings in a moist mixture of half sand and half soil, and keep out of strong light. When the cuttings have developed roots, transplant them to the outdoors, 16 inches apart on all sides.

• Seeds should be sown ¼ inch deep and about 1 inch apart in rows 16 inches apart.

Germination Time

• Seeds germinate in 10 days.

Care During Growth

• When the seedlings are about 3 inches high, thin them to stand 8 inches apart for summer savory, 16 inches apart for winter savory.

• Very little cultivation or care is needed, beyond seeing that the plants are kept slightly moist, particularly during dry periods.

• • •

Maturation Time

• Plants reach maximum development in 45 days for winter savory, 60 days for summer savory, but leaves can be used throughout the growing season.

Harvesting

• Tender leaves and stems can be removed to be used fresh throughout the growing season, without disturbing the main plants.
• To harvest for drying, cut 6 to 8 inches of the top growth when blooming just begins.

Storing

• Spread cuttings to dry on wire mesh or a screen where it is warm, dry, and shaded.

• Remove the dried leaves from the stems before storing, and enclose them in airtight containers.

Garden Tips

• A row of savory plants spaced 3 to 4 inches apart will form a low, fragrant hedge around a flower garden or along a walkway.
• Savory is said to deter bean beetles and is therefore a good companion plant for beans. It is also said to be beneficial to the growth of onions.

Kitchen Tips

• Add chopped leaves of fresh-picked summer savory to room-temperature butter for a marvelous spread.
• Fresh savory is wonderful in omelets.

Scab

Scab is a set of diseases caused by either bacteria or fungi, producing crust-like, irregular patches on the surfaces of leaves, fruits, shrubs, and certain vegetable roots and stems, especially tubers. It's one of the most common potato diseases but is also seen on beets, carrots, radishes, rutabagas, and turnips. Some growers believe an alkaline soil, as well as a soil that's too dry, promotes scab, especially in potatoes. The organisms are often brought to the garden in fresh manure. Since the damage caused by scab is usually primarily on outer coverings, fruits can still be eaten if the warty portion is removed.

Manifestation

• Scab on edible tubers and fruits starts with small raised spots that slowly expand and thicken into corky patches.

To Combat

• Don't let the soil dry out, especially around potatoes. It's particularly important to give plants adequate moisture when the tubers are developing—about 6 weeks after planting.

• Keep the soil slightly on the acid side—most tubers prefer this anyway.

• If scab has affected one of your vegetables, don't plant the same kind in the same bed the next year.

• Never use fresh manure in the garden bed where you grow any of the plants vulnerable to scab.

• At the end of the season, remove all old vegetation.

• When sectioning mature potatoes for planting, never use any from a crop that has shown any incidence of scab.

• There are several scab-resistant varieties of potatoes—check for them when purchasing seed potatoes.

Scale Insects

There are numerous species of these minute, hard, oval, sap-sucking insects, all falling within two major types. Their bodies produce secretions that form either shieldlike ("armored") or waxy-powdery ("cottony-cushioned") coverings. Although scale insects attack mainly the barks and leaves of trees, they can also infest many garden shrubs, chiefly blueberries, currants, gooseberries, grapes, and raspberries. Like aphids, scale insects secrete honeydew, which attracts ants. If unchecked, the insects can kill bushes and, in extreme cases, trees.

Manifestation

• The first signs of scale are usually ashy or dark-colored, gradually spreading patches on stems and leaves. Their appearance can be like a pale powder or a scaly bumpiness. Leaves become speckled, yellowed, and wilted, and sometimes fall. Both stems and fruits may become spotted. A sooty-colored mold often grows on

the sticky honeydew exuded by scale insects.

To Combat

• If you catch it early, you can try removing the scale with a brush or cotton swabs dipped in alcohol. But this process is difficult because the insects stick firmly to leaves and stems.

• Birds—particularly chickadees, titmice, and wrens—devour scale insects.

• Lacewings eat the cottony-cushioned types.

• Spray affected plants with a mixture of 1 teaspoon each liquid detergent and rubbing alcohol dissolved in 1 quart of water.

• Both pyrethrum and rotenone sprays are effective against scale insects.

Scallions

See *Onion*

Scorzonera

See *Salsify*

Seeds

Most seeds germinate best at a soil temperature of around 70°F. Anything lower than 68°F hinders germination. Generally, seeds should be covered to three or four times their own thickness. But tiny seeds need light to germinate: Cover them very lightly with fine soil or not at all, and be sure to keep the bed moist at all times. Seeds with very hard coats will germinate faster if you cover them with warm water and let them stand 24 hours before you plant them. Once a germinated seed is allowed to dry out, it will die. To increase the viability of any seeds you're storing over the winter, refrigerate them in a dry, covered jar.

Indoor Sprouting

• Pasteurize garden soil before using it for indoor potting. Spread it over a shallow pan and put it in a preheated 150° oven for 45 minutes.

• Most seeds to be started indoors should be sown about 6 weeks before the last frost date in your area.

• Some plastic pots release a vapor that may harm seedlings. Try using starter pots of other materials, such as peat.

• The skin of a juiced half orange or half grapefruit, filled with soil, makes a nice pot for planting seeds indoors. When the seedlings are ready for transplanting in the garden, sink the whole thing in the ground—the "pot" will compost in short order, adding nutriment to the soil.

• If the soil in which you're growing seedlings is kept too wet and the room too cold, the seedlings may damp off.

• After planting seeds, slip the flats or containers into clear plastic bags. At the first sign of germination, take them out of the bags and move them to a slightly cooler place, but one with plenty of light.

• Seeds to be sprouted indoors do best with strong overhead light.

• Seedlings grown indoors by natural daylight won't need turning if you set them before a mirror, which will reflect the outdoor light back on them.

Outdoor Sowing

• Don't plant seeds too early in the season, regardless of the weather. Too-cold garden soil hinders germination and may even rot the seeds.

• Early planting of seeds doesn't necessarily lead to early maturity. Seeds planted later almost always catch up in development with the early-sown ones, without the risk of loss in a cold snap.

• Never sow seeds in water-saturated soil. Test the soil by picking up a handful and squeezing it. If it sticks together in a soggy lump or water runs from it, wait a week or two for the soil to drain before planting.

• For faster outdoor germination, you can prewarm the soil before sowing seeds: Cover it with sheets of black plastic for a week or so.

• If your garden soil is on the heavy side, plant seeds a little less deep than is recommended. Conversely, and especially if the weather is quite warm, plant seeds a little deeper if the soil is light.

• Small seeds, or seeds that you have soaked before planting, are easier to distribute if you mix them with dried used coffee grounds, a little sand, fine soil, perlite, or vermiculite. Or—for extra-fine seeds—use a saltshaker to distribute them evenly.

• A good rule of thumb for planting seeds in rows: Place 3 seeds very close together or even in the same hole. When the seedlings are 1½ to 2 inches high, remove all but the sturdiest one at each location.

• If seeds planted at one time in the garden sprout irregularly, they were probably sown at uneven depths.

• Be on the alert to provide moisture to planted seeds if there's any danger of the soil drying out.

• Try planting seeds outdoors in very small cans from which both ends have been removed. Allow 1 inch of the can to protrude above the surface of the soil—this can serve both as a reservoir that you can fill with water as needed and as a cutworm collar.

• • •

Shallot

Shallots, sometimes called eschalots, are small, papery, onionlike bulbs that have a mild onion flavor. When planted, each clove (also called a bulb or a set) produces a cluster of seven to ten additional bulbs, somewhat as garlic does. Shallots are hardy, and their cultivation is similar to that of onions, although they stand dry weather better. There are red, yellow, and gray varieties. The shallot bulbs you buy in the market are fine for growing in your garden. You can plant any size bulb.

When to Plant
• Sow sets, starting as early in the spring as the ground can be worked, up to late spring.

Where to Plant
• Choose a sunny site. Shallots will grow in almost any garden soil, but you'll get more flavorful and bigger ones in a compost-rich, moist soil that's well drained. Moisture is very important, but so is drainage. Shallots thrive on phosphorus and potassium (add bonemeal and dried fish meal) and prefer a mildly acid soil (pH around 6).

How to Plant
• Weed the soil well first. Sow the sets pointed ends up, about 1 inch deep and 6 inches apart. Allow 12 inches between rows.

Germination Time
• The sets will send up green spears in 10 to 14 days.

Care During Growth
• Keep the bed weed free.
• From time to time throughout the season, feed with a solution of fish emulsion, and make certain the bed is always slightly moist (but avoid waterlogging). Stop watering when plants reach full size.

Maturation Time
• Shallots are ready for harvesting 2 to 3 months after planting.

Harvesting
• You can pull shallots any time they reach eating size, or even pull them early to use as you would bunching onions or scallions.
• To harvest the bulbs when they reach maximum size, wait for the tops to dry and turn brown. At this stage you must protect them from any moisture, including rain: They should be allowed to dry out in the soil for about 2 weeks (cover the bed with plastic if rain seems imminent). Then

pull the clumps to the surface, and let them cure in the sun for a few days. If shallots get wet at this time, they'll begin to sprout again and you won't be able to store them.

• You can also mulch the shallot bed in the fall and leave the bulbs in the ground over the winter for harvesting in the spring.

Storing

• Separate the bulbs from their clumps, and lightly wipe off any loose skins. Store shallots as you would onions: in a cool (40°F), fairly dry place. They can be piled lightly in baskets or laid out shallowly on newspapers on a shelf. They should last the winter through.

Diseases and Pests

• Fusarium rot, onion fly maggots, thrips.

Garden Tip

• Keep moving the shallot bed every year because of onion fly maggots, which may attack shallot seedlings but which spend their life cycle in a very small area.

Kitchen Tips

• Don't try to store double bulbs—they don't keep well. Use them in the kitchen first.

• You can chop shallots and freeze them. You can also peel them, put them in jars, and cover with oil.

• Plant some shallots in pots to keep in your kitchen. They'll send up green shoots rather like those of chives, which you can keep snipping off to use in the same way.

• Shallots are the only members of the onion family that lose most of their flavor when chopped and dried.

Slugs (and Snails) 🐌

Slugs and snails are mollusks. So far as their garden activity goes, there is little difference between them, except that slugs are more numerous. They are, in fact, snails without shells. Slugs are soft bodied and slimy, usually gray, sometimes brown to near black. They vary in size, depending on age and variety, from ¼ inch long (the very young) to 1½ to 2 inches (usually), although they can be much longer.

Slugs are found in most gardens, from early spring to late fall. They need cool, moist shade during the day, and, unless the days are rainy and overcast, are active only at night. Besides attacking foliage and many garden flowers, slugs devour cabbage, lettuce, potatoes, strawberries, and tomatoes. To be fair, one must say that slugs feed mainly on decaying vegetable and animal matter and are part of what is known as the decomposer chain, which is very important in nature. Unfortunately, they don't limit themselves to this valuable activity.

Manifestation

• Slugs relish many seedlings and young shoots. Although they can climb, they tend to attack the lower parts of many edible plants and low-growing fruits. Leaves close to the ground are left with large holes in them.

To Combat

Every gardener seems to have devised a way of combating slugs. Here are several recommended methods, all of which work, according to their devotees:

• Coat the soil liberally around the stems of any affected plants with ground oyster shell (you can buy this at garden supply houses—ask for poultry-grade oyster shell) or crushed eggshells. The sharp edges deter the soft-bodied slugs.

• Slugs are reported to hate dry wood ashes. Sprinkle these liberally around your plants. You may need to repeat this after a rain.

• At night set wide cans half-filled with any of the following into the ground so that the tops of the cans are at ground level: beer, a milk and water mixture, or a yeast and water mixture. Slugs are said to love all of these; they crawl in and drown.

• Slugs will congregate under the damp surfaces of boards, shingles, bricks, and so on, in or near the garden. Set these out as traps, and, at various times during the day from morning on, lift them, pick up the slugs, and drop the creatures in a can of soapy water or water mixed with an equal amount of ammonia or alcohol.

• Two more things that can be used as traps for slugs: raw potatoes and banana peels. Slice potatoes in half, and at night place them here and there, cut side down, in the garden. Do the same with banana peels, placing strips with the inner skin down. Go out early in the morning with a container of soapy water, lift the traps, and drop the slugs in the water. You can do this several nights running.

• Spraying wormwood tea (see *Repellents* for how to make) over the soil early in the spring and again in the fall is said to repel slugs strongly.

• You can make slug barriers around plant stems by sinking small cans with both ends cut out into the soil so that about 2 inches protrude above ground level. Or make ventilation holes in clear plastic highball glasses, invert each glass over a seedling, and either push the glass 1 or 2 inches into the ground or hold the glass in place with a stone on top.

• Cut squares of screening, and make

holes in them so that the ragged edges point upward. Arrange each square around a plant, especially strawberry plants.

• Take a flashlight and a saltshaker into your garden at night and sprinkle salt on any slugs you see feeding. Salt demolishes slugs speedily.

• Hand picking is probably the most successful method of ridding your garden of slugs. An excellent way to keep them in check is to go outdoors after a rain, preferably in the morning, and examine the ground and lawn for slugs. You'll see plenty of them. Pick them up and drop them in a can of alcohol or ammonia mixed with water. You'll find fewer and fewer as the season progresses. You might want to wear rubber household gloves for this task; handling slugs is unpleasant. Or don't bother picking them up—reach down with a small pair of scissors kept for this purpose among your garden tools and cut the slugs in two wherever you see them.

• If you have irises, cut them to the ground late in the fall. Slugs love to winter over in them.

• Firefly grubs and ground beetles are great eaters of slugs. So are ducks.

Soil 🗲

Garden soils are generally classified into three broad groups: sandy, loamy, or clayey, depending on the preponderance of those substances in them. Most soils are a combination of two or even all three in different proportions. Sandy soils are fine or coarse grained and will fall apart readily after being squeezed. Extremely sandy soils cannot hold moisture and contain a minimum of nutritive matter for plants. For garden use they must be built up by the addition of organic matter. Loamy soils (what good garden soil should be) contain plenty of organic matter, are very dark, are moist yet crumbly, and have a pleasant woodsy smell. During periods of dryness they do not become hard or unduly crusty. Clayey soils are dense and heavy. They hold much more water than other types of soil and therefore have fewer air spaces. This consistency interferes with a plant's ability to absorb the water.

You can increase the humus content of soil by planting buckwheat and then plowing it back into the garden. You can do this twice in one season.

Earthworms are extremely beneficial for soil. They aerate it and enrich it with their castings.

Spade and turn your garden soil before cold weather in the fall—this helps to expose insect eggs to the winter cold; also, winter weathering benefits soil texture.

If you have a heavy clay soil, add lots of decaying organic matter to lighten it. Clay soil can also be much improved by the addition of peat moss, sand, or both. A little lime added to heavy clay soil improves its texture, allowing better aeration and drainage.

The heavier the soil (the more clay it contains), the longer it takes to warm up in the spring. A heavy soil tends to become crusty, dry, and hard after very heavy rains. This makes it difficult for many seedlings to surface from germinating seeds.

The more organic matter in your soil, the better the drainage. The deeper you prepare soil for planting, the better drainage you'll have, and the deeper your plants will root. Deeper roots mean a better supply of moisture and nutriments.

It's essential that bulbs, roots, tubers, and perennials of all kinds be planted in well-drained soil. Otherwise the roots are likely to rot. Well-broken-up bits of plastic foam—drinking cups, supermarket meat trays, and so on—make excellent drainage material to mix with heavy soil around plants. (Bits of plastic foam are also fine for potted plants.)

Soil pH is a chemical symbol denoting hydrogen ion concentration. On a scale of 0 to 14, a pH of 0 is extremely acid, or "sour." A pH of 14 is extremely alkaline, or "sweet." A pH of 7 is "balanced" or neutral. Most plants, including most vegetables, grow well in soil whose pH is between 6.0 and 6.9. A form of sulfur added to soil will increase its acidity, and a form of lime will increase its alkalinity. It's easy to test the acidity or alkalinity of your soil with an inexpensive pH kit, available at garden supply stores. Or send samples of your soil in clean containers to the agricultural extension service in your state. There is usually no charge for this analysis.

Most of the organisms that break down organic fertilizers and make them usable to plants thrive in slightly acid soil. Texturally, peat is very good for soil, although it contains very little plant food. It is also acid. Soils that are high in salt are generally alkaline. To raise acidity (lower the pH) in soil, add any of the following: aluminum or ferrous sulfate, cottonseed meal, peat and peat moss, pine needles, rotted manure (except chicken manure), sawdust, shredded mountain laurel or oak leaves, unused paper matches (bury these near plants), used coffee grounds, and used tea leaves.

To raise alkalinity (raise the pH) in soil, add any of the following: bonemeal, chicken manure, ground limestone or marble, poultry-grade ground oyster shell, wood ashes. You can substitute wood ashes for lime in alkalinizing soil—use three times more wood ashes than you would limestone. The finer the grind of limestone you use, the sooner it will be integrated into the soil. It takes at least 6 months for the addition of limestone to strongly affect the pH of soil, so apply lime in the fall to get the full benefits during the coming growing season.

Southern Corn Rootworms

See *Cucumber beetles*

Soybean

See *Bean*

Spearmint

See *Mint*

Spider Mites

See *Mites*

Spinach

See also *New Zealand spinach* and *Tampala*

Common garden spinach is a low-growing, hardy leaf vegetable that loves cool weather. Because it is extremely sensitive to heat and bolts to seed in hot weather, it is usually grown as a spring and again as a fall crop. Once matured, the plants don't stay in good condition very long, so it's advisable to make continuous sowings during each growing period to have successive harvests.

When to Plant

• Sow spinach seeds as early in the spring as the ground is workable—they'll germinate in temperatures as low as 45°F. As soon as you see the first seedlings, make another planting, and continue this way until late spring.

• For fall harvesting, sow seeds in late summer, when the main summer heat is past. You can make continuous plantings, as in the spring, up to the beginning of midfall.

• It's also possible to plant seeds in the fall before a freeze and cover the bed with a thick mulch. This will give you an early-spring harvest.

Where to Plant

• Spinach likes a nitrogen-rich soil that holds moisture well, a pH from near neutral to lightly alkaline (6.5 to 7.5), and plenty of light. A little cool shade will help your last spring planting grow into early summer.

How to Plant

• Sow seeds ½ inch deep, 3 inches apart, in rows 18 inches apart. Or broadcast seeds over the spinach bed and cover with 1 inch of soil. For summer plantings, mist the seedbed well every morning to cool the soil and aid germination. If the ground seems too warm (seeds won't germinate well in hot soil), cover the seedbed after planting with a mulch of hay or straw or even some light brush, which you can remove when the seedlings are up.

Germination Time

• Seeds germinate in 7 to 10 days.

Care During Growth

• If they are planted in rows, thin seedlings to 6 inches apart. If sown by the broadcast method, thin seedlings so they're roughly 10 to 12 inches apart on all sides.

• Because spinach is a heavy nitrogen user, give it periodic feedings of manure tea or a fish emulsion solution.

• Be sure the plants get plenty of water, particularly the late-summer planting.

• Spinach will have a new spurt of growth in the cool weather of September, so keep up the fertilizing and watering.

Maturation Time

• Spinach can be harvested 30 to 45 days after the sowing of seed.

Harvesting

• Don't harvest spinach until the plant has grown at least six regular leaves. Spring-planted spinach that matures after the middle of June isn't very good. Once you see the leaves beginning to toughen, cut spinach at once—it won't remain edible long.

• The harvest period for any one planting usually lasts about 2 weeks.

Storing

• Once cut, spinach will generally keep for about 1 week. Wash it, shake it dry, and keep it as close to 32°F as possible, but don't let it freeze.

Diseases and Pests

• Cabbage loopers, damping off, flea beetles, green peach aphids, leafhoppers, leaf miners.

Garden Tips

• Cut spinach to the ground in the late fall, leaving the roots in, and mulch deeply. It will often survive very cold temperatures and yield fresh new growth in the early spring.

• You can also sow spinach seeds in the late fall and cover them with a mulch. It's taking a chance, but they may well sprout in the spring and give you an extra-early crop.

• For warm-weather planting (for a fall crop): Chill spinach seeds in the freezer for 1 week, then plant. They'll sprout more readily.

• Or soak seeds for planting in warm soil for half a day, roll them up in moist paper towels placed in a plastic bag, and keep them in the refrigerator for a few days. Then plant them.

• Try interplanting spinach with tomato plants. You'll finish harvesting the spinach before the tomatoes take over. This is a good idea if your garden space is limited.

• Spinach is said to be a good companion plant for corn and strawberries.

Kitchen Tips

• Don't cook spinach in iron or aluminum pots or serve it in a silver dish—all these give it a metallic taste.

• Spinach, rinsed well but with no water added, cooks, covered, in about 6 minutes. But lift the cover a few times so the spinach will keep its green color.

• Add some fresh mint to the pot the next time you cook spinach.

• Tender baby spinach leaves are delicious in salad.

• If fresh spinach begins to wilt, sauté it lightly with a very little bit of bacon fat and serve hot. Or chill it after sautéing, add croutons, and serve as a salad.

Spinach Leaf Miners

See *Leaf miners*

Squash

See also *Pumpkin*

Squashes are heat-loving, frost-sensitive plants that require a fairly long growing season. If you can't depend on up to 120 days in your area, instead of sowing seeds directly in the garden, either start them early indoors (see "When to Plant") or buy transplants.

Every squash plant produces both male and female flowers, with the male blossoms usually appearing first and always outnumbering the female flowers. Male flowers are narrow and straight and have longer stems; the smaller female flowers show a swelling at the base, which will develop into fruit if the flowers are fertilized.

Squashes are divided into summer and winter types:

Summer squashes are soft-skinned bush types that don't form vines. They're easy to grow, fast maturing, and very productive (5 or 6 squash per plant are often produced weekly during the growing season). Although new varieties and hybrids appear each year, the most common types are crookneck, pattypan (also called scallop or scallopini squash), straight-neck, vegetable marrow, and zucchini.

Winter squashes are hard shelled and generally long vined, thus requiring more room unless you trellis them. The chief types are acorn, buttercup, butternut, gourds, Hubbard, and vegetable spaghetti (also known as spaghetti squash). New Asian varieties are also now coming onto the market. Most winter squashes don't mature until late summer and fall, although acorn, butternut, and Hubbard types can be picked when about half grown and prepared as summer squashes are.

All squash plants will be more productive if you pick the fruits as soon as they mature, thus stimulating the plants to produce more.

When to Plant

• If you are starting seeds indoors, plant them in early to midspring, or 5 to 6 weeks before the soil warms to about 60°F and there is absolutely no danger of frost. Transplant the seedlings to the garden in late spring or early summer, when they are 3 to 4 inches tall.

• If you are sowing seeds in the garden, wait until early summer begins, when the soil is 60°F or warmer.

• You can make a second sowing of

summer squashes in midsummer, to assure a crop until frost.

Where to Plant

• Squashes need deep, rich soil with plenty of organic matter mixed into it (compost, humus, leaf mold, aged manure). The soil should be moist but well drained. Squashes like a slightly acid to neutral soil (pH 5.75 to 7.00) and lots of sun.

How to Plant

• All squashes: Plant 4 seeds 1 inch deep to form a square, 3 inches long on all sides, the squares 42 inches from one another on all sides.
• Or plant seeds 1 inch deep, 6 inches apart, in rows 4 feet apart for summer squashes, 7 feet apart for winter squashes.

Germination Time

• Seeds germinate in 7 to 12 days.

Care During Growth

• If you planted in squares, thin to the 2 strongest seedlings per square when they are 2 to 3 inches high.
• For seeds sown 6 inches apart in rows, thin to about 20 inches apart when the seedlings are 2 to 3 inches tall.
• If the nights begin to turn cold after seedlings are up or after transplants are in, mulch with clear or black plastic or black paper to keep the soil warm. A gravel mulch also attracts heat during the day and holds it overnight. Stones set on top of the plastic, around the plant openings, will hold the plastic down.
• When the first fruits appear, side-dress with compost or feed with liquid manure or leaf mulch tea. From this point on, a steady supply of water is necessary—be on the alert, especially during dry spells. Any time the leaves of squash plants show signs of wilting before 11:00 A.M., they're telling you they need water. (A little afternoon wilt in hot weather is normal.)
• Most vining winter squashes can be trained up a trellis or other support. This saves garden space and increases air circulation, preventing mildew. It also makes harvesting easier (see "Garden Tips").
• Once 6 or 8 fruits per plant (of winter squashes) have set, remove all further blooms as they appear. By the end of August there won't be time for new fruits to complete development. Tip pruning is also a good idea at this time; it pushes plants into putting their energies into developing the fruit already set.
• Fertilize again with liquid manure in early fall.

Maturation Time

• *Summer squashes:* 44 to 62 days to first harvest, depending on variety.

• *Winter squashes:* 50 to 120 days, depending on variety (the earlier maturing time is for acorn, butternut, and Hubbard varieties, which can be harvested when young and treated as summer squashes).

Harvesting

• All summer squashes should be harvested when young and tender, while the rinds are still soft enough to be easily pierced with a fingernail. They should never be more than 8 inches long—shorter is even better. Pattypan types are best when about 3 to 4 inches across.

• Don't pull squashes from the vine, but cut with a sharp knife, leaving about 1 inch of stem on the fruit. The harvest period for summer squashes lasts 6 to 8 weeks. The plants will produce more if you pick them frequently.

• For finest flavor and ability to withstand storage, harvest winter squashes as late as possible, either after the vines have died down or just before a hard frost. If a light frost occurs, harvest them immediately afterward. The rinds should be quite hard, resisting piercing with a fingernail. Acorn squashes should have a very dark green rind; spaghetti squashes should be completely yellow. Leave on about 4 inches of stem, and be very careful not to bruise the squashes, or they won't store well.

Storing

• Squashes that aren't mature won't store well.

• Summer squashes should be stored in temperatures from 45° to 55°F. They will keep for a few weeks, but they're not the long keepers that winter squashes are.

• With the exception of acorn squashes, all winter squashes intended for storage should be cured first, to harden the rinds: Keep them for about 10 days in a very warm place (80° to 85°F is ideal), either outside in the sun or indoors. Then store them in a cool (45° to 55°F), dark, well-ventilated, moderately dry place, arranged in single layers but not touching.

Diseases and Pests

• Aphids, armyworms, bacterial diseases, blossom-end rot, corn earworms, cucumber beetles, damping off, fusarium rot, leafhoppers, mosaic virus, powdery mildew, squash bugs, thrips, vine borers, whiteflies.

Garden Tips

• Don't start squashes too early indoors—once they become spindly and lanky, they won't take well to transplanting.

• Squash roots are unusually fragile—handle delicately when transplanting.

• After transplanting squashes, cultivate lightly around the stems every few days—aeration helps prevent damping off.

• If the weather turns cold after transplanting, cover the seedlings with cloches of any type (cans are good: Remove one end and pierce the other here and there to let air in). Remove these during the warmer part of the day. (Even a light frost will kill squash seedlings.)

• Bees are nature's pollinators of squash blossoms. Lure them to your garden by planting herbs and flowers nearby. If you think you're short of bees, pollinate by hand: Carefully break off a male blossom, tear off the petals, and dab the pollen-carrying portion around the inside of the female flower.

• Pruning improves the quality of winter bush-type squashes: Remove all but about 4 developing fruits per plant.

• For a sweet, tasty, tender vegetable, pick acorn squashes about 3 days after the female blossoms appear.

• Zucchini and other summer squash plants become great producers if the fruits are picked frequently. Allowing them to remain on the vines until they grow large will cause the plants to bear fewer fruits.

• The more mature the plant, the greater its eventual fruit production. Keep squash plants from setting fruit for the first 3 weeks by removing the female flowers when they appear.

This way you'll have later-yielding but more productive plants.

• In the height of the season, summer squashes can grow an inch a day!

• Squashes greatly benefit from animal fertilizer (cow, horse, or sheep), but be sure it's well aged first.

• Fencing or trellising squashes saves many square feet of garden space, as well as protects the squashes from ground rot. Most varieties of vining squashes will readily cling to latticework or poultry wire attached to poles. Use plant ties or a double skein of soft yarn to help anchor vines to supports. The stems of heavier squashes accommodate to the weight by becoming thicker, but sometimes making slings to hold up the heavy fruit will prevent the vines from being pulled downward. Slip each squash into a nylon stocking, and attach the open end of the stocking to the trellis or fence. It easily expands as the fruit grows.

• As soon as the plants develop a dozen or so true leaves, water at ground level instead of spraying from above, to avoid foliar diseases, such as mildew.

• Look for insect eggs on the undersides of leaves during June and July. Look also at ground level, at the bases of the stems, for the red or orange eggs of borers. Remove all these with cotton swabs dipped in alcohol.

• Wood ashes sprinkled around the bases of squash plants are effective in keeping stem borers away.

• Another method of repelling borers is to spread aluminum foil under the plants. The reflected light is said to bother them.

• Cover parts of squash vines with soil, stimulating them to root. Then if borers invade some stems, the plants will have subsidiary roots to keep other parts alive.

• In general, foil or white plastic mulches (use recycled aluminum foil or white plastic trash bags) keep away many squash pests, including aphids.

• Place boards, bricks, or rocks under developing fruits to raise them from the ground and lessen chances of fusarium rot.

• Butternut squash is very resistant to borers and many squash plant diseases.

• Gourds are grown like winter squashes, their vines spreading to about 12 feet. They do well on trellises.

• A sharp frost will hinder the keeping quality of any squash.

• At the end of the growing season, pull up all squash plants and bag or burn them—they may carry insect eggs.

• To remove all possible contamination of surface bacteria just before storing winter squashes, wipe them with a mild solution of bleach and water. Be sure they're well dried before storage.

• Examine your stored squashes in midwinter to make sure they're all sound. Remove any that show spoilage.

• Some gardeners report that catnip or tansy interplanted with summer squashes repels cucumber beetles.

• Other good companion plants for squash are borage, corn, and radishes.

Kitchen Tips

• Squash blossoms are delicious— dip them in batter and fry them. You can do this even during the early part of the season without harm to productivity if you pick only male flowers (leaving a few, of course, to fertilize the female flowers).

• Winter squashes are often hard to cut when raw. A small serrated meat saw does a better job than a knife and is safer because it's less likely to slip.

• You can use the flesh of any winter squash in place of pumpkin in a pie.

• A little grated raw winter squash is a fine extender for meat loaf or hamburger.

• Winter squashes have an affinity for ginger. Butternut squash is delicious served peeled, boiled, and mashed with a heaping tablespoon of ginger marmalade mixed well into it (no butter needed). You can also scrub an acorn squash, cut it in half lengthwise, seed it, and put the halves in the oven with a teaspoon of ginger marmalade in the center of each. Bake until the flesh is soft.

• Use winter squash as a substitute for carrots in carrot cake.

• You can pickle any type of winter squash (or pumpkin) just as you do watermelon rind. But you have to pare off the hard outer shell and pickle the flesh in chunks. Use the same spices and technique as for watermelon rind, and heat the pieces in the pickling liquid until they become translucent.

Squash Bugs

These ½-inch-long, flat, brownish-black insects with yellow underbodies fly into gardens in late spring. The females lay oval, bright yellow eggs, which turn dark brown in a few hours, in geometric patterns on the undersides of leaves. The eggs hatch in a week or two into green nymphs with red legs, which feed in groups on vine crops: chiefly cucumbers, melons, pumpkins, and winter varieties of squash. They molt several times throughout the season before becoming winged adults. The insects hide under leaves and boards at night and spend the winter in similar places. They give off an unpleasant odor when crushed.

Manifestation

• As they feed, squash bugs inject a poisonous substance into plants, causing vines and leaves to wilt, turn dark, dry out, and die. If there is a large infestation, the plants will produce no fruit.

To Combat

• Destroying squash bug eggs is your best defense: Look for the egg clusters on the undersides of leaves. Remove the eggs with a cotton swab dipped in alcohol. Or pick off the affected leaves and drop them, eggs and all, into soapy water.

• Handpick the adult bugs. You can provide boards as traps. Lift the boards around noon, remove the bugs, and drop them into soapy water or an alcohol-water mixture. Also, look for squash bugs on the ground, under withered leaves.

• Look for the nymphs (which resemble the adults but are smaller) and the adults on your plants. It's possible to handpick them successfully if you move fast. Early in the morning is a good time to do this.

• If your garden has squash bugs, avoid straw and hay mulches; their depth and coolness provide shelter for the bugs. Mulch instead with compost, which they don't like.

• Gardeners report that squash bugs are repelled by wood ashes—sprinkle these over vines and leaves after a rain or a watering. Repeat each time it rains.

• Keep your plants as vigorous and healthy as possible so that parts not attacked will continue producing.

• Nasturtiums, pink petunias, and radishes have been reported as effective against squash bugs. Interplant these among your vegetables.

• At the end of the season, burn or compost your vines to keep the bugs from breeding or overwintering in them.

. . .

Squash Vine Borers

See *Borers*

Squirrels

Squirrels aren't usually offenders in a home garden, but there have been reports of their getting into the corn patch and wreaking havoc. They also have been known to go after tomatoes.

To Combat

• It's said that squirrels won't go under dense foliage. Try using thick-foliaged plants—rhubarb, for example—as a border around your garden plot.

• Human or dog hair can be used as a squirrel deterrent. Place hair and fur trimmings around the garden, close to the attractive plants, either loose or tied in netting bags.

Stem Borers

See *Borers*

Sterile-Plant Virus 🐞

Also called nubbins, sterile-plant virus is a disease of blackberry plants.

Manifestation
• The plants, although they appear vigorous and have many blossoms, produce either tiny, nondeveloping nubbins or no berries at all.

To Combat
• There is at present no cure for this disorder.

• Dig up and burn affected bushes, as well as any suckers that may appear later.
• Don't plant blackberry bushes in an infested spot for at least 1 year. You can, though, use the plot for other annual garden flowers or vegetables.
• Make sure the blackberry bushes you buy are guaranteed to be virus free.

Strawberry

There are 3 main varieties of strawberries: the June bearers (also called early bearing), which produce a single large crop in early summer; the everbearers (or alpine strawberries), which actually yield two harvests, a large one in spring and a second from late summer to fall; and the day neutrals, which produce throughout the season but blossom and set fruit only when the weather is warm and sunny.

Most strawberry plants multiply by sending out runners, which will produce fruit the next year; everbearers produce fewer runners than other types, some producing no runners at all. Strawberry plants produce fruit for 2 and sometimes 3 years, although the best harvest is in the first season after planting. Many growers start each season with new plants only.

You can either purchase seedlings or, more economically, plant seeds early indoors (see "How to Plant") and move the transplants to the garden in the spring. If you have bought transplants, plant them as soon as possible. If you must hold them for a while, slip them into plastic bags and refrigerate them.

When to Plant
• If you have midspring frosts, sow seeds indoors in late winter for transplanting to the garden in midspring.

• Set transplants into the garden around early spring, or as soon as the ground can be worked, provided danger of frost is past. A good rule of thumb is to plant seedlings outdoors when leaves on the trees begin showing green.

• In cold areas, you can also start new strawberry beds (usually with rooted runners that have developed from established plants) in early winter, provided you mulch them well with high-nitrogen materials, such as sawdust or straw.

Where to Plant

• The best site for a strawberry bed is a south-facing gradual slope that gets full sun. The plants do best in light-textured, organically rich, sandy soil with excellent drainage. If your soil seems heavy, consider raised beds, which are ideal for strawberries. It's advisable to fertilize the soil before planting strawberries. Mix in any or several of the following: bonemeal, compost, leaf mold, peat moss, rotted leaves, well-rotted manure. Strawberries do best in slightly acid soil (pH 5.5 to 6.5).

How to Plant

• *Indoors:* Fill a 6- or 8-inch flowerpot with potting soil mixed with a little sand, and sprinkle strawberry seeds over the surface. Cover with ¼ inch of soil mixture. Keep the soil lightly moist, always watering from below. When the seedlings develop their first set of true leaves, transfer them carefully to individual peat pots or other small containers, setting the plants at the same depth they were growing at before. Keep them moist, and give them plenty of light.

• *Outdoors:* Strawberry plants are generally spaced 18 inches apart in rows either 2 or 4 feet apart, depending on which of the following methods you use:

The single-row system, where the rows are 2 feet apart, concentrates on the plants themselves, with all runners nipped off as they appear.

The matted-row method, where the rows are 4 feet apart, allows runners to fill in both sides of each row until the rows grow to about 2 feet wide at the end of the first season. Fruit is harvested from the mother plants, with the runners becoming mother plants the next year, producing fruit and runners in their turn. This method, although it continually produces more plants, requires more work (former mother plants must be removed each year), and many gardeners today prefer the single-row system.

It's a good idea to bring strawberry plants to the garden set in a container with a little water. Any roots longer than 5 inches should be trimmed back. Dig each hole deep enough and wide enough that the plant can be set in with its roots spread, fanwise, as far as possible and with the crown (where the stems meet the root) level with the surface of the soil. Press the soil down firmly against the roots, and water well at once. You can add some fish emulsion or manure tea to the water.

Germination Time
• Seeds germinate in 10 to 14 days.

Care During Growth
• From the time of transplanting onward, take care that the plants get plenty of water. Never let them dry out. They especially need water when they're fruiting.
• An early mulch of well-rotted manure and sawdust is a good idea, particularly to help the plants through the cold nights of early spring. If frost threatens, you can also weight down pieces of newspaper with stones as a protective mulch. Once all danger of frost is past, you can remove the mulches.
• Nip off the first blossoms of everbearing varieties until the beginning of early summer. The plants will then set more and bigger fruit.
• If you decide to use matted-row planting, remove all the flowers from the mother plants the first season and let the plants put their energies into producing runners. The next year you'll have bumper crops.
• Many strawberry gardeners say you should not let new runners fruit the first season they appear. Keep picking off the flowers. The runners can

either be left in the bed as they develop or moved to new beds just before autumn sets in. This will give them time to get established before frost. This is a good time to add some bonemeal, compost, or aged manure to the new bed.
• Everbearing strawberries should be well watered and fertilized with fish emulsion solution or manure tea after harvest. At this time the plants are forming the next year's buds, so they need moisture and nutrients.
• Mulch strawberry plants after the first fall frost—5 inches of manure mixed with straw, oak leaves, pine needles, or salt-marsh hay is excellent. Leave the mulch on all winter and remove, a little at a time, when spring comes. Allow some to remain until all danger of frost is past.

Maturation Time
• Early-bearing (June-bearing) strawberries produce fruit from early to late June, approximately 10 weeks after transplants have been set out, or 120 days from the indoor sowing of seed.
• Everbearing varieties have a quicker yield: 5 or 6 weeks after transplanting to the garden.
• All strawberry plants produce a little earlier if they have wintered over.

Harvesting
• For best flavor (and immediate use), pick berries when they are quite

ripe—bright red. Take care not to press the berry itself, but put your fingers behind the calyx (the small ring of tiny green "leaves" surrounding the base of the berry) and pull forward. A ripe berry will detach easily, bringing the calyx with it.

• All strawberry plants, after the final harvest, should have their foliage cut to about 1 inch above the ground.

Storing

• Refrigerated, ripe berries will stay in good condition no more than 3 or 4 days. Spread them on paper towels on a cookie sheet so they don't touch one another. Wash only before using; otherwise they'll become soft.

• To freeze, wash the berries, blot them dry, and arrange them directly on cookie sheets without using paper towels. When they have frozen, pop them into a plastic bag and return them to the freezer.

Diseases and Pests

• Bacterial diseases, birds, Botrytis blight, corn-root aphids, flea beetles, fruit flies, leafhoppers, mealybugs, powdery mildew, slugs, tarnished plant bugs, thrips, verticillium wilt, whiteflies.

Garden Tips

• Because certain wilt diseases that attack the following plants may remain in the soil where the plants grow, don't plant strawberries in beds formerly occupied by eggplants, melons, okra, peppers, potatoes, raspberries, or tomatoes.

• Strawberry plants have shallow roots, so the soil in which they are planted must hold moisture well without becoming waterlogged.

• The plants are most susceptible to frost at their budding and flowering stages. Be ready with hot caps or cloches if the weather turns cold at these times.

• Cut all the runners off your strawberry plants and you'll get a larger yield and bigger berries.

• Try thinking of strawberry plants as annuals, pinching off runners, harvesting your berries, and starting each season with new plants.

• Occasional spraying of strawberry plants with a fish emulsion solution will make them produce more.

• You can place everbearing strawberry plants along driveways and sidewalks or use them to make borders for flower or vegetable beds.

• A single strawberry plant generally needs replacing after the third season. Dig it up or, if there's been no sign of disease, plow it under. Set out new plants the next season, or cultivate the runners from the mother plants.

• If your winters are severe, push snow up around the plants and over the mulch. This will usually protect strawberries nicely.

Kitchen Tips
• Don't let picked berries become warm—refrigerate them quickly.
• Wash strawberries before removing the caps, otherwise water will get into the berries, diluting their flavor and making them mushy.
• Putting sugar on strawberries softens them. To sweeten them, add the sugar shortly before—or as—you serve them.
• To give not-so-sweet strawberries a richer flavor, wash them quickly in cool water, pat dry with a towel, remove the hulls, and stand the berries, hulled sides down, on a tray that has been sprinkled with white granulated or light-brown sugar. Cover lightly with paper towels, and let stand at room temperature for a couple of hours.
• To prepare strawberries for a pie, always wash and pat them dry with a towel, remove the hulls, and set them to drain on layers of paper toweling. This will rid them of excess moisture so your pie won't be mushy.

Summer Savory

See *Savory*

Summer Squash

See *Squash*

Sunberry

See *Huckleberry*

Sunchoke

See *Jerusalem artichoke*

Sunflower

Annual or perennial herbs, sunflowers are now popularly grown for their edible seeds, which are dried and roasted, as well as for their attractive blossoms. Certain species are raised for their oils, but these aren't of garden significance.

Sunflowers grow easily and rapidly and can reach heights of 2½ to 15 feet, depending on variety and growing conditions. Their large, golden-yellow, daisylike flowers bloom from July until fall but require an 80- to 120-day growing season. Besides yielding seeds, sunflowers make excellent hedges, windbreaks, and back borders for gardens.

When to Plant

• Sow seeds outdoors in late spring.

Where to Plant

• Sunflowers are heavy feeders: The soil in which they're planted should have a pH of 6.0 to 7.5 and be well mixed with blood meal, compost, fish meal, or well-rotted manure, then loosely tilled. Sunflowers do best in full sun.

How to Plant

• Sow seeds 1 inch deep, 8 inches apart, in rows 2 feet apart. If you want very large heads with larger seeds, plant the seeds 1 foot apart in rows 2 feet apart.

Germination Time

• Seeds germinate in 10 days.

Care During Growth

• A mulch of compost and grass clippings is a good idea, as is plenty of water, especially during the 3 weeks when the flowers are developing. Water at the base of the plants, trying not to wet the heads or the foliage. Tall varieties need staking to prevent them from toppling as the heads become heavier. If you're after maximum flower size, water occasionally with manure tea and side-dress with aged manure of any kind.

• As the heads become ripe, you might want to protect them from birds (who love the seeds) by wrapping them loosely in netting, cheesecloth, or a piece of nylon stocking (too-tight wrapping may invite decay).

Maturation Time

• Sunflowers mature in 80 to 120 days, depending on variety.

Harvesting

• Harvest sunflowers when the backs of the heads become dry and begin to turn brown and the heads themselves tip downward. Be sure to get them before the seeds start to shatter. Cut off each head with about 1 foot of stem attached, and hang them to dry in a well-ventilated place. You can also let the heads dry in the garden— cover them with netting to protect against birds and to keep the seeds from falling.

Storing

• Once the seeds are dry, store them in open containers or in paper bags, where air and slight warmth can get at them. You can roast and salt them slightly if you like, or crack and eat them as is.

Diseases and Pests

• Birds, mildew, rust, verticillium wilt.

Garden Tips

• Take care not to overwater sunflowers. And water from the bottom, or mildew may develop.
• A good companion planting for sunflowers is cucumbers, which will climb sunflowers' tall staked stalks.

Kitchen Tips

• To deseed the flower heads, try scrubbing them across an old washboard.
• Sunflower seeds are nutritionally rich and particularly high in protein.
• Use hulled, dried or undried sunflower seeds as a substitute for nuts in almost any recipe.

· · ·

Sunscald ⚜

Sunscald of certain fruits (peppers and tomatoes are more prone to this) results when the weather is dry and hot and there is prolonged exposure to the sun. It is a plant's version of sunburn. Normally, foliage shades and protects fruits from strong direct sunlight. Insect and disease depredations of leaves can interfere with this protection, exposing the fruits to long periods of intense sunlight.

Manifestation

• White or yellow patches, like papery blisters, develop on the skins of the fruit. These may later turn brown, and they sometimes become infected by fungi. Tomatoes can be ruined by sunscald.

To Combat

• Be sure plants have ample water during long dry periods.
• Increase nitrogen in the garden soil, especially after plants begin setting fruit. This stimulates foliage production to shade the fruits.

- Shade the plants with a light covering of straw during intense sunny periods, or cover them lightly with cheesecloth.

- If sunscald is frequent in your garden, try growing susceptible plants in areas that receive some shade.

Sweet Balm

See *Lemon balm*

Sweet Marjoram

See *Marjoram*

Sweet Potato

Until recently sweet potatoes were considered growable only in warm areas, those with a long growing season. But there are now cultivars that can be grown in the North, although they must be treated as very tender annuals still requiring a long, warm growing season. Some varieties can actually stand early frosts. Growing them in raised beds and mulching with plastic mulch also increase the success of the crop in colder climates.

Sweet potatoes are extremely easy to grow, although they need approximately 100 warm, frost-free days and nights. They flourish even in very dry seasons. You can buy slips (sprouts) or start your own indoors. A single sweet potato can give rise to a multitude of plants (see "How to Plant"). The dark-orange-fleshed tubers commonly called yams are cultivated like sweet potatoes.

When to Plant

- *Indoors:* Set sweet potatoes to sprout in early to midspring, or about 8 weeks before setting out the slips.
- *Outdoors:* Set the slips you have grown or purchased in the garden in late spring or early summer, when the soil has become thoroughly warm. Any frost at this period of the tubers' development will very likely kill them.

Where to Plant

• *Outdoors:* The soil shouldn't be too rich in nitrogen—avoid compost and manures. In fact, sweet potatoes do well in very ordinary soil. Some wood ashes are desirable and perhaps a little bonemeal. The soil itself should be light, sandy, well drained, and on the acid side (pH 4.5 to 6.5). Some gardeners raise sweet potatoes successfully on clay soil. A sunny location is best. Raised beds are fine if your climate is inclined to be cool in early summer or early fall.

How to Plant

• *Indoors (to get slips for later planting outdoors):* Suspend each sweet potato in a jar or glass by means of three toothpicks, with the stem end up and the other end submerged in about 2 inches of water. Be sure to keep the water level constant. Set on a sunny windowsill or under constant grow lights. Warmth is essential. Each "eye" will sprout a slip, so a single sweet potato can produce 30 or more slips, easily enough for any home garden. You can snap off each slip when it is 4 inches long; at this point it can be set straight into the garden to form roots. Or, if it is too early to place them in the garden, plant the slips 2 inches deep in pots filled with half sand, half soil, and keep them under constant light, watering as needed, until the time for outdoor planting.

• *Outdoors:* If you're starting with purchased plants, or slips that have already developed roots, soak the roots in water for 1 hour before planting. Place the plants deep enough so that the roots are well covered, 18 inches apart, in rows 36 inches apart.

• For your own slips that have not yet developed roots, plant outdoors 2 inches deep, 18 inches apart, in rows 36 inches apart.

• Some gardeners plant slips in 1-foot-high ridges of soil, with the ridges 3 feet apart, claiming that these give the developing roots more room and allow for moisture conservation.

• After planting, firm the soil thoroughly around the plants and water them. Unrooted slips should be kept lightly moist. If you can, keep the newly planted slips shaded for a few days.

Care During Growth

• Sweet potatoes grow best at soil temperatures between 70° and 80°F. Mulching with plastic mulch helps preserve warmth; it also keeps weeds at bay.

• Pinch out any roots sprouting from stems that lie on the ground; otherwise they'll produce many small, unwanted sweet potatoes.

• Be sure the plants get plenty of water while they're forming fruit, particularly during dry weather.

Maturation Time

• Sweet potatoes are ready for harvest in 90 to 120 days, depending on variety and the warmth of summer days.

Harvesting

• Sweet potatoes grow quite close to the soil surface. Dig up a couple in early September to check their size. But you can wait until the first light frost. Then you *must* dig them up: Exposure to further cold reduces their storage life. Dig carefully to avoid bruising—they're very delicate at this stage and have almost no skin. Each slip you planted should give you several pounds of roots.

• If you damage any sweet potatoes, don't try to store them. Use them right away.

Storing

• Sweet potatoes must develop a protective skin before being stored. Keep them covered in a warm place (80° to 85°F if possible) with high humidity for 1 week. They'll then be covered with fairly tough skins.

• The flavor of sweet potatoes improves with storage—they become sweeter. Store them where it's dark, with fairly high humidity (to keep the skins from shriveling) and at a temperature between 55° and 60°F (no lower). A good method for storage is to wrap them individually in sheets of newspaper, then lay them on top of one another in cardboard boxes.

• Any sweet potatoes stored in the refrigerator should be used within a week.

Diseases and Pests

• Sweet potatoes have very few enemies. Occasionally, bacterial diseases, flea beetles, mealybugs, nematodes, thrips, or whiteflies.

Garden Tips

• Harvesting will be easier if you pull off all the vines first. Use a digging fork or a firm rake to unearth the sweets carefully.

• If your stored sweet potatoes become woody, it's probably because the storage temperature was too low.

Kitchen Tips

• Sweet potatoes won't turn dark after they're peeled if you plunge them into salted water—use 1 tablespoon salt to 1 quart water.

• You can remove the strings from cooked, mashed sweet potatoes or yams if you beat them with an electric mixer. The strings will adhere to the beaters.

• You can make an interesting sweet potato flour if you peel, then slice sweet potatoes very thin and dry them in a low oven until they're as crisp as potato chips. Then grind them in the blender. Store in jars.

Substitute this flour for a portion of the white or whole wheat flour when you make bread, muffins, or other baked goods.

Swiss Chard

Also called chard, this is a spinachlike green related to beets. It is hardy, easy to grow, and will give you a crop from late spring right through to fall frost. It stands both hot and cold weather well and in many ways could be called a gardener's dream. There are green, crinkly-leaved varieties and some with bright red stalks. The young leaves are used in salads, very much as young spinach is, and the larger ones—also as spinach is—are served as cooked greens.

When to Plant
• Since the seedlings are fairly tolerant of light frosts, you can plant chard seeds as early in the spring as the ground can be easily worked.
• If you want young plants later in the season, sow seeds again at the beginning of late summer for fall harvesting.

Where to Plant
• Swiss chard prefers sandy, well-drained soil (pH 7.0 to 7.5) that's rich in nitrogen: Till in composted grass clippings, leaves, and well-rotted manure. Although it likes sun, it grows well in partial shade.

How to Plant
• Sow seeds ½ inch deep, 3 inches apart, in rows 18 inches apart.

Germination Time
• Seeds will germinate in 7 to 12 days.

Care During Growth
• When the seedlings are 3 inches high, thin them to about 6 inches apart.
• Little care is needed during growth, since chard thrives even during hot, dry spells without much watering. But if you've sown seeds in midsummer for fall harvesting, keep the seedbed moist until the seedlings are up and flourishing.

Maturation Time
• Chard reaches full maturity 55 to 60 days after seeds are sown, but you can begin harvesting tender leaves in as little as 30 days.

Harvesting
• You can harvest Swiss chard the whole season long: Begin when the leaves are 3 to 4 inches long, and use them in salads. When they reach 8 inches in length, they're right for

cooking. Your plants will continue to produce if you keep cutting off the outer leaves. You can also cut off the entire plant, leaving about 2 inches above the crown: As long as the root is undamaged, new leaves will continue to be produced.

Storing

• Wash chard before storing, and keep it very cold—as close to 32°F as possible, without freezing. It will last for a week or so.

• For long-term storage, freeze chard. It freezes very well and can be used in cooking all winter long.

Diseases and Pests

• Leaf miners, tarnished plant bugs.

Garden Tips

• Don't try to transplant the seedlings when you thin your plants—Swiss chard doesn't take well to being moved. Discard the thinnings, or use them in salads.

• Don't use any leaves that are longer than 10 inches—they're tough and bitter. If your whole plants grow too tall, cut them to 1 inch or so above ground level and tender new leaves will grow.

Kitchen Tips

• Remember, the only chard worth cooking and eating is young, fresh, and crisp. Discard any leaves that are rubbery or wilted.

• Like spinach, chard needs no cooking water except what clings to the leaves when they're washed. But it needs slightly longer cooking than spinach.

• Don't use salt when cooking Swiss chard—it darkens the leaves.

Syrphid Flies

Sometimes called syrphus flies or hover flies, wasplike syrphid flies can often be seen above blossoms, drinking nectar from the plants. Adult flies also eat the honeydew of aphids. The larvae of syrphid flies eat aphids, scales, and other soft-bodied insects. Plant flowers here and there near or among your vegetables to attract these valuable predators.

Tampala

Tampala, an edible variety of a popular garden annual, is also known as amaranth spinach, edible Amaranthus, hinn choy, and vegetable amaranth. It's often thought of as a hot-weather substitute for spinach; unlike spinach, it isn't at all bothered by summer heat. It is used exactly as spinach is: the tender, growing tips in salads, the more mature leaves cooked. Its flavor somewhat resembles that of an artichoke.

When to Plant
• Sow seeds early in the spring, after danger of hard frost is past.

Where to Plant
• Tampala grows well in ordinary garden soil (pH 6 to 7). If the soil is very rich you'll get larger leaves, but this isn't necessarily desirable. Tampala needs full sun.

How to Plant
• Sow seeds ¼ inch deep, 6 inches apart, in rows 18 inches apart.

Germination Time
• Seeds germinate in 7 days.

Care During Growth
• When the plants are 3 inches high, thin them to 18 inches apart. The thinnings can be transplanted elsewhere, at 18-inch distances.

• Tampala needs practically no care unless your season is extra dry, in which case a little watering now and then is helpful.

Maturation Time
• For salad use, the first leaves are ready in about 40 days, when the plants are about 8 inches tall. For cooking like spinach, the plants are ready in 60 to 70 days.

Harvesting
• Tampala will produce all summer. You can cut off the leaves as needed (as you do with Swiss chard), leaving the rest of the plant to continue producing.

Kitchen Tip
• You can also use tampala stems in cooking—treat them as you would asparagus.

Tarnished Plant Bugs

These ¼-inch long, yellowish brown, oval insects suck sap from buds, leaves, and fruits, injecting a toxic substance into plants as they do so. The adults overwinter in garden debris, becoming active in early spring and laying eggs in all parts of the host plants. They attack beans, beets, cabbage, cauliflower, celery, cucumbers, potatoes, strawberries, Swiss chard, and turnips, as well as many flowers and trees. They are extremely active bugs.

Manifestation
• The feeding of tarnished plant bugs causes great distortion in plants. Leaves are deformed, stems are discolored and wilted, the tips of new shoots are blackened, flowers fall from the plants and thus don't produce fruit, and what fruits there are, are often dwarfed and pitted.

To Combat
• Keep weeds down in the garden— the bugs feed and breed in them.

• When you see new shoots or leaf tips blackening, spray with pyrethrum, rotenone, or sabadilla sprays once a week.
• Covering vegetables with fine netting will keep these bugs off.
• Remove all debris from the garden in the fall to prevent the bugs from overwintering there.

. . .

Tarragon

Also known as French tarragon, or estragon, this is a semihardy, vigorous, perennial herb whose long, narrow leaves have an aniselike flavor and are used fresh, dried, or frozen in salads, soups, as a flavoring for vinegar, and as a garnish. Tarragon rarely forms seeds and is propagated by either root divisions or cuttings. It grows to a height of about 2 feet.

When to Plant
• Either divide rootstocks and replant them or place new tarragon plants in the garden in early spring, after the last frost.

. . .

Where to Plant
• Tarragon grows best in poor soil that is not too acid (pH 5.5 to 6.5). The leaves are most flavorful when the plants are grown in stony or sandy soil and with not too much moisture. It will grow in full sun or partial shade.

How to Plant

• Set root divisions or plants 1 foot apart in rows 2 feet apart. If you're rooting cuttings indoors, place them in moist sand under filtered light. Gradually increase the light as the roots become well formed, and, when the seedlings look quite sturdy, place them in the garden.

Care During Growth

• Tarragon needs practically no attention. It rarely even needs watering.

• If your winters are very cold, it's a good idea to cut the plants to the ground before frost and cover the bed with a light mulch of leaves or straw.

Harvesting

• You can pick off leaves at any time during the growing season; you can also make several harvests of the tender top growth during a single season. The plants renew themselves.

Storing

• Tarragon leaves freeze very well. Wash them quickly, blot dry, spread them on a cloth, and place in the freezer. Once frozen, the leaves can be stored in a freezer jar.

• To dry tarragon leaves for storage, place them singly and loosely on a screen or piece of coarsely woven material and keep them in a dark place with good air circulation. Stir the leaves lightly once a day. When they're thoroughly dry, put them in airtight bottles or jars.

Garden Tips

• Never use fertilizers, manure, or other nutrient enhancements on the tarragon bed. Growing in rich soil reduces the fine flavor of the leaves.

• Once every 3 years, dig up your tarragon plants and divide the rootstocks into several sections, planting each separately. You'll have tarragon plants forever.

• Tarragon is said to be an excellent companion plant for every vegetable in the garden!

Kitchen Tips

• One of the finest vinegars for all kitchen uses is tarragon vinegar. Put several sprigs of fresh tarragon in a bottle, add white wine vinegar, and let the mixture steep for a few days before using. You can leave the tarragon in the bottle—it will continue to add its flavor to the vinegar.

• Add finely chopped, fresh tarragon to all kinds of sauces, especially cream sauces, and to fish and egg dishes.

• Tarragon is one of the best herbs to use with chicken. Soak 1 teaspoon of dried tarragon in ½ cup dry white wine for ½ hour. Pour this mixture over the chicken, then cook it any way you want.

Thrips 🦗

Thrips are ¹⁄₁₆-inch-long insects with specialized mouth parts for rasping plant tissues and sucking out the juices. The adults are dark yellow to brown (when you can see them), have fringed wings, and are extremely active. The females lay white, oval eggs in the interiors of leaves and stems. The eggs hatch into pale, wingless nymphs that immediately start feeding. There can be as many as eight generations within a single season. They appear in late spring and remain numerous into midsummer.

Some thrips are adapted to particular plants only; others attack many kinds indiscriminately, injuring leaves, flowers, stems, and bark. Among vulnerable edible plants are beans, blueberries, cabbage, carrots, cauliflower, celery, collards, corn, cucumbers, grapes, leeks, lettuce, melons, onions, peas, potatoes, pumpkins, shallots, squashes, strawberries, sweet potatoes, tomatoes, and turnips. These insects can be quite injurious—onions, particularly, can suffer great damage from them. In addition, thrips can carry viral diseases from plant to plant.

Manifestation

• Leaves develop brown or yellow, sometimes silvery, blotches, or turn wholly white. Leaves and branches wilt. Occasionally the entire plant withers and falls over.

To Combat

• Sheets of shiny aluminum foil laid down as a mulch are said to confuse and repel thrips from plants in the vicinity.
• Since thrips proliferate rapidly, check several times a week for them.

If you see any, a hard spray with a hose will dislodge them. Do this daily for a while.
• Some gardeners report that frequent spraying with soapy water keeps thrips off plants.
• Pyrethrum spray, used frequently, is effective.
• Natural enemies of thrips are lacewing larvae, ladybugs, syrphid fly larvae, and toads. Eggs of the first three of these are obtainable from many garden supply houses.

Thyme

There are many scented varieties of thyme (lemon thyme, oregano thyme, and others) but *Thymus vulgaris*, also known as common thyme, English thyme, or French thyme, is the most common in culinary use. It is a semihardy, perennial, bushy herb that generally grows 6 to 10 inches high. It can be grown from seed or by root division and is largely pest free. It may die back in very cold winters unless it is mulched.

When to Plant
• Plant seeds outdoors as early in the spring as you can, after danger of frost has passed.

Where to Plant
• Thyme likes a light, slightly sandy, and very well-drained soil a little on the alkaline side (pH 7.5 to 8.0). It also needs plenty of sun.

How to Plant
• If you think your soil is too acid, dig in some wood ashes before planting. Sow seeds, or set out transplants, 12 inches apart in rows 15 inches apart.

Germination Time
• Seeds germinate in 7 to 14 days.

Care During Growth
• Keep cultivating lightly around the plants, and remove all weeds as they appear. Thyme is rather slow growing, so be patient.
• If your winters are cold, it's safer to mulch the plants before the first sharp frost.

Maturation Time
• Cut leaves anytime. Established plants mature in 50 days.

Harvesting
• Harvest thyme leaves throughout the growing season, stripping leaves from the stems when they are about ½ inch long, preferably early in the morning.

Storing
• To dry thyme leaves for storage, strew them loosely over a screen and keep them in a dark place with good air circulation. Stir the leaves lightly once a day. When they're thoroughly dry, put them in airtight bottles or jars.

Garden Tips
• Thyme plants tend to become woody and produce coarser leaves when they get to be 3 or 4 years old. Dividing the plants and planting the divisions separately will take care of this. Or plant new ones every third or fourth year.
• Thyme, with its delicate, pink-violet blossoms, makes a very attractive edging plant.
• Thyme is very attractive to bees.
• Thyme is said to deter cabbage-worms, so plant it among your cabbages.

• • •

Kitchen Tips

• The way to add thyme to any food is to rub it well between your palms and let the pieces drop into the dish or pot.

• Manhattan clam chowder (the chowder made with tomatoes) just isn't chowder without thyme.

• Add thyme to any meat stew, particularly lamb.

• Because lamb has such an affinity for thyme, you should rub it well over a leg of lamb before roasting.

• • •

Tipburn 🐞

This is a disease of lettuce, in which the ends of the leaves turn brown and wilt. It is thought to be the result of a calcium deficiency in the soil. If you see evidence of tipburn in your lettuce, mix into the soil some finely ground eggshells, oyster shell, dolomitic limestone, or wood ashes.

Toads 🐞

The common garden toad (*Bufo americanus*) found in many gardens eats thousands upon thousands of insects over a summer, as well as quantities of ants, armyworms, caterpillars, cutworms, mosquitoes, and slugs. If your garden has reasonably moist areas you may already have a toad or two. Provide moisture by sinking a shallow pan in a shady and sheltered area. You can bring a few toads in from lakes, ponds, and swamps, or purchase them from some plant nurseries.

Tobacco Budworms

See *Corn earworms*

Tobacco Mosaic Virus

See *Mosaic virus*

Tomato

Tomatoes are a tender crop; they love heat and are very sensitive to frost. Once they get started and the weather is warm, most varieties yield continuously until the end of the season. Because they need warm soil, a black plastic mulch can get them off to an early start.

There are determinate and indeterminate types of tomatoes. Determinate types may be best if you live in a short-season area. These are generally early tomatoes that form compact plants and finish producing once the fruits have set. Their yields are high, but their flavor isn't considered the best. The more common—and tastier—tomatoes are indeterminate. Their vines continue growing throughout the summer, and, though fruiting starts a little later than in the determinate types, they produce all season long, until frost. Common tomato varieties, unless stated otherwise, are indeterminate.

Many gardeners start tomato seeds indoors for later transplanting outside, but most seeds can be sown directly in the garden once the soil has warmed. They'll grow more slowly to begin with, but they almost always catch up with transplants. Some varieties are more cold resistant than others and can be planted earlier in the spring.

Try staking tomatoes if you're pressed for space. The plants can be grown closer together, giving high yield in a small area. Tied loosely to trellises or poles, they receive more sun and air, are less prey to insects and disease, and are easier to harvest.

When to Plant
• *Indoors:* Sow seeds in early spring, or about 7 weeks before the most likely frost-free date.

• *Outdoors:* Plant seedlings when day and night temperatures are above 55°F, usually in late spring or early summer.

• The best soil temperature for quick germination of tomato seeds is 70° to 80°F.

• Purchased seedlings have usually been hardened off. Those you've grown yourself should be hardened off beginning in late spring by being introduced to the outdoors daily, during the warmest part of the day, for a few hours.

Where to Plant
• Choose a warm site for tomatoes— a southern slope or a raised bed is best—and a location that receives full sun. The soil should contain humus and be loose, deeply worked, and well drained, with plenty of phosphorus but not too much nitrogen at

the beginning. It should also be on the acid side (pH 5.75 to 6.75).

How to Plant

• Indoors

Fill flats (trays) or small pots with moist, sterilized potting mixture. In flats, sow seeds ⅓ inch deep, 1 inch apart. In pots, plant 3 seeds equidistant from one another, around the center of each pot.

Grow seeds on a warm, sunny windowsill or under grow lights turned on at least 12 hours a day.

After planting, and before the seeds sprout, you can prevent the soil's drying out and avoid further watering by covering the flats or pots with clear plastic or slipping them into plastic bags. Leave room for a little air to enter so the soil surface won't mildew. Remove the plastic when the seedlings appear, but continue to keep the soil lightly moist.

• Outdoors

Sow seeds ⅓ inch deep, 3 inches apart, in rows 24 inches apart.

For transplants, choose a cloudy day for setting into the garden. Dig the holes 2 feet apart on all sides, and deep enough for the plants to be set in about 1 inch deeper than they grew in their pots (to force more roots to grow and give

sturdier plants). After burying the roots and part of the stem, make a circular depression around the base of each plant to be used for watering—this both saves water and keeps the foliage from getting wet. Follow the transplanting with a light application of fish emulsion solution, then water daily.

You can save lots of garden space by staking, caging, or trellising tomato plants. Space them 1 foot apart in rows 3 feet apart. If you are using stakes (4 feet is a good height), drive each one about 5 inches into the ground at 1-foot intervals, then plant a seedling beside it. Caging can wait until the plants are about 1 foot high. If you're trellising, place seedlings at 1-foot intervals, 2 inches in front of the trellis.

Germination Time

• Seeds germinate in 5 to 12 days.

Care During Growth

• Indoors

Keep the seedlings in full sunlight as long as possible, at daytime temperatures of 70°F or above, and nighttime temperatures above 60°F. When seedlings in flats show two pairs of leaves, transplant them to 4-inch pots, 1 plant per pot. At this time, seedlings you've already grown in pots should be thinned to the 1 sturdiest plant per pot.

If indoor-grown seedlings seem ready for the garden before warm weather comes, replant each one to a still larger pot, a little deeper than it grew before. Continue to keep them where it's moist, warm, and light.

• Outdoors

When seedlings are 3 inches tall, thin them to stand 2 feet apart.

It's essential that tomato plants receive a constant water supply during fruiting (but avoid wetting the foliage). Give the plants a boost of manure tea every 2 or 3 weeks. When you see fruits beginning to form, add a top dressing of soil mixed with compost or cottonseed meal, or a 2-inch mulch of grass clippings, hay, peat moss, or strawy manure. Many gardeners favor aluminized plastic film during the hottest part of the summer—as do the organic mulches just listed, it cools the soil, keeps weeds down, conserves water, and protects the fruit from soil contact.

Do a little pruning of suckers at the joints between the main stems and branches to keep the plants from putting too much energy into side foliage production and let more light penetrate to the interior. Determinate varieties don't need pruning.

If you are staking or trellising your tomato plants, tie them to the supports loosely; soft yarn or torn strips of sheeting are best, but you can use twist ties if you don't fasten them too tightly. Or use wire cages for less work. Staked plants receive better ventilation and more sunlight, but they need mulching more than those allowed to sprawl, since they dry out more quickly.

About 1 month before the first expected frost, pinch off the tips of all tomato vines and remove any marble-sized fruits (these won't have time to mature). These measures will speed ripening of the larger green tomatoes.

To protect plants from light frosts in the fall, cover them at night with plastic bags, newspapers, or even light blankets. Remove these during the day when the sun warms things up.

Maturation Time

• Tomatoes can take 52 (early tomatoes) to 100 days from seed to harvest, depending on variety. It takes about 40 days for a harvestable tomato to develop from a blossom.

Harvesting

• A tomato is usually ready to pick about 6 days after it shows the first sign of red. Harvest promptly to stimulate further production. A ripe tomato will stay in good condition on the vine for only about 2 or 3 days.

• For canning, pick tomatoes at the moment of ripeness—don't let them get soft.

• Pick the last tomatoes of the season (you can pickle green ones, or cook them, or use them in salads) before the first killing frost. A frost will ruin them.

Storing

• Only green (unripe) tomatoes, and those without any blemishes, can be stored for any appreciable time. You · can delay ripening for 3 to 4 weeks by keeping them at 50° to 55°F; at 65° to 72°F, they'll ripen in about 2 weeks. Keep them in the dark, either wrapped individually in newspapers or placed so they don't touch each other. Check weekly, removing any that show signs of ripening, and keep those at room temperature until they're usable.

Diseases and Pests

• Alternaria disease, anthracnose, armyworms, bacterial diseases, birds, blister beetles, blossom-end rot, borers, Botrytis blight, cabbage loopers, Colorado potato beetles, corn earworms, cutworms, damping off, flea beetles, fusarium wilt, green peach aphids, hornworms, leafhoppers, mealybugs, mosaic virus, nematodes, slugs, squirrels, sunscald, thrips, verticillium wilt, whiteflies.

Garden Tips

• Plum tomatoes are more meaty, and best for making tomato paste or puree.

• Beefsteak tomatoes are among the most flavorful, but they don't store well.

• Cherry tomatoes, because of their thicker skins, repel corn earworms (also called tomato fruitworms).

• At the most, 12 tomato plants will give more than enough fruit for an average family, including plenty for canning and storing. But plant more seeds than you think you'll want—not all make it to transplant size.

• If you are planting seeds indoors, keep them away from a gas stove or gas heater: The tiniest amount of gas will kill tomato seedlings.

• If indoor seedlings are becoming spindly, either they're not getting enough light or they're getting too much heat.

• It's best to move your tomato patch each year.

• A couple of weeks before transplanting seedlings to the outdoors, cover the tomato bed with black plastic. This warms the soil.

• When you buy transplants, look for stocky ones that are wider than they are tall.

• Don't smoke tobacco either before or while you handle tomato plants—

you may transmit tobacco mosaic virus to them.

• If a transplant is tall and gangly, dig a long, 4-inch furrow and gently bend the plant over, along the furrow, so that much of the stem (except the top 6 inches) can be covered with soil. New roots will grow from the buried portion, and you'll have a higher-producing plant.

• If cutworms are a problem in your garden, remove both ends of small cans—small cans of frozen orange juice concentrate are excellent—and half-fill them with soil. Sink each can into the garden with the top 2 inches above ground level. Set a seedling in each can, and fill with soil. Water well. Leave the cans as you have set them— the cutworms can't climb the barriers of their sides, and the plants will grow fine inside.

• Avoid putting too much nitrogen in the soil before tomato plants set fruit—it promotes heavy foliage development and delays fruiting. But once fruiting starts, nitrogen is needed. An occasional wetting with manure tea is fine at this time.

• Banana peels contain phosphorus and potash, valuable to tomato plants. Cut a few into small pieces, and bury them in your tomato patch.

• Tomato flowers are easily pollinated by wind, insects, or even a passing jostle.

• The larger suckers that you cut off tomato plants can often be planted right away in the garden. Bury them up to their first leaves, then water well. It may take several days for them to perk up, but they generally survive and thrive.

• Tomatoes that ripen in full sun have more flavor and vitamin C than those grown in the shade of their leaves.

• Among vine-ripened tomatoes, the smaller ones generally have more flavor.

• An occasional spraying with diluted fish emulsion will increase the yield of tomato plants.

• Excess heat in the height of summer will cause fewer fruits to set and may produce leathery patches on the bottoms of tomatoes. To avoid this, do more watering and mulching.

• The low temperatures of early fall can cause tomatoes to crack.

• Like corn, tomatoes begin to lose flavor the moment they're picked.

• If a frost is imminent, pull up your tomato vines and hang them, roots up, in a warm place. The tomatoes that are mature will ripen slowly, even though the plants wilt.

• Good companion plantings for tomatoes are said to be asparagus, basil, cabbage, carrots, celery, chives, endive, lamb's-quarters, lettuce, lima beans, marigolds (which are said to deter tomato hornworms), mint, nasturtiums, onions, parsley, radishes, and spinach.

• Do not plant kohlrabi or potatoes among your tomatoes.

• If you want to attract bees, plant borage among your tomatoes.

• Hornworms are attracted to four-o'clock flowers: Plant a border of them around your patch as a trap crop; the worms are easier to see and pick off from the flowers than they are from the tomato plants.

• Many gardeners plant borage, which is said to repel hornworms, among their tomatoes.

• Tomato leaves are poisonous if eaten.

Kitchen Tips

• Vine-ripened tomatoes are much more flavorful than those picked green and then ripened.

• Don't put green tomatoes in the sun to ripen—they often soften before they get red. Instead, put them in a brown paper bag and set in a dark spot at room temperature for 3 or 4 days.

• A tomato won't ripen properly once it's been refrigerated. And a ripe tomato loses flavor if it's refrigerated for more than 2 hours.

• You can freeze whole tomatoes or tomatoes cut in quarters. Place them in a single layer on a cookie sheet, set in the freezer, and when they're frozen solid transfer them to a plastic bag and keep frozen. (Hold a frozen tomato under cold water for a few seconds and the skin will slip off.)

• To peel tomatoes: Bring water to a boil, turn off the heat, and place the tomatoes in the water. Remove with a slotted spoon after 1 minute or so, pierce the center top with a sharp knife, and peel the skin down in strips.

• To prepare tomatoes for stuffing, peel, seed, and salt and pepper them, then turn them cut side down on a plate and chill well. This process will remove all excess water and make them easier to handle.

Tomato Fruitworms

See *Corn earworms*

Tomato Hornworms

See *Hornworms*

Transplanting 🔙

If you're raising seedlings indoors, use individual peat pots rather than flats—there'll be less root damage when you transplant. Before burying the peat pots with their seedlings in the garden, carefully cut out the circular bottom of each pot with a pair of scissors, being sure not to cut the roots. Or make holes through the walls of the pot here and there with a sharp-pointed pencil.

Don't transplant seedlings in the morning—it's often hard for them to face up quickly to the bright sun later in the day. The best time to transplant seedlings to the garden is late in the afternoon or on a mild, cloudy day with little wind.

When removing a plant from its earlier location for transplanting, take plenty of the surrounding soil with it to disturb the roots as little as possible. Never expose the roots of transplants to dry air. Always water seedlings before transplanting. Some gardeners swear by dipping the roots in a mild fish emulsion solution before transplanting.

The day before transplanting seedlings to the garden, make a compost or manure tea; at transplanting time, fill the planting holes with the strained tea and do your transplanting when the tea has drained out of the holes. Your seedlings will get off to a better start. If you have a heavy clay soil, dig planting holes extra large and fill in with humus-rich soil around the transplants.

Place each seedling in its planting hole about ½ inch deeper than it grew indoors. Water seedlings immediately after transplanting with a very mild solution of fish emulsion, manure tea, or other liquid plant food. Shielding each newly transplanted seedling with an inverted flowerpot for a couple of days helps it adjust to its new location. Be sure the bottom of the pot (now on top) has a hole in it.

Trellising 🔙

Tying plants to grow vertically lets you squeeze more plants in less space. Trellising exposes more leaves to sunlight and air, and makes harvesting easier. Any plant that vines—cucumbers, muskmelons, peas, pole beans, pumpkins, squashes, even watermelons—can be trained to grow up a fence or trellis. Just tie them loosely here and there. The heavier fruits can be supported by slings made of nylon stockings, which expand as the fruits grow. Dried sunflower stalks from the season before can be used as poles to form tepee-style trellises for peas and beans.

Trichogramma Wasps

These are very minute chalcid wasps and are famous for laying their eggs inside the eggs of a multitude of harmful insects, thus killing them before they hatch. They help keep the following in check: armyworms, cabbage loopers, cabbageworms, codling moths, corn earworms, cutworms, gypsy moths, hornworms, and Oriental fruit moths, among others. You can buy trichogramma wasp eggs from many nurseries and garden supply houses.

Turnip

Turnips are a hardy crop that grows best in cool weather. They take light frosts easily—in fact, as with rutabagas, their flavor improves after frost. These vegetables are grown for both their roots and their green tops, which are delicious when cooked. Turnip greens can be harvested continuously from the growing roots; they replace themselves until after the first frost.

A variety of turnip called broccoli raab is grown mainly for its greens and, when overwintered in the ground, is highly prized for the delicate seedstalk it sends up.

When to Plant
• In early spring, sow seeds directly in the garden as soon as the ground can be worked, or about 1 month before the last expected frost. For a fall crop, sow seeds 7 to 8 weeks before the first expected frost.
• You can also sow seeds every 2 weeks, beginning with the first spring planting, until late spring, to get successive crops; then make a fall planting, as just described.

Where to Plant
• Turnips do best in deeply spaded, organically rich garden soil with plenty of phosphorus and potash. They prefer slightly acid soil (pH 5.50 to 6.75) and tolerate partial shade.

How to Plant
• Spade the bed about 1 foot deep, and plant the seeds ½ inch deep, 5 inches apart, in rows 15 inches apart.

• Or sow seeds thinly but evenly along the row for thinning later.

• After sowing seeds, keep the bed moist by daily misting, especially if the weather is warm.

Germination Time

• Turnip seeds will germinate at temperatures in the 20s—and as high as 100°F! And they are quick to sprout, usually in less than 1 week.

Care During Growth

• Thin turnip plants to 6 inches apart when they are 3 to 4 inches high (use the thinned tender leaves for cooking or in salads).

• Turnip plants need no particular care while they're growing.

Maturation Time

• Turnip greens can generally be harvested 30 days after seeds are sown, as can the roots of some quick-growing varieties of small turnips. Other turnips are ready for digging in 35 to 80 days, depending on variety.

Harvesting

• Turnip roots are mature when they're 2 inches or more in diameter. Dig them out carefully to avoid cutting or bruising them, especially those you plan to store. Cut off the tops, leaving about 1 inch of stem.

• Turnips are sweeter and have much more flavor if you harvest them after

a sharp frost. The harvest period generally lasts 2 to 4 weeks.

Storing

• Turnips store very well. Be sure the roots are dry, and also be sure they have no cuts or bruises. They should be kept where it's dark and cold (32° to 40°F) and—this is very important—in high humidity; otherwise they'll shrivel and become useless. Properly stored, they'll keep for several months.

• Turnips can also be stored right in your garden. Once frost hits, cut the tops down to a couple of inches and cover the whole area with at least 5 inches of mulch—hay, shredded leaves, or straw are good. Snow also makes an excellent added mulch. It's a good idea to mark the rows with stakes so you'll know where the turnips are when you want to dig them up through the winter.

Diseases and Pests

• Aphids, bacterial diseases, blackleg, cabbage loopers, cabbage maggots, cabbageworms, clubroot, cutworms, flea beetles, scab, tarnished plant bugs, thrips.

Garden Tips

• If the soil is warm when you plant turnip seeds, don't be surprised to see them sprout in a day or two!

• Try planting turnip seeds between rows of corn—this arrangement is a great space saver.

• If you have occasion to transplant turnips, remove the lower leaves first. The transplanted roots will recover faster if they don't have too much top growth to nourish at the outset. Good companion plantings for turnips are said to be beets, celery, dill, lavender, mint, onions, peas, rosemary, sage, and thyme.

Kitchen Tips

• Turnips are an undeservedly much-neglected vegetable! You can boil them and mash them with butter and nutmeg. Or cube them and serve them with or without cubed carrots.

They're also great in stew, and delicious sautéed with a little onion.

• Boiled turnips are sweeter if you don't skin them before cooking.

• If you find the consistency of mashed turnips a little thin, mash in a boiled potato.

• Turnips with a strong flavor can be made milder if you parboil them in salted water for about 4 minutes, then drain and continue as your recipe directs.

• Add a little sherry to mashed turnips.

• Turnips and pork go together. Add some turnips to the pot 45 minutes before a pork roast is done, cover, and continue roasting.

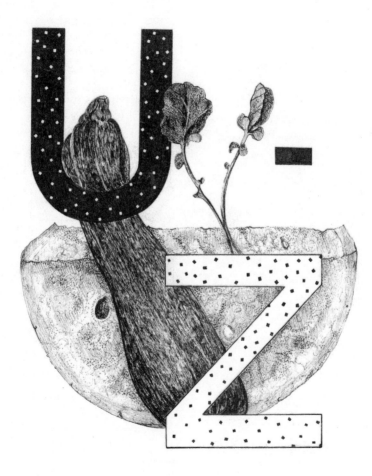

Upland Cress

See *Garden cress*

Vegetable Oyster

See *Salsify*

Vegetable Spaghetti

See *Squash*

Verticillium Wilt 🕷

This is a soil-borne fungal disease that afflicts many plants, especially when there is a prolonged stretch of wet, hot (75°F or more) weather. The fungus interferes with the transfer of water through plants' vascular systems. The spores tend to persist in the soil, although they decrease in number when no host plants are present. Edible garden plants most frequently affected are eggplants, okra, peppers, potatoes, strawberries, sunflowers, and tomatoes. Verticillium wilt may not kill a plant, but it reduces its vigor and the size and number of its fruits.

Manifestation
• Older (bottom) leaves wilt, turn yellow, then become dry and brown. Younger leaves lose their luster and often curl. The tips of new shoots may wilt. Many plants will lose most or all of their leaves. Strawberries or tomatoes may show an ash-gray mold.

• If a plant shows any of these symptoms, cut through a stem and examine it: If the interior is dark brown or black, verticillium wilt is probably the cause.

To Combat
• To lower the infestation in the soil, practice crop rotation: Avoid planting vulnerable hosts in the part of your garden where verticillium wilt has struck for 2 to 3 years. Plant nonsusceptible crops in these beds.
• Destroy diseased plants by burning them.
• Avoid high-nitrogen fertilizers, which stimulate fungal growth.
• Don't crowd your plants—see that they get plenty of aeration.
• Look for wilt-resistant varieties when buying plants.

Vine Borers

See *Borers*

Watercress

An extremely hardy aquatic perennial, watercress belongs to the mustard family. It grows primarily in slow-running water, such as a stream or brook. Grown elsewhere (as in the garden), it should be treated as an annual, since it can't survive a winter unless covered with water. Watercress can take light frosts.

When to Plant
• *Indoors:* Plant seeds in very early spring, or start root cuttings about 2 weeks later.
• *Outdoors:* Set out seedlings or already-rooted plants in late midspring, or when danger of hard frost is past.

Where to Plant
• Watercress grows best in the shallow edges of clean, flowing fresh water, where it gets some shade. It's often possible to grow watercress in your garden if you have a very moist, shady spot where the soil is sandy, with pH of 6.0 to 6.5.

How to Plant
• Indoors
   Fill a flowerpot with sandy soil and set it in a pan of water in a cool spot with filtered light. Sow seeds

thickly, ¼ inch deep. Keep water in the pan at all times. When the seedlings are 1 inch tall, thin them to stand about 1 inch apart.

Or, insert broken-off stems of watercress in a pot of wet sand in semifiltered sunlight. They'll develop roots if you keep the sand wet at all times.

• Outdoors

Transplant seedlings when they're 3 inches tall, or cuttings that have developed strong roots, in a shallow stream where the water doesn't flow too fast.

Or place seedlings or cuttings in a moist, sandy, shady spot in your garden.

Germination Time
• Seeds germinate in 12 days.

Care During Growth
• Apart from seeing that the ground never dries out where you've planted watercress, it needs no care.

Maturation Time
• A watercress plant will reach full growth in 50 days, but stems and leaves can often be harvested much earlier.

Harvesting
• You can cut stems when they're 4 to 6 inches long, both in the spring and in the fall.

Garden Tip
• Watercress is at its best and most piquant during cool weather, when the leaves and stems are a bright green.

Kitchen Tips
• Watercress is thought by many to be an appetite stimulant.

• Wash watercress, then stand it upright in a glass of cold water. Wrap glass and all in a plastic bag and refrigerate. Fresh cress will keep for about 1 week this way.

• Watercress is particularly delicious minced and cooked in cream soups or clear bouillon.

• Watercress makes one of the finest herb butters. Chop the watercress (not too fine), and mix it well into butter at room temperature. Use this as a sandwich spread or for a sauce over baked potatoes or other hot vegetables.

• • •

Watering 🦫

Don't water your garden during midday, especially in hot weather—doing so can cause petal or leaf burn. The best time to water is in the late afternoon, but early enough so moisture on the leaves will evaporate before the sun goes down. Wet foliage at night is an invitation to damping off, mildew, and other plant diseases.

When watering tiny seeds, use a mist spray if possible; otherwise you risk flushing the seeds out of the ground.

In the absence of rain, a garden should be watered thoroughly twice a week. Give it 1 inch of water each time: You can measure the water by setting a pan under the sprinkler near one of the plants in the garden bed; leave the sprinkler on until there's an inch of water in the pan. If you're watering by hand, do only a few plants at a time to ensure that each of them gets enough. Too-shallow watering encourages roots to grow close to the surface, where they can easily dry out. Avoid keeping soil waterlogged—constant water in the soil prevents the plants from absorbing oxygen through their roots.

Bulbs or plants going into the ground in the fall should be watered at the time of planting and weekly thereafter, until the ground freezes. The same is true for all the perennials in your garden—they need watering up to the time the ground is hard frozen.

Tap water is generally too cold for growing seedlings indoors. Let it come to room temperature before using.

Watermelon

See *Melon*

Weeding ⌐🥄

The most important time to weed your garden is early in the spring: before planting seeds, and during the two weeks following seed planting. After that, just an occasional weed-pull will do the job. The main thing is to keep weeds from becoming established.

Sheets of black plastic can cover your whole garden bed and totally eliminate weeds, which cannot grow when light is cut off. Just make holes for your plants, and anchor the sheets with stones.

Use a kitchen fork to stir the soil, not too deeply, around seedlings. This method can catch weeds before they get too large or deeply embedded. Be careful not to damage the seedlings' roots. Here's a quick way to weed without disturbing the soil around fragile seedlings: With a small pair of sharp-pointed scissors, go around your garden bed snipping the young weeds off just below the soil line. They seldom come back. Leave the carcasses where they fall— they'll become mulch.

A deep mulch around plants also helps eradicate weeds.

It has been reported that pouring boiling water over poison ivy plants where they emerge from the ground makes them disappear entirely. Another method of eradicating poison ivy is to cut the vine at ground level and put a large stone over the stump. This cuts off light, so the plant can't survive.

Are tough weeds hard to pull up? Try using pliers.

Dandelion roots, which are deep, can be more easily removed if you make a small excavation around each stem and let your garden hose slowly and thoroughly drench the root area. After this soaking, the long taproot will come out very easily with a slow, steady pull.

Quack grass releases toxins into the soil that inhibit the growth of other plants. Get rid of it early, and keep it out of the garden thereafter; the toxins can remain in the soil even after the weed has been eliminated.

Any hardy, persistent weed, such as quack grass, can be removed permanently if you cut the stem flush to the ground, leaving no green whatsoever aboveground, and repeat this once a week or so until the stored nutriments in the roots are depleted. Continuous attack of this kind—depriving the tiniest emergence of green stem from receiving sunlight—will eliminate the weed.

But not all weeds are obnoxious! Some have beautiful foliage and/or blossoms. You can leave attractive ones in some spots of your garden if you have unused space.

White Cabbage Butterflies

See *Cabbageworms*

Whiteflies

These barely visible, sap-sucking insects covered with a white or gray waxy powder are related to scale insects and, like them, secrete honeydew on leaves and stems. They not only suck the sap from plants but may also carry viruses from plant to plant. They congregate in great numbers under leaves, from which they burst in swarms when disturbed. Female whiteflies lay twenty-five or so minute eggs in a circle under a leaf, and from these pale green nymphs emerge and immediately start feeding. Later the nymphs pupate, giving rise to more whiteflies. The insects can infest beans, cabbage, collards, cucumbers, eggplants, grapes, lettuce, melons, peas, peppers, potatoes, pumpkins, raspberries, squashes, strawberries, sweet potatoes, and tomatoes.

Manifestation

• Leaves wilt, get white spots, then turn yellow and brown and dry out. The leaves and stems of infested plants are often coated with the honeydew whiteflies exude, on which a sooty black fungus frequently grows. Fruits are paler and smaller than normal.

To Combat

• Whiteflies are less likely to infest plants where there's plenty of air circulation. So don't crowd your plants.
• The flies are attracted to the color yellow. You can make effective traps by smearing molasses on bright yellow cardboard and posting this near infested plants. Yellow flypaper will also work. Shake the plants to dislodge the insects, which will rise up in a cloud, and many will settle on the traps.
• Sprays are very effective: Liquid soap or detergent (1 tablespoon to 1 gallon of water) works well. Be sure to spray both the upper and undersides of the leaves. Do this every few days, as long as you see whiteflies on your plants.
• Both pyrethrum and rotenone sprays kill the insects on contact.
• Catnip, which whiteflies are said to love, can be planted near tomatoes as a trap crop.
• Gardeners also report that cabbage interplanted among tomatoes deters whiteflies.

Whortleberry

See *Blueberry*

Wilt

See *Bacterial diseases*; see also *Fusarium rot*; *Verticillium wilt*

Winter Savory

See *Savory*

Winter Squash

See *Squash*

Witloof

See *Endive*

Wonderberry

See *Huckleberry*

Yam

See *Sweet potato*

Yellow Jackets

Yellow jackets are a kind of wasp, fond of nectar and therefore important as pollinators. However, to the gardener they are equally important as predators. In order to supply food to their growing larvae they inject a paralyzing fluid into hornworms and other caterpillars, transferring the worms, piece by piece, to their nests. They are attracted to many garden flowers and herbs, including lovage and Queen Anne's lace.

Youngberry

See *Blackberry*

Zucchini

See *Squash*

...And a Few
Random Hints

One of the most common causes of trouble with home gardening is planting fruits or vegetables where they don't get enough daily sunlight. Keep a log, at various times of day, of where the sun lights particular areas in your garden. Do this off and on every couple of weeks through one entire season (the sun changes position relative to the earth as the season continues, but these positions are constant at any particular time, year after year).

The best time for garden chores is in the early morning, before the sun gets too hot.

For very useful garden "gloves," cover your hands with old nylon stockings cut to elbow length and anchored with rubber bands. These are surprisingly serviceable.

You can make a good disposable garden smock by cutting holes for neck and arms in a large plastic trash bag.

Minnow traps, which you can purchase at fishing-gear shops, make fine soil sifters.

You won't have to worry about mosquitoes laying eggs in rain barrels if you keep the barrels stocked with goldfish. The fish usually survive the winter, too, when the water freezes, just as they do in ponds. In addition, the goldfish enrich the water for use in your garden.

To turn a piece of lawn into an easily worked garden plot, some time around January cover it with black plastic. By spring the grass, roots, and leaves below the plastic will have composted and the soil can be easily worked.

To warm up any garden bed quickly in the spring, spread a sheet of black or clear plastic over it, holding it down with stones. Let this stand for about 1 week.

Discarded automobile tires placed around small garden beds help the soil to warm earlier in the spring.

Buildings and stone walls hold and reflect heat: Gardens planted close to these can be sown earlier in the spring.

Garden beds sloped to the south receive the maximum amount of direct sunlight in spring and can thus be planted earlier in the season.

If your garden area gets some but not full sun, space plants farther apart than normal so they won't shade one another.

If your garden is on a slope, plant rows transversely rather than up and down to help prevent erosion.

You can also save a sloping piece of land from erosion by planting asparagus on it. The plants have deep and widespread root systems that hold soil firmly.

Plant taller crops (corn, Jerusalem artichokes, sunflowers, and so on) toward the north end of your garden so the shorter ones in front of them get the sun they need.

Instead of planting all of one kind of vegetable at one time, make successive sowings at intervals of 1 or 2 weeks. You can thus avoid having too many of the same kind mature at once.

Plant more than one kind of vegetable in the same garden bed. You'll have more variety, you can make more frequent sowings and thus have a more continuous supply, and you can plant more varieties in less space.

To help keep many kinds of insects from your garden plants, interplant with chives, garlic, leeks, marigolds, mint, nasturtiums, onions, and petunias.

When covering indoor-growing seedlings with plastic, be sure no parts of the plants touch the covering, or they will rot.

Once indoor-grown seedlings appear, feed them weekly with a weak solution of fish emulsion, compost tea, manure tea, or seaweed emulsion.

Seedlings growing under fluorescent lights should be placed so their tops are about 2 inches below the tubes.

After seedlings emerge from the ground outdoors, it's a good idea to surround them lightly with compost to spur their growth and strengthen their stems.

Growing young plants in the garden under cloches (hot caps or grow tunnels) lets you get plants started earlier in the season.

Inexpensive clear-plastic highball glasses make very useful cloches for tender plants in early spring. Make holes in the sides with a hot awl or ice pick, invert the glasses over the plants, and place a stone on top of each for stability. This way light and air can enter (slugs can't).

You can protect seedlings and delicate plants from the cold and wind of early spring by surrounding each with a large can that has had its top and bottom removed. Push the can into the ground deep enough so it stays in place.

You can also use coffee cans with their tops and bottoms removed as permanent enclosures around plants (one can per plant). Sink the cans halfway into the ground. They will act as barriers against slugs and ground-creeping bugs of all kinds and make fine moats for watering.

Another protective cover for plants when temperatures are low is a gallon or ½-gallon plastic milk jug, or a 2-liter clear-plastic soda bottle, with the bottom cut out and cap left off.

The fastest developers in a vegetable garden are the leafy greens.

Pod- and fruit-producing plants need more light and warmth than leaf and root vegetables.

It's the leaves of fruit-bearing plants, not the fruits themselves, that need the sun.

Be merciless when your crops need thinning. Plants grown too close together will not develop well.

If any of your plants show mottling, spotting, or wilting in the spring, remove and destroy them before whatever is attacking them can spread to your other plants.

If the stem of a growing plant is partially broken, don't assume it's a total loss. Sometimes the break will heal: Try taping it with adhesive tape, staking the stem if necessary. This often works!

A wide ring of wood ashes around tall plants such as corn will strengthen the stalks.

If you want continuous production from your garden, pick the fruits as soon as they're ripe. Fruits left on plants or vines inhibit further production.

In mid- or late summer, cut off the yellowing, spent leaves from bean, cucumber, or squash vines; they'll often put forth new growth at these spots, producing more fruits when you'd thought the plants were through.

At the end of the summer, bring some of your garden herbs indoors to grow over the winter. Remove each plant from the garden with a wide enough root-and-soil ball to fit comfortably into an ample pot, and tamp in well with rich soil.

You can leave edible roots and tubers in the ground up to the time the soil freezes, regardless of what the leaves and stems look like.

After harvest in the fall, dig a hole near your house deep enough to sink a large metal trash can or barrel, with a cover, with about 4 inches of the rim extending aboveground. Use this as a root cellar for storing root crops (apples too) over the winter. Interlayer with hay or peat moss, put the cover on, and over this spread a plastic or other waterproof sheet. Help yourself to your crops throughout the winter.

You can store many root vegetables for months where it's cool and dark if you place them in wide-mouthed containers and cover lightly with earth. Sprinkle with water about once a month, and leave them exposed to air.

Use wood ashes instead of salt (salt damages soil) on paths and driveways each winter.

A Gardener's Glossary

Annual: a plant that starts and ends its life cycle (growing, flowering, and setting seeds) in a single season.

Axil: the point at which a branch or leafstalk diverges from the stem to which it is attached.

Biennial: a plant with a two-year life cycle; it produces roots, stems, and leaves the season the seeds are sown but doesn't bloom and set seed until the next year.

Blanching: cutting off light from a plant or part of a plant to make the covered section pale or white.

Blood meal: the ground, dried blood of animals, used as a high-nitrogen fertilizer.

Bolting: the formation, usually in a plant grown for its edible leaves and stalks, of a seedstalk that flowers and produces seeds, rendering the edible parts of the plant bitter.

Botanicals: substances derived from plants, for example, insecticides produced by pulverizing certain roots or flowers, as opposed to those produced from synthetic chemical compounds.

Brassicas: a vegetable group that includes broccoli, Brussels sprouts, all cabbages including kale and Chinese cabbages, cauliflower, collards, horseradish, kohlrabies, mustard, radishes, rutabagas, and turnips.

Bulb: a circular underground plant portion consisting of modified leaves or scales, in which food is stored, surrounding a bud in embryo; for example, an onion.

Castings: in a garden sense, the excreta of earthworms, very beneficial to garden soil.

Caterpillar: the immature, wormlike stage of a butterfly, moth, or sawfly.

Clay: a kaolinite-containing material present in varying amounts in many soils. Because of its ability to retain water, a small amount is beneficial to soil, but if it is present in too-large amounts the soil tends to clump when wet and become hard when dry. Soils containing clay in varying amounts are often referred to as sandy clay, clay, or silty clay soils. Most plants don't grow well in heavy clay soils unless some sand and loam or humus are added.

Cloche: any protective covering of a plant or group of plants that allows air, light, and moisture to penetrate but protects against cold, wind, and battering rains. When designed for an individual plant, a cloche is often called a hot cap; if made to enclose a long line of plants, it is called a tent or a grow tunnel.

Cold frame: a bottomless, boxlike structure with a removable transparent top in which tender plants are grown before they would normally be set in the garden or to extend their season in the fall. Interior heat is supplied by the sun, and the temperature is modified by raising or lowering the lid.

Cole crops: a vegetable group that includes broccoli, Brussels sprouts, cabbage, cauliflower, collards, horseradish, kale, kohlrabi, mustard, radishes, rutabagas, and turnips.

Companion plants: plants of different species grown in the same bed, at least one of which is benefited by the presence of the other; often they are mutually beneficial.

Compost: a fertilizing mixture containing decayed organic (usually vegetable) matter that has gradually turned into humus.

Compost tea: a mixture of compost and water, strained and used as a liquid fertilizer.

Corm: a bulblike underground stem that stores food for the plant that will rise from it and from the base of which roots will grow.

Cover crop: a planting of any of various crops (alfalfa, barley, buckwheat, clover, cowpeas, oats, annual or winter rye, vetch) to prevent erosion, to enrich the soil, or to improve its tilth. The plants are plowed under before they flower or go to seed.

Crop rotation: the successive planting of a different crop each year on the same land. At the least, no one crop is planted two years in succession in the same place. (see *Monoculture*)

Crown: the point in a plant where the stem meets the root; or the upper part of a root from which a stem will grow.

Crucifers: plants of the mustard family: broccoli, Brussels sprouts, cabbage (all kinds), cauliflower, garden cress, horseradish, kohlrabi, mustard, nasturtiums (Indian cress), radishes, rocket, rutabagas, turnips, and watercress.

Cucurbits: cucumbers, melons, pumpkins, and squashes.

Cultivar: a plant resulting from selective breeding and cultivation, as opposed to a variety that appears in the wild. Most cultivars will not maintain themselves without human care (but see *Escape*).

Cultivate: to till the soil around a plant in order to break up the crust, increase aeration, conserve moisture, and keep weeds down.

Cure: to harden the surface of a fruit or vegetable before storing (for example, the sweet potato).

Cutting: see *Slip*

Deadheading: removing faded blooms to prevent seed-head formation.

Deciduous: referring to perennial plants or trees that lose their leaves at the end of their growing season (in the Northeast, this is usually in the fall).

Determinate: having a restricted growing season, as in some tomato varieties, which concentrate their fruit set in a certain period, then cease growth and production. (see *Indeterminate*)

Diatomaceous earth: a talclike powder made from the petrified shells of ancient one-celled organisms. It contains tiny "needles" of silica, which, when dusted around plants and on soil surfaces, pierce the bodies of scales, slugs, and all types of soft-bodied insects. It can be handled safely, and does not injure earthworms.

Dioecious: referring to individual plants that produce either male flowers only or female flowers only. (see *Monoecious*)

Drill: a trench or excavated row in which seeds are planted.

Earthworms: long, slender, brown worms very desirable in gardens for aerating the soil and increasing its fertility. Their presence in a garden is testimony to the goodness of the soil.

Escape: a cultivated plant that has run wild and maintains itself on its own; also, a plant that has sprung up from the self-sown seed of a cultivated form.

Espalier: a plant, usually a shrub or tree, trained to grow laterally, along a fence, railing, or trellis.

Everlastings: flowers, shrubs, or grasses whose blossoms, leaves, plumes, or fruits hold their colors when dried, for use as winter decoration.

Fish emulsion: a concentrated high-nitrogen solution of fish residues and water which, when mixed with additional water, makes a valuable food for both plants in gardens and houseplants.

Flat: a shallow box or other low-sided container used for growing seedlings.

Forcing: artificially causing plants to develop or come into blossom sooner than they normally would, usually by simulating the climate and conditions that would be several months away.

Frass: the excrement of insect larvae, often visible on or below attacked plants.

Friable: easily crumbled.

Frost date: the date on which the last spring frost would normally be expected in an area in a given year; also, the date when the first sharp fall frost would be expected. These dates can more or less be determined by calling your local agricultural extension service.

Green manure: any fast-growing plants—such as alfalfa, buckwheat, cowpeas, clover, vetch—that are grown and plowed under while green to enrich the soil and increase its water-holding capacity.

Green manure tea: a solution of chopped green plants steeped in water until slight fermentation occurs, then strained and used as a liquid fertilizer.

Greensand: a sandy mineral substance containing glauconite that can be dug well into garden soil to provide a rich source of potassium.

Grow lights: an incandescent or fluorescent lamp, used alone or in combination, for growing plants indoors.

Grow tunnel: see *Cloche*

Grub: the larval stage of a beetle.

Hardening off: before outdoor transplanting, exposing indoor-grown seedlings to full sun outdoors, at slightly lower temperatures and less moisture than they were accustomed to, for progressively longer periods until they have acclimated to garden conditions.

Heaving: caused by the alternate thawing and freezing of the upper layers of moist soil, the pushing up of perennial plants in early spring, exposing their roots to cold and dryness. This is not likely to happen to perennials properly (deeply and firmly) planted in soil where moisture does not collect.

Herb: a plant with a stem of soft tissue that dies down to the ground at the end of the season, as opposed to a plant with a persistent woody stem, such as a shrub or tree.

Hill: a group of seeds planted around a hill of soil; also, a group of seeds planted in a ring. Hilling, or hilling up: mounding soil around the base of a plant, as is generally done with corn or potatoes.

Host, Host plant: a plant in or on which parasites grow.

Hotbed: a heated cold frame.

Hot cap: see *Cloche*

Humus: brown or black material consisting of partially or totally decomposed organic matter; the organic portion of soil.

Indeterminate: continuing to grow and produce fruit throughout the growing season, usually up to frost. (see *Determinate*)

Larva: the immature, wingless form of an insect, usually wormlike.

Layering: a method of inducing new roots to grow from a stem, either by bending the stem down to the soil, making an incision, then anchoring it and covering that portion with soil; or by making an incision in an upright stem, inserting a wooden match or toothpick to hold the incision open, packing sphagnum moss around the wound, and covering with plastic, tied above and below with only enough opening to allow for watering. This second method is often called air layering.

Leaf mold: a form of humus; soil composed chiefly of decayed leaves.

Leggy: applied to plants, usually seedlings, whose stems are too elongated, usually because of a struggle for more light or because of overheating or overfeeding.

Legume: generally, a plant with edible roots, or with seeds contained in pods, such as beans, lentils, and peas. Also, alfalfa and clover.

Lime: a calcium compound that, for garden use, is derived chiefly from ground limestone or ground oyster shells. It is used to add calcium to the soil and to reduce soil acidity or to increase soil alkalinity.

Liquid manure: see *Manure tea*

Loam: a friable soil mixture of relatively equal proportions of clay, sand, and organic matter, such as humus.

Maggot: the larva of a fly.

Manure tea (liquid manure): an infusion made by steeping fresh or dried manure of any kind in water for about a week, then diluting to a pale tea consistency to use as a liquid fertilizer.

Mildew: a powdery or downy growth on the surface of plant tissue caused by fungi.

Monoculture: the growing of the same plant or closely related plants in the same place, year after year. (see *Crop rotation*)

Monoecious: referring to plants that produce separate male and female flowers on the same plant. (see *Dioecious*)

Mulch: any substance (grass, leaves, manure, paper, plastic sheets, peat moss, pine needles, sawdust, straw, and others) spread over the ground to protect the roots of plants from heat, cold, and dryness, or to keep fruits from direct contact with the soil.

Naturalizing: creating a natural effect in a garden, as when spacing plants to appear as though they are growing in the wild.

NPK ratio: the proportion by weight, relative to one another and to the total contents, of nitrogen, phosphorus, and potassium in any given mixture, as in a bag of fertilizer. The marking 5-10-5 on a bag or box of fertilizer means that 5 percent of the contents is nitrogen, 10 percent is phosphorus, and 5 percent is potassium (K is the chemical symbol for potassium). The remaining 80 percent of the contents is mainly inert ingredients, acting as a carrier for these plant nutrients (which in their pure form are very strong).

Nymph: the immature stage of an insect, usually closely resembling the adult form except in size and the absence of wings.

Organic matter: dead plant or animal tissue (grass, hay, leaves, stems, straw, insect and animal refuse, and so on).

Peat: partially or wholly decomposed plant matter. The term is often used interchangeably with *humus*, although decomposition is usually further advanced in peat. There are different kinds of peat, depending on plant origins and the stage of decomposition.

Peat moss (also called sphagnum moss): peat derived from a type of bog moss.

Perennial: a plant capable of blooming year after year, although each season's blooming period may last only a few weeks. (A perennial is not immortal, however.)

pH: a chemical symbol denoting hydrogen ion concentration in soil. On a scale of 0 to 14, a pH of 0 is extremely acid, or "sour." A pH of 14 is extremely alkaline, or "sweet." A pH of 7 is "balanced," or neutral. Most plants grow well in a soil whose pH is between 6.0 and 6.8. A form of sulfur added to soil will increase its acidity, and a form of lime will increase its alkalinity.

Phosphorus: a very important chemical required by plants, available in the form of phosphates. Bonemeal, fish emulsion, and finely crushed rock phosphate are the most common sources of phosphorus for garden use.

Pinching, Pinching off: removing shoots or buds from a plant to channel the plant's energies into the shoots or buds that remain. Where there are several buds on the same plant, pinching off some or most of them (or in certain cases all but one) will make the remaining ones larger. Pinching off unwanted shoots will strengthen those left. Pinching off the upper 2 or 3 inches of a plant will cause it to develop more heavily at the base.

Potash: potassium carbonate, a necessary plant food, good sources of which are dried fish scraps or fish emulsion, greensand, dried or well-rotted manure (especially poultry manure), seaweed, and wood ashes.

Potting soil: a pasteurized blend of soil, organic compounds, and drainage materials. If you wish to make your own potting soil, use these rough equivalents: 2 parts garden soil; 1 part compost, humus, or leaf mold; and 1 part sand, vermiculite, or perlite. To each quart of this mixture add 1 tablespoon of bonemeal. Mix well, spread evenly in a large oven pan, and put in a preheated 150° oven for 45 minutes.

Pricking out: see *Thinning*

Pruning: removing branches, twigs, and so on from a plant to promote the health and vigor of the remaining branches and fruit, or to make the plant more shapely.

Pupa: a developmental stage of an insect, usually in a chrysalis or cocoon, between the larval and the adult forms.

Raised bed gardening: growing crops along the flattened tops of elongated mounds of soil or in beds entirely elevated a foot or more above ground level. This method increases drainage, allows roots to grow longer, and warms up the soil earlier.

Rhizome: also called rootstock, an elongated, thickened, horizontal, underground stem that sends out a series of roots from its lower surface and a series of leafy shoots along its upper surface. The rhizome acts as a food storage repository for the plants until the lower roots are established.

Root crops: a term commonly used for all underground vegetables, including beets, carrots, onions, parsnips, potatoes, rutabagas, salsify, sweet potatoes, and turnips.

Rooting powder: a substance (which can also be used in solution) into which cuttings are dipped before planting to induce or hasten rooting. The powder usually contains one or more fungicides to prevent damping off and several hormonelike substances to stimulate root growth.

Rootstock: see *Rhizome*

Rotation: see *Crop rotation*

Salt hay (also called salt-marsh hay): a grass growing in salt marshes, valuable for mulches because it doesn't pack down like ordinary hay or straw, contains relatively little salt in spite of its habitat, and is quite free of weed seeds.

Sand: loose grains formed by the disintegration of rocks, larger than the particles that form silt. Sand is a component, in various proportions, of most soils and contributes to their drainage capabilities.

Seed leaves: the first set of leaves that appear after germination. These wilt and are discarded shortly after the more permanent leaves (known as true leaves) appear.

Sets: a word usually applied to onions, meaning small bulbs (or bulblets) planted for developing into larger, edible bulbs.

Shattering: scattering of seeds that results from the bursting open of a seed pod, or the dropping of seeds from ripe or overripe fruits or flowers.

Side dressing: see *Top dressing*

Silking: in corn, the appearance of the long, silky threads that are actually prolongations of the ovaries of the female flowers.

Silt: loose sedimentary material consisting of rock particles that are larger than the particles that make up clay but smaller than those making up sand. Almost all soils contain some proportion of silt.

Slip: a cutting, as of a sprout, shoot, or stem, removed from the parent plant to be induced to form roots and become a separate plant. Also, any new plant developing from a bud at the base of a fruit, as in the pineapple. The term *slip* is frequently used for softwood or soft-stemmed plants; *cutting* is the corresponding term for hardwood plants.

Sod: also called turf, the upper layer of soil in a lawn, filled with the roots of grasses.

Specimen plant: a plant grown for exhibit or special individual display, as distinguished from plants grown in beds or as borders.

Sphagnum moss: see *Peat moss*

Stratification: the temporary placing of seeds in layers of damp sand, peat moss, sawdust, or other growing medium, and then burying the layers outdoors to subject the seeds to the action of frost over the winter. For certain seeds, this treatment induces germination when they are dug up and replanted in the spring.

Straw: the dried stems and leaves of grains or grasses that have had their seed heads removed.

Succession planting: the planting, in a single season, of one crop in a bed immediately after another crop has been harvested.

Succulents: plants, usually with swollen-looking or fleshy stems or leaves, that store water in their cells to tide themselves over arid periods; also, certain plants that have developed drought resistance through their own chemistry, without noticeable means of water storage.

Suckering: removing suckers, or small side branches, that arise from the leaf axils of plants such as tomatoes; or of new canes that arise from the roots of plants such as red or yellow raspberries. Suckering forces a plant to put its growth and vigor into already developing portions of the plant and to grow upward rather than sideways.

Taproot: a long, main, sturdy root growing straight downward, which some plants have instead of the succession of the smaller, lateral roots characteristic of most other plants. Many herbs, including dandelions, and certain trees and shrubs have taproots. Such plants are hard to transplant since they have fewer feeder roots to depend on while adjusting to a new location.

Tea: see *Compost tea*; *Green manure tea*; *Manure tea*; *Wormwood tea*

Thinning: removing excess plants from a garden bed to give more room to those left behind. If those removed are to be planted elsewhere, the thinnings are taken out with care so that the roots are not harmed. This thinning is known as pricking out. (see also *Pruning*)

Tilth: in common garden use, the character of soil that has been cultivated and prepared for planting, its degree of readiness for garden use.

Tipping, Tip rooting: the sprouting of roots from the ends of long canes (as black raspberry canes) that bend over and grow into the ground. This is a natural form of propagation.

Top dressing (also called side dressing): adding compost, fertilizer, or other nutriment enhancements to the soil adjacent to growing plants, usually by lightly raking in without disturbing the roots and without allowing any fresh manure or raw fertilizers to come in direct contact with the plants.

Trap crop, Trap plant: a crop attractive to certain insects that is planted to lure those insects away from other nearby or later crops.

Trellis: a frame of latticework, slats, or wires used as a support for climbing plants.

True leaves: the leaves of a plant that appear after the first set of leaves (known as seed leaves) has developed.

Tuber: a short, fleshy, usually underground stem bearing buds or "eyes" from each of which a shoot grows upward. Tubers are characteristic of plants such as Jerusalem artichokes and potatoes.

Tunnel: see *Cloche*

Turf: see *Sod*

Vertical gardening: the training of plants to trellises, fences, walls, or other supports.

Volunteer: a plant that appears, uninvited, at a particular site. It may arrive as a seed brought by wind, water, or bird or by an extension of an underground root.

Wormwood tea: an infusion made by covering chopped wormwood with boiling water and allowing the mixture to steep until it starts to ferment. Used as an insecticide in the garden.